Rockhounding and Gems

Unlocking the Secrets of Rocks, Gems, Minerals, Agates, and Fossils for Enthusiasts and Beginners

© Copyright 2024 – **All rights reserved.**

The content contained within this book may not be reproduced, duplicated, or transmitted without direct written permission from the author or the publisher.

Under no circumstances will any blame or legal responsibility be held against the publisher, or author, for any damages, reparation, or monetary loss due to the information contained within this book, either directly or indirectly.

Legal Notice:

This book is copyright protected. It is only for personal use. You cannot amend, distribute, sell, use, quote or paraphrase any part or the content within this book, without the consent of the author or publisher.

Disclaimer Notice:

Please note the information contained within this document is for educational and entertainment purposes only. All effort has been executed to present accurate, up-to-date, reliable, and complete information. No warranties of any kind are declared or implied. Readers acknowledge that the author is not engaging in the rendering of legal, financial, medical, or professional advice. The content within this book has been derived from various sources. Please consult a licensed professional before attempting any techniques outlined in this book.

By reading this document, the reader agrees that under no circumstances is the author responsible for any losses, direct or indirect, that are incurred as a result of the use of the information contained within this document, including, but not limited to, errors, omissions, or inaccuracies.

Your Free Gift
(only available for a limited time)

Thanks for getting this book! If you want to learn more about various spirituality topics, then join Mari Silva's community and get a free guided meditation MP3 for awakening your third eye. This guided meditation mp3 is designed to open and strengthen ones third eye so you can experience a higher state of consciousness. Simply visit the link below the image to get started.

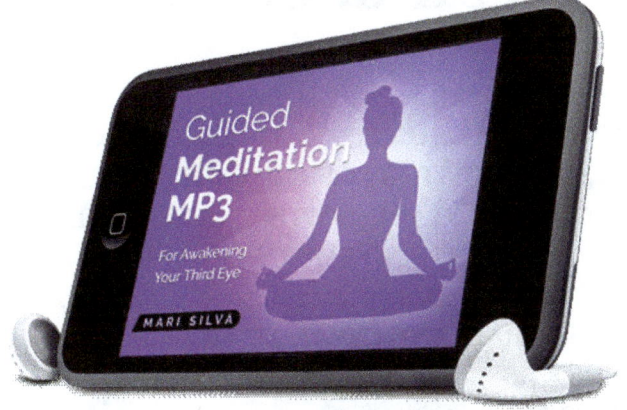

https://spiritualityspot.com/meditation

Or, Scan the QR code!

Table of Contents

PART 1: ROCKHOUNDING 1
    INTRODUCTION 2
    CHAPTER 1: A BRIEF HISTORY OF THE EARTH 4
    CHAPTER 2: GETTING STARTED WITH ROCKHOUNDING 14
    CHAPTER 3: EQUIPMENT AND SAFETY TIPS 23
    CHAPTER 4: GEMSTONES 37
    CHAPTER 5: MINERALS AND CRYSTALS 49
    CHAPTER 6: ROCKS 61
    CHAPTER 7: FOSSILS 75
    CHAPTER 8: SPECIMEN CLEANING AND CARE 86
    CHAPTER 9: YOUR FIRST ROCKHOUNDING TRIP 97
    CHAPTER 10: LEGAL CONSIDERATIONS 105
    BONUS: GROW YOUR OWN CRYSTALS 111
    CONCLUSION 123
PART 2: ROCKS, GEMS, AND MINERALS 125
    INTRODUCTION 126
    CHAPTER 1: THE BASICS OF ROCKS, GEMS, CRYSTALS, AND MINERALS 128
    CHAPTER 2: IGNEOUS ROCKS 138
    CHAPTER 3: SEDIMENTARY ROCKS 149
    CHAPTER 4: METAMORPHIC ROCKS 163
    CHAPTER 5: MINERALS AND CRYSTAL SYSTEMS 176
    CHAPTER 6: QUARTZ 185

CHAPTER 7: CHALCEDONIES AND AGATES 197
CHAPTER 8: PRECIOUS GEMSTONES 206
CHAPTER 9: SEMI-PRECIOUS GEMSTONES 214
CHAPTER 10: METEORITES AND TEKTITES 222
APPENDIX: A-Z OF ROCKS, CRYSTALS, GEMS, AND MINERALS 228
CONCLUSION 230
HERE'S ANOTHER BOOK BY MARI SILVA THAT YOU MIGHT LIKE 232
YOUR FREE GIFT (ONLY AVAILABLE FOR A LIMITED TIME) 233
REFERENCES 234
IMAGE SOURCES 239

Part 1: Rockhounding

The Ultimate Beginner's Guide to Finding and Studying Rocks, Gems, Minerals, Agates, and Fossils

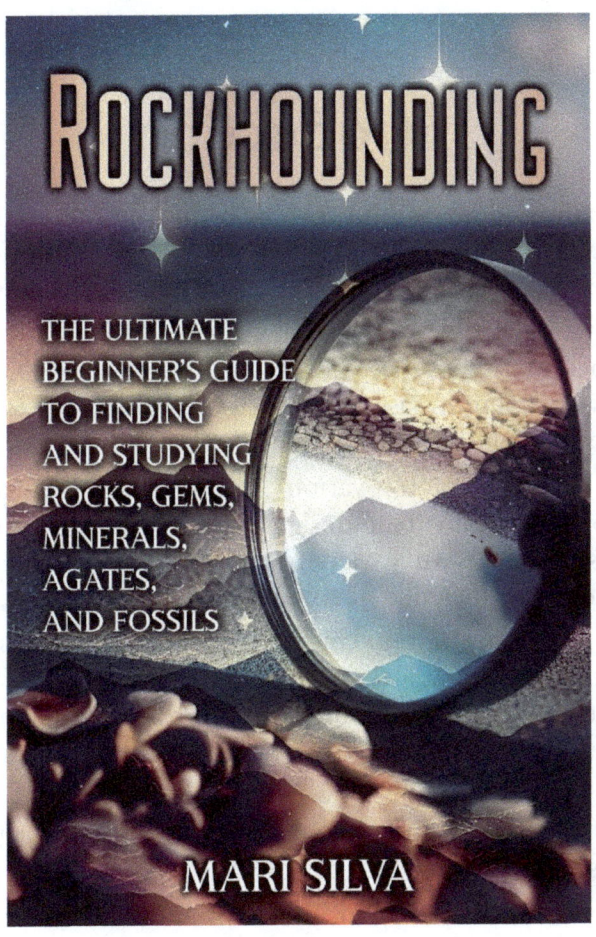

Introduction

If you've ever admired a beautiful rock or gem and pondered its origins or formation, then rockhounding may be the perfect pastime for you. It involves the exploration and study of rocks, gems, minerals, agates, and fossils, offering a fascinating activity that anyone can enjoy.

Though rockhounding may not be as popular as it once was, it continues to attract enthusiasts due to the opportunity to visit diverse natural landscapes while seeking unique specimens.

People are drawn to it for various reasons. Jewelers can search for stones to incorporate into their designs, while history and geology buffs might be seeking hands-on experience with regional gemstones. Some people love the extra challenge of going hiking or trekking.

For many, collecting, identifying, refining, and acquiring gems goes beyond a hobby – it can also be a lucrative endeavor. The value of gemstones and minerals is significant, and rockhounds may not only amass specimens for personal enjoyment but also profit from their passion by selling rocks to fellow enthusiasts.

Regardless of the motivation, rockhounding is a captivating and rewarding pursuit for many.

This book serves as a helpful guide for those interested in learning more about this enjoyable activity. Designed with the understanding that you may not be familiar with rocks, it avoids complex terminology and scientific jargon. Instead, it uses easy-to-understand language and helpful illustrations to clarify concepts.

Ideal for rock hunting novices, the book covers the basics, such as the different types of rocks, minerals, and gems and where to find them. It also provides guidance on essential equipment, supplies, and safety tips for rockhounding.

Included are methods for identifying the rocks and minerals you've found, maintaining and cleaning your collection, and creating your own personal treasury of gemstones.

One of the most exciting aspects of rockhounding is making new discoveries, and this book will teach you how to determine whether you've found something truly exceptional. It also instructs you on responsible and safe rock hunting practices and how to utilize various resources to learn more about your specimens.

This book is a valuable resource that will teach you a great deal and inspire a lifelong love for rockhounding.

Chapter 1: A Brief History of the Earth

The earth is billions of years old. During this time, it has undergone many changes, including rock formation and species' evolution. This makes the earth's history an interesting story of change and adaptation. This chapter will examine the earth's history and how scientists discovered what happened.

Geology studies the earth's physical structure, history, and formation. Geologists strive to understand how the earth worked in the past and how it will work in the future. They do this by looking at rocks, minerals, and other things that make up the planet and by studying things like earthquakes, volcanic eruptions, and the movement of the earth's plates.

The geological time scale is important in studying the earth's history because, without it, it will be hard for people to understand how long the earth's been in existence. Geologists use different ways, like radiometric dating, to figure out how old rocks and minerals are, and they do this to learn more about how the earth's history fits together.

The principle of uniformitarianism is another big idea in geology. It means things that changed the earth in the past are still happening. Uniformitarianism allows scientists to study what's happening now and figure out what happened in the past.

By the end of this chapter, you'll have understood geology, geological time scale, the principle of uniformitarianism, and plate tectonics.

Basic Geological History

Some major concepts can help you understand how the earth works. These concepts are outlined below.

Geology

The earth is very old (more than 4.5 billion years), and geology sheds light on how it evolved through time. It is a field of science that looks at the earth and everything in it (rocks, mountains, and volcanoes) using logic and scientific methods.

Geology is also useful in preparing for catastrophic events like earthquakes and landslides. Geologists can help mankind prepare for these disasters by researching how the earth moves and its structure.

However, geology isn't just about disasters. It also uncovers important resources like oil, coal, and metals.

Geological Time Scale

The notion of time is fundamental to the study of geology. Geological processes and changes can take millions of years to occur. Even little geographical changes, like a chemical reaction on a rock, can take millions of years.

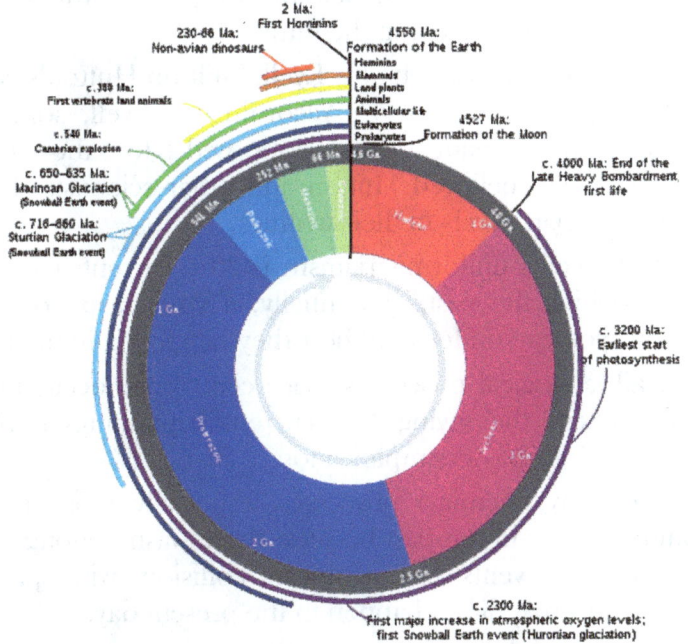

Geological clock with events.[1]

Geologists utilize the geological time scale to help them study the earth's evolution. This method divides time into distinct periods based on significant events in the earth's history. They don't use numbers to talk about different times. Instead, they use "era" and "epoch" to delineate between the different periods.

Seeing how there are always new discoveries, the geological time scale is always evolving. For example, it is now known that big creatures lived on earth much earlier than previously imagined.

Even if no one knows the precise age of rocks or fossils, the geological time scale sheds some light on their relative age.

Uniformitarianism

According to uniformitarianism, the same geological processes occurring today have occurred in the past. Although it might not seem that significant today, when humans first learned about it, they believed the earth to be just a few thousand years old. For others, it was difficult to understand that it was considerably older than that, especially since that put their religious beliefs into question.

James Hutton, a Scottish geologist, is the founder of uniformitarianism. He wrote about it in a book he published in 1788. Hutton said that observing current events makes it possible to gain knowledge of earlier events and make predictions about the future.

A fellow Scottish geologist, Charles Lyell, built on Hutton's concepts in his work "Principles of Geology." According to Lyell, some people's religious convictions made them opposed to the notion of uniformitarianism. He believed Hutton and other scientists should have used more images than words in their writings.

The tenet of Lyell's uniformitarianism is "the current happenings are the key to unlocking the past." Essentially, if you grasp how things are going right now, you can understand how they happened in the past.

Since not all geological processes that occur today occur in the past, some people believe the saying "the current happenings is the key to unlocking the past" is an oversimplification.

Many present-day chemical processes, especially those that require oxygen, couldn't occur in the past because there wasn't enough oxygen in the air. Also, certain events, like significant collisions with space objects, occurred in the past that didn't happen in the present day.

However, there are still certain areas on earth where you can learn about the things that occurred a long time ago, even if the circumstances were different in the past. You only need to be cautious of the changes that have happened between the past and the present.

Plate Tectonics

The earth's outer layer comprises numerous massive sections known as tectonic plates that move around on the surface. Think of these plates like jigsaw puzzle pieces that fit together to make up the earth's crust.

Tectonic plates fit together like a puzzle.[3]

The movement of these plates is caused by the flow of molten rock underneath the earth's crust, called magma. This movement is responsible for creating many of the earth's features, like mountains, volcanoes, and earthquakes.

Three types of tectonic plate boundaries exist: divergent, convergent, and transform.

Plate tectonics is a way for scientists to learn about the Earth's past, present, and future. Scientists can predict and prepare for natural disasters like earthquakes and volcanic eruptions by looking at how tectonic plates move. They can also learn more about how the earth has changed over time.

The Most Important Events in Earth's Geological History

Several major events in Earth's geological history explain the planet's formation, living organisms, and how these organisms have evolved. Seven of these events are outlined below:

1. Formation of the Earth and Moon

Scientists want to know how the earth and moon came to be because it tells them how the solar system was made and what makes a planet suitable for life. According to them, the Earth and other planets were tiny bits of dust and gas circling the sun. These particles came together a long time ago and formed rocks, which grew into bigger rocks called "planetesimals."

The planetesimals crashed into each other and became Mars-sized rocks called "protoplanets." Finally, a huge collision called the "moon-forming impact" created the moon. The impact was highly forceful, causing certain substances to vaporize from both Earth and the object. Over time, this vapor cooled and transformed into the moon.

The most widely held theory of the moon's origins postulates that it resulted from a catastrophic impact between Earth and a protoplanet called "Theia." Lunar meteorites and rocks brought back by astronauts allow scientists to learn more about the moon's history.

Scientists examine these rocks to learn more about the moon's composition and formation.

2. The Emergence of Life on Earth

The subject of life's emergence on Earth continues to puzzle the scientific community. Despite several theories, none have been verified, and scientists are still intrigued about the circumstances that led to the genesis of life. The components that may have started life's development, like water, chemical reactions, and temperature cycles, are difficult to comprehend since they occurred during Earth's early life, about which we know nothing.

At the University of Chicago, the Miller-Urey research was carried out to demonstrate the origin of life's key building blocks in a "primordial soup."

According to this experiment, life is believed to have begun at least 4.5 billion years ago because the earliest known fossils of living organisms date back 3.7 billion years. But life might have emerged many times during the 600-million-year period. Cataclysmic collisions could have wiped it out with asteroids and comets.

The earliest zircons contain retained carbon clues going back 4.1 billion years, which living creatures require. However, this is insufficient evidence of life's presence at that early age. Two possible places where life began on Earth are hydrothermal environments on land and at sea, like hot springs and deep-sea hydrothermal vents.

It's possible that tiny pieces made of natural substances were created inside some types of mud, which might have made a good home for keeping things safe. The things needed for life to thrive on earth are a continuous energy source, organic compounds, and water. The energy from the sun fuels photosynthesis, which is essential for life. Meanwhile, nutrients on the ocean floor are provided by geothermal energy. Elements like carbon, hydrogen, oxygen, nitrogen, and phosphorus are also crucial, but it remains a mystery how they were able to come together on Earth. This is because carbon and nitrogen should not be present on a planet that is so close to the sun. Carbon is not commonly found on the earth's surface as it often bonds with iron instead of rock. The origin of water on the earth's surface remains unknown, but one theory suggests that it may have come from carbonaceous chondrites, a class of meteorites that formed outside the sun's proximity and were capable of delivering water to our planet.

3. Formation of Oxygen in the Atmosphere

Oxygen is vital for life on Earth. It makes up a major part of the air living organisms breathe, around 21%, to be precise. So, how did it end up in the atmosphere? It's quite a complex story involving life's evolution and many geological processes.

Photosynthesis is the way plants and other organisms convert sunlight into energy. It's a complicated chemical process, but the basic idea is that the energy from sunlight gets used to make oxygen and glucose out of carbon dioxide and water.

Cyanobacteria, tiny creatures that lived in the ocean around 2.5 billion years ago, were probably the first organisms to carry out photosynthesis. They made oxygen as a byproduct, but it took a long time for it to build up in the atmosphere.

The oxygen created by these cyanobacteria reacted with iron in the oceans to form iron oxide. This then settled to the bottom of the ocean and created the banded iron formations seen today. It's proof that oxygen was slowly built up in the atmosphere over billions of years.

Around 2.4 billion years ago, there was a "Great Oxidation Event." This event led to a significant increase in oxygen levels in the atmosphere. This paved the way for more complex life forms to evolve. Scientists still debate what caused this event, but they think it was related to the earth's crust changes and photosynthetic organisms' evolution.

Eventually, land plants evolved around 500 million years ago. They were able to use sunlight to create energy, which increased oxygen levels even more. Today, there's still oxygen being produced in the atmosphere, and it's affected by changes in the environment and the evolution of life on Earth.

4. Cambrian Explosion

One of the biggest mysteries in the discussion of life on Earth is the "Cambrian Explosion." This happened about 542 million years ago, and it was a time when new kinds of creatures appeared on the planet. This was surprising because only a handful of species existed before that.

There are two main theories on why this happened. One is that the earth changed a lot, which created new places for creatures to live and made it easier for them to evolve. The other is that more kinds of creatures existed before the Cambrian explosion.

Some fossils scientists found before the Cambrian explosion are strange and hard to classify. They're called the Ediacaran Fauna. These creatures didn't fossilize well, making it even harder to know exactly what they were like.

The Cambrian explosion is important because it's when many of the major groups of animals known today first appeared, like mollusks, arthropods, and chordates. It's also when creatures started to evolve things like hard shells and exoskeletons, which helped them survive better.

Some scientists think that the Cambrian explosion was like an arms race, where creatures had to evolve quickly to keep up with each other. This led to many new and interesting adaptations, like eyes and ears.

5. Mass Extinctions

Mass extinctions have significantly impacted the history of life on Earth. An event like that occurs when a large number of different species die at the same time for the same reason. Temperature fluctuations, volcanic eruptions, and changes in water and air quality are some possible causes of extinctions.

Roughly 440 million years ago, the first significant extinction occurred. It was caused by a severe frost, which changed ocean levels and removed a major percentage of the food supply. Nobody knows why this happened; however, some speculate that it may have been related to the development of a massive mountain range.

The Devonian era saw the second great extinction catastrophe. This was due to many plants sprouting, which caused a significant quantity of algae to begin growing in the water. Several species died due to the algae consuming all the water's oxygen.

The third great extinction event occurred at the conclusion of the Permian period, and it was exceptionally devastating. It is believed that around 90% of the world's living creatures died as a consequence. This might be because numerous volcanoes erupted at the same moment, releasing carbon dioxide into the atmosphere. This caused a rise in global temperature as well as precipitation acidification, both of which were very harmful to the world's waters.

The Triassic period saw the fourth major extinction catastrophe in Earth's history. No one knows what caused this, but it was most likely due to many volcanoes erupting and emitting a large amount of carbon dioxide. As a result, the climate transformed, making it far more difficult for any living being to breathe.

These massive extinctions were disastrous for the previously existing life on Earth. They were responsible for the extinction of numerous distinct species of living creatures and entire groups of living organisms in certain situations.

6.Evolution of Mammals

Around 252 million to 201 million years ago, mammals came to be during the Triassic period. Synapsida was one of the first reptilian groups known. They were related to the therapsids, although at that time, the therapsids weren't as impressive as other reptiles.

It wasn't until the Permian period, which occurred between 299 million and 252 million years ago, that the therapsids became the dominant reptiles. Interestingly, some of them were herbivores, while others were carnivores.

As time passed, therapsids evolved specialized teeth and improved how they moved their limbs. They also developed a hard palate, separating the passages for food and air, making breathing easier for them to breathe while eating.

Modern mammals have many features that set them apart from modern reptiles. These features evolved at different rates, many related to the fact that mammals are very active. For example, they have a four-chambered heart, which helps them circulate blood more efficiently.

They also have a special type of blood cell that lacks a nucleus and is shaped like a disc, which allows for more efficient movement of oxygen. They also have hair, which helps them maintain their body temperature.

During the time when mammals were evolving from reptiles, some animals had features of both groups. This is called a mosaic pattern of evolution, and it is common when new types of animals are evolving. Some scientists suggest that the main characteristic that separates mammals from reptiles is how their jaw bones are articulated. Some of the bones in their jaw move in a way unique to mammals.

Using this characteristic allows scientists to classify different animals as either mammals or reptiles.

7. Human Evolution

It took millions of years for human evolution to take place. It started with primates that no longer exist, eventually leading to humans. Humans are the only ones left from this group, called Hominini. Before that, there were other groups like Ardipithecus and Australopithecus, and humans lived with the Neanderthals. Humans have always shared the earth with other apelike primates, like the gorilla.

There was a common ancestor millions of years ago that led to different groups. It's like a big family tree, but there are many branches instead of a straight line. It's hard to figure out exactly how everything happened because there are a lot of different ideas.

The best way to learn how humans evolved is by looking at fossils. They can show you what kind of species there were and when they lived. You can't always figure out why they evolved or what happened to them. Scientists have to guess based on what they know about the fossils and where they were found.

Most experts agree that the first Hominin came around during the Pliocene Epoch about 5.3-2.6 million years ago. Before that, some other primates might have been related to them, but scientists aren't exactly sure. Some of the ones they've talked about include Kenyapithecus,

Griphopithecus, and Dryopithecus.

Geology studies the earth's history and processes. This field of study has created three big ideas: geological time scale, uniformitarianism, and plate tectonics.

The geological time scale refers to the earth's different time periods, each with distinct geological and biological events. Uniformitarianism says the earth's geological processes have always been the same. The plate tectonics theory explains how these plates' movement and interaction cause earthquakes and geological features like mountains and ocean trenches. The chapter has provided numerous examples to help you better understand the various processes and events.

Seven major geological events have shaped the earth and influenced life's evolution. These seven events encompass the formation of the earth, the development of life, the Cambrian explosion, the five great extinction events, the production of oxygen in the atmosphere, and the evolution of animals and humans.

Understanding earth's geological history allows humanity to appreciate its natural processes and diverse life. The study of geology remains vital to our knowledge of the earth and the future consequences of humanity's actions.

Chapter 2: Getting Started with Rockhounding

Are you intrigued by the prospect of becoming a rock and mineral collector but uncertain about where to start? Have you developed an interest in rockhounding but feel overwhelmed by the information available? You're in luck. This chapter is designed specifically to guide you.

It will begin by acquainting you with the fascinating world of rockhounding and its historical development, culminating in the popular hobby it represents today. You will also discover rockhounding's numerous advantages and rewards for its enthusiasts.

By the end of this chapter, you will be equipped with essential tips and strategies to kickstart your rockhounding journey with confidence and success.

What Is Rockhounding?

Looking for and gathering rocks, gems, fossils, minerals, or crystals is commonly called rockhounding and is sometimes referred to as *geology for beginners* or *collecting rocks and minerals*. A rockhound is someone who can't resist picking up specimens of interesting rocks and minerals whenever they go on rock-hunting trips. Their natural inclination is to pause, pick up specimens, and examine them closely.

Rockhounding is the process of looking for and gathering rocks.[a]

Rockhounding is a popular and enjoyable hobby, particularly among those who like being outside, going on hunts, and people that are interested in geology. People of all ages continue to be drawn to it because it allows them to travel across a wide range of terrain, searching for rocks and minerals of interest.

Any of the following describes the actions of a rockhound on a rock-hunting trip:

- Hunts for natural stones and gather them
- Collects certain rocks and minerals
- Collect fossils, minerals, or gemstones

Historical Background and Development of Rockhounding

Before the development of technology, rockhounding was a common pastime. It was first widely recognized in the 1930s. People roamed around the desert or mountains. They often picked up stones like jasper, petrified wood, and agate. This was common among native Americans and amateur geologists.

However, a new era began during the Great Depression, when rock collecting became an even bigger deal. Due to the high unemployment rate, many folks scoured fields, canyons, and quarries for valuable stones that they could sell for a little extra cash. This resulted in the establishment of rock shops along the roadside in an attempt to draw tourists' attention to their discoveries.

There are numerous reasons why people are interested in rockhounding right now. Some people love the added difficulty of a hiking trip searching for rocks, while others want a hands-on experience because of their interest in geology and local history. There are also jewelry makers looking for that one stone that will complete their collection. It doesn't matter what motivates you to go rockhounding; you'll quickly learn that the experience is satisfying on many levels.

Benefits of Rockhounding

Since rocks and minerals can be found everywhere, rockhounding can be done just about anywhere. Considering the exploratory nature of rockhounding, here are some of its advantages:

- It allows you to investigate the formation of crystals and minerals, which can lead to learning more about the subject.
- Rockhounds can obtain diverse rocks and minerals that will amaze the rockhounding community.
- You will gain a better understanding of the various components that comprise the planet. Learning about geology and the natural world will also increase your knowledge and appreciation of the earth and how it works.
- Hiking and exploring different parts of nature are two of the best ways to get some exercise, and rockhounding provides both. =
- One of the best aspects of rock collecting is that it can help you feel less stressed and more relaxed. When you find a great specimen, you feel a great sense of accomplishment.
- It leads to positive social interactions. This is a great way to meet new people and connect with them. Many rockhounding enthusiasts belong to the same clubs or social circles, sharing common interests and knowledge.

- Financial gain is another benefit of this activity because precious stones have a monetary value. As a result, many professional rock hunters make a living by selling the rocks they find to tourists and shops.
- Hunting for rocks and minerals stimulates the mind because it requires a certain level of expertise and knowledge. When you set out to learn about different rocks, minerals, and their geological formation, you keep your brain active and engaged. This stimulation aids in the prevention of age-related cognitive decline.
- It gives you a sense of responsibility. Rockhounding's aims are not just to collect shiny rocks and place them in a jar. It involves cleaning the rock you spent time hunting for, storing it in a safe place, and ensuring that it remains intact. As a result, you develop a sense of responsibility and ownership over your possessions.

Perks of Rockhounding

The following are some added perks of rockhounding:

- **No prior experience is required:** You don't need a degree or experience to pick up rocks from the ground, and you don't need any training to become a rockhound. You only need basic knowledge, get your tools, go outside, and start digging.
- **It is all around you:** You don't have to travel far to become a rockhound. Many rock species you were unaware existed just outside your house or on the road leading to your home.
- **Quality time spent in nature:** This is a two-for-one offer. You get to spend time in nature while looking for a rock or mineral specimen.
- **Low-budget hobby:** Rockhounding is a low-budget hobby. Like any other hobby, rockhounding can be as cheap or expensive as you want. It has taken some people worldwide in search of rocks, while others stay close to home.
- **Getting outside:** One of the most enjoyable aspects of rockhounding is that it gets you and your family outside. It allows you to get fresh air and spend quality time outside.

Getting Started with Rockhounding

Here are some helpful tips to consider as you plan your rockhounding trip.

What Are You Looking For?

What kinds of minerals, fossils, or stones are you looking for? Before you go hunting, do some research on the minerals you want, their gemological information, history, properties, and where you can find them.

Are They Available in Your Area?

You must first know your area to determine if the types of minerals or rocks you are after are available. This is where the internet comes in.

If you're curious about rocks, minerals, and gemstones, you may want to check out websites or social media pages belonging to agencies in your state or nearby areas. These sources can provide you with more information and tips about rockhounding.

As you browse the search query results, remember the following things.

- Private lands are only accessible if you have permission from the owners.
- Beginners may enjoy visiting dig sites and paid mines, as these places are likely to have more predictable and familiar rocks and minerals.

Is the Area Beginner-Friendly?

It's also helpful to research which areas are beginner-friendly, with paid sites and mines being good options. This way, you can explore new territory with guidance from those familiar with the land.

Rock and Mineral Clubs

Connecting with local rock and minerals clubs is the best way to access your area's quality and valuable rockhounding information. You'll also get to meet like-minded people who share the same hobby and are just as passionate as you.

As a beginner connecting with the local club near you, you'll likely meet an experienced member who will take you under their wing and teach you all they know. Also, you're more likely to learn about group rockhounding trips you can participate in.

When you join a club, you gain access to a wealth of information you might not have had otherwise, like reprints of classic works or copies of rare books that are unfortunately no longer in print but still in the hands of a member. You can even stumble upon interesting materials that reveal the geology of your location.

Being in a local rock club offers you the opportunity to gain experience using rockhounding equipment from others who are ahead of you in their usage. You can even get a fair deal on purchasing such equipment from a club member and be allowed to borrow equipment from the club.

You can Google the local rock and minerals clubs in your location. Go through the time allotted for the meeting and the location. Also, contact the head representatives of the clubs to confirm their meeting structure and time.

Useful Rockhounding Tips

Time Management

As a beginner, understanding how to manage your time is as important as the rockhounding activity itself. Some rock hunters set alarms to keep them in check regularly. When they have spent a long time at one spot, the alarm serves as a reminder to move on to the next spot, especially if the first spot has produced no results. The purpose of setting the alarm is to assist you in keeping track of time so that you do not spend more time than was initially planned.

Route Knowledge and Field Research

The first thing you should do when starting a rockhounding activity is research. Look at your environment and consider the rocks and minerals present there and the best possible route to get to it. You will reduce your chances of going down the wrong path when you understand what is around you, where to get what you're after, and how to use the tools you have.

Using the internet, you can properly investigate and unravel the path you need to take to discover the rocks or minerals you seek.

Books and Magazines

Your local library contains precious knowledge concerning the geology of your area, allowing you to become astute in your newfound passion for rocks. Your library card can also grant you access to additional online resources like academic articles that can guide you on your way.

If you cannot find the materials you are looking for, do not hesitate to ask the librarians for assistance. They will gladly assist you by pointing you in the right direction.

Local bookstores are the best places to look for anything in your area because they are more likely to stock local titles than large corporate bookstores. Local bookstores can assist you by locating or helping you to purchase the book of your choice if it is not currently in stock.

Specialized bookstores can be a great resource for acquiring hard-to-find books containing valuable information.

State Natural Resources Agencies

In the majority of states, there is a mining and geology department. You can be sure to find the information you need for the minerals, rocks, fossils, or diamonds you're looking for.

Some of these agencies may not have a physical location, but they will definitely have websites you can access.

Museums

Numerous countries have museums dedicated to natural history and geology, offering educational programs alongside their exhibitions.

Local Universities

Nearby universities can also offer opportunities to explore departments like geology, mineral engineering, and paleontology. You will undoubtedly find the necessary information to support your rockhounding hobby.

Rock Shops

Visit shops with high-quality jewels, minerals, or rocks to learn more about your interests.

Rock shop employees are knowledgeable and can provide you with information on local rock clubs and rockhounding locations. Tourist-friendly shops often employ staff who are well-versed in local geology and can help you find the perfect rock for your collection.

Rocks, Gems, and Minerals Shows

Even though the entrance fees to these rock shows are quite low, you get to experience a wide range of rocks, gems, and mineral specimens.

Rockhounding Backpack

The right backpack is important if you want to enjoy rockhounding activities. You must consider durability, comfort, and the right size when looking for one. Other factors to consider include the ability to adjust the straps, having enough pockets and compartments to store your items, and ensuring sufficient space to hold all your gear.

Only use the backpack with the following qualities for rockhounding.

Comfort

Because you will be carrying your tools and specimens for hours, ensure that your backpack fits properly and is designed for comfort. Also, make sure that it has adjustable straps. A bag with straps for the shoulders and chest can offer enhanced comfort by evenly distributing its weight.

Durable and Waterproof

Seeing how you might be packing pointy tools or sharp rocks, ensure your backpack is durable and tear-resistant. Also, it should be waterproof just in case it rains when you're out and about.

Space and Compartments for Your Gear

The amount of time you intend to spend in the field should determine the size of the backpack you choose. A thirty-liter backpack should be enough for a day. If you are staying longer, go for a 40 to 50-liter backpack. You'll need your clothing, tent, and sleeping bag to fit inside; anything less than that might not be sufficient.

So, consider how often you'll be in the field and opt for a backpack that can hold your food, specimens, safety equipment, and drinking water.

Consider using backpacks with external pockets that are easily accessible. You don't have to stop to get your gear because you can do it on the go with this.

What Needs to Fit in Your Rockhounding Backpack

To make enough room for your specimens, limit your gear to 10 pounds. Your rockhounding style determines the equipment you will take with you. If you just stay for a day, you will need the following essentials:

- Essential items like a magnet, rock hammer, wedges, toothbrush, chisel, foldable shovel, small broom or paintbrush, and a hand trowel
- Cellphone. This will be your alarm, compass, and camera
- Bear repellant spray
- Insect repellant
- Flashlight
- A bottle of water for washing rocks.

- Paper towels and newspaper to wrap your specimens
- Hat and sunscreen
- Safety glasses
- Drinking water
- Work gloves
- Whistle
- First aid kits
- Ziplock bags for small rocks; use film containers or pill bottles.
- Waterproof poncho
- Pry bar
- Sieve or colander

What to Avoid Carrying

When spending several hours investigating rocks and minerals in the field, it's important to invest in a high-quality backpack. A rucksack or old-school backpack is not recommended as they are not designed for these activities and can cause more harm than good. Instead, opt for a comfortable and sturdy backpack specifically designed for outdoor activities.

Rockhounding is a fun activity that anyone can enjoy. If you're not convinced, consider attending the Tucson Gem and Mineral Show, which attracts visitors from all over the world each year. To start rock hunting, you only need to step outside your house and explore the outdoors. With the right backpack and a love for adventure, anyone can enjoy the thrill of discovering new rocks and minerals.

Chapter 3: Equipment and Safety Tips

Embarking on the journey of discovering and collecting rocks and minerals is both thrilling and fascinating. This pursuit has captured the interest of many enthusiasts, and embracing this passion is something no one will fault you for. While rockhounding shares the excitement of outdoor sports, it also comes with its unique set of risks and hazards. This is why it is vital to be equipped with the appropriate gear and knowledge.

The intention here is not to deter or overwhelm you but to empower you with the necessary information, ensuring you are well-informed and can fully immerse yourself in this delightful hobby. This chapter aims to provide comprehensive guidance on having a secure and enjoyable rockhounding experience, along with essential safety measures.

You will uncover the must-have rockhounding equipment for a fruitful venture into nature, safety, and self-defense strategies to help you sidestep potential dangers. Additionally, you will acquire a wealth of knowledge for an exceptional rockhounding experience, ranging from fundamental rock and gemstone identification tools to recommendations on assembling your first aid kit.

Basic Rockhounding Equipment and Tools

Before rock hunting, you must ensure you're as prepared as possible. Whether you're a novice or a seasoned rockhound, these items are essential for collecting specimens and ensuring your safety. You'll have a great time if you have the right tools and know the proper safety precautions.

Starting with the fundamentals: what equipment do you need for rockhounding?

1. Rock Hammer

A rock hammer is an essential tool for rockhounding.'

The first item on your list should be a good rock hammer, which breaks rocks into more manageable pieces. This is an essential tool for rockhounding because it allows you to easily break apart rocks to reveal hidden treasures without damaging the specimens. If you're just starting, you need to get one that fits you and your plans for rockhounding. Here are some of the considerations you need to make:

- **Size and weight:** The weight of a good rock hammer is among its most important characteristics. A heavier hammer can deliver a more powerful blow and break through harder rocks, but it is also more tiring to use for long periods. A lighter hammer, on the other hand, can be easier to use but may not be as effective on harder rocks. As a result, it's important to choose a hammer with a weight that feels right for you.

- **The type of hammerhead:** The hammer's tip is also important. It should be sharp and strong enough to pierce rocks without bending or breaking. A flat-tipped hammer is useful for chiseling

or cracking open larger rocks. In contrast, a pointed tip is better for precision work, like cracking open smaller rocks.
- **The handle:** This is another crucial component of a quality rock hammer. The handle should be easy to hold and provide good control. The material can also influence how it feels in your hand. For example, a rubber or plastic handle can be more comfortable than a wooden handle, especially if you use it for extended periods.

Selecting the Right Rock Hammer

When choosing a rock hammer, there are a few factors to consider.

- You should consider what kind of rockhounding you want to do. This will influence your choice. A solid hammer, one not as heavy as the ones you would need to collect specimens like hard rocks or minerals, is necessary if you want to focus primarily on collecting fossils. This is because you only need something lightweight and sturdy to collect fossils.
- Should you choose affordability over effectiveness? While selecting a hammer model with a lower price can be tempting, you should choose a high-quality one because it is more effective, lasts longer, and will not wear off in the long run.
- What about brand reputation? You should consider what others have said about the brands you're thinking of. A hammer from a well-known and respected brand could cost more, but it will most likely be of higher quality and come with a warranty.

A good rock hammer can mean the difference between a successful and frustrating day of rockhounding. As an aspiring rockhound or someone with some experience, you must understand the significance of having the right rock hammer. The right rock hammer will allow you to access difficult-to-reach areas like crevices and outcrops. A good rock hammer is also long-lasting and comfortable; if your hands and wrists start to hurt after a few uses, this is not the hammer for you!

Using a rock hammer safely and effectively is essential for your health and productivity. Hold it with both hands and swing it down in a controlled motion, using your arms and shoulders for power. Swinging with your wrists can result in strain and injury.

2. Apparel

You will also need a good pair of hiking boots. Because you'll be walking on uneven terrain, they must be sturdy, comfortable, and provide good ankle support. You'll also need a high-quality backpack to transport your gear, snacks, and water. Wear a hat, sunglasses, and sunscreen to protect yourself from the sun's harmful rays.

Hiking boots can help you navigate difficult terrain.[5]

3. Gear for Carrying Tools, Identifying Specimens, and Navigation

When rockhounding, you should always bring the proper gear, which includes more than just your hammer. These are the basics:

- **Backpack:** A sturdy backpack is essential for carrying all your rockhounding equipment and tools. It should be comfortable to carry and have enough space for your equipment, snacks, and water when you get hungry or tired.

A sturdy backpack will help you carry your tools.[6]

- **Gloves:** A pair of gloves will come in handy when rockhounding. When working with rocks and minerals, gloves protect your hands from sharp rock edges, debris, and other hazards.

Gloves and eye protection are necessary for rockhounding.[7]

- **Eye protection**: Safety glasses or goggles are important to protect your eyes from flying rock fragments or other debris.
- **Chisel:** A chisel is useful for prying rocks loose from their surroundings, mainly used to extract wedged rocks. It is also used to delicately chip away at rock surfaces to reveal hidden mineral specimens or fossils.

Chisels and sledgehammers can help you break up large rocks.[8]

- **Sledgehammer:** Sledgehammers are larger, heavier hammers that break up large rocks or boulders. It is typically used in more difficult rockhounding locations with larger rocks.
- **Prybar:** A pry bar is also used to extract rocks that have become wedged. It is a long, thin metal bar that pries loose rocks and boulders from the ground. It is especially useful for moving larger rocks too large to move by hand or with a chisel.
- **Water bottle:** As a rockhound, you do not want to overlook this. It is vital to stay hydrated during any outdoor activity, especially in hot weather. Every rockhound should have a refillable water bottle.
- **GPS:** When rockhounding, it's vital to know where you're going at all times, especially in remote areas.

A GPS can help you navigate your trail.[9]

- **Field guides:** Field guides are excellent for identifying various rocks, minerals, and fossils you might encounter on your rockhounding excursions.
- **Hand lens:** A hand lens or magnifying glass is useful for closely inspecting small rocks and minerals. It can also assist you in identifying minerals or fossils that are difficult to identify with the eyes.

A hand lens can help you inspect small rocks and minerals.[10]

- **A handheld brush and heavy-duty trowel**: The brush will remove dirt from specimens before placing them in your bag, allowing you to get a better look at them. The heavy-duty trowel is for digging and sifting.
- **Streak *plate***: This is a small piece of unglazed porcelain or ceramic called a streak plate used to examine the color of a mineral's streak. When a mineral is rubbed on the surface of the plate, it leaves behind a powder. This powder is an essential aspect of inspecting the color of the mineral's streak.

A streak plate can help you inspect the color of a mineral.[11]

- **Hardness tester**: A *Mohs hardness scale* can determine how hard a mineral is compared to other minerals. This can also be done by scratching the mineral with other series of minerals.

- **UV lamp:** Many minerals can give off a visible glow when exposed to UV light. This will allow you to identify them.
- **Magnet:** Magnets can be used to find magnetic minerals like magnetite that might be hiding in geological samples. If a rock or soil sticks to a magnet, it probably has magnetic minerals.

Magnets can help you find minerals like magnetite.[12]

- **Maps:** Maps are among the most important rockhounding tools because they show where different kinds of rocks, minerals, and gemstones can be found. Some of the maps you need are topographical maps, geologic maps, and mining claim maps. Each one has its level of complexity and detail, which is why they are so important for a successful rockhounding trip.

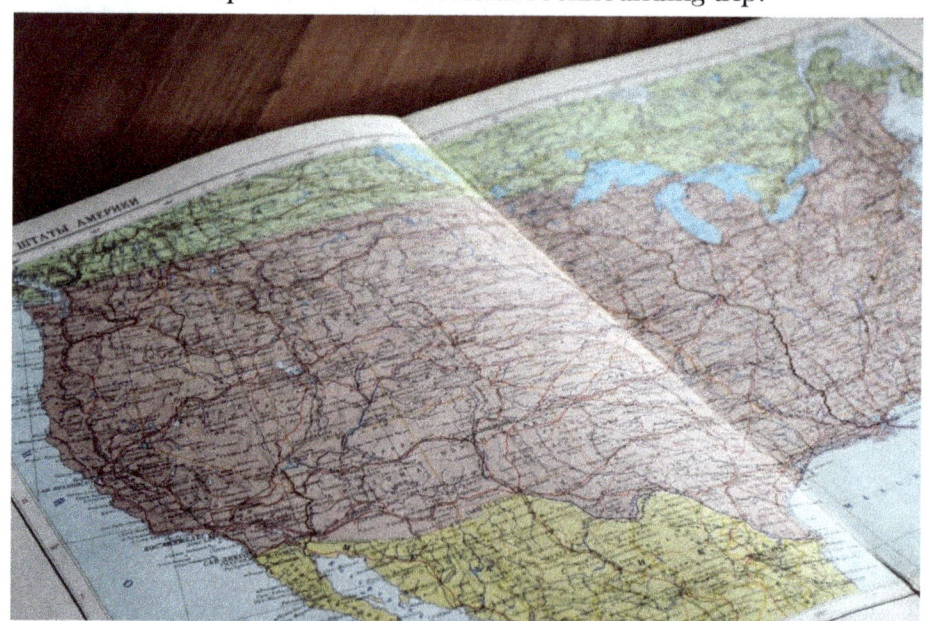

Maps can show where different rocks and minerals are.[13]

- **Compass:** A compass is a simple but very useful tool for rockhounding. With one, you can figure out where you are going and where you are in the landscape around you. This makes it easier to find specific rock formations and mineral deposits.

A compass will help you recognize which direction you should go.[14]

- **Altimeter:** This measures your height above sea level, which can be helpful when exploring mountainous areas. That allows you to find your way to specific heights where you might find certain rocks or minerals.

Binoculars will help you get a closer look at rock formations.[15]

- **Binoculars:** Binoculars are another useful tool for rockhounding because they let you get a closer look at interesting rock formations, cliffs, and other things. They can help you find interesting places and learn more about them, whether trying to get through rough terrain or find hidden treasures.

- **Headlamp:** A headlamp is also an important tool for getting around when it's dark. It allows you to see what's around you and avoid obstacles at night or when there is insufficient light.

Headlamps will help you get around when it's dark.[16]

Safety Tips for Rockhound

Although rock hunting can be a fascinating and rewarding hobby, you should always put your health and safety ahead of your enthusiasm. Here are a few things to keep in mind before you start:

1. Research the Area

Researching the area will give you a better idea of what you may find.[17]

Before you go rockhounding, do some research on the area. Before stepping outside, figure out what kind of specimens you will collect. Research the location you intend to explore; this will ensure you have the necessary equipment when the time comes. Familiarizing yourself with the area, potential hazards, and special regulations will be a good way to prepare for a successful and safe journey.

2. The Right Equipment

You should wear sturdy, closed-toe shoes and a hat if it gets too hot or cold. Sunscreen, hand warmers, flashlights, snacks, and plenty of water are also recommended. Don't forget to bring gloves for handling sharp rocks or tools.

3. Let Someone Know

Ensure someone knows where you're going and when they should expect you to return. If something goes wrong while you're out rockhounding, they'll know where to look for you.

4. Take Someone Along

Whether you're experienced or not, it is preferable to go on such trips with someone. Being in a group of at least two people is always preferable. If you must travel alone, leave a message with someone, and let them know where you'll be, so they can raise the alarm if they don't hear from you in a while. Having someone else accompany you on the trip can ensure your safety and provide an extra pair of hands to make the process go more smoothly. Also, the extra company can make things even more enjoyable.

5. Be Prepared

Prepare for unpredictable weather conditions and possible wildlife encounters. Learn how to assess the demeanor of various wildlife so you know how to respond safely if you encounter anything dangerous. Always keep a first-aid kit on hand.

6. Research Any Hazards in the Area

Preparation is the cornerstone of a safe and successful rockhounding trip. By planning ahead and gathering information, you can avoid potential hazards and enjoy a more rewarding experience. Here are some key aspects to consider when preparing for a rockhounding adventure:

- **Weather Warnings and Natural Hazards**: Before setting out, it is crucial to check local weather forecasts and be aware of any weather warnings or natural hazards in the area. This can include

storms, floods, landslides, or extreme temperatures. By staying informed, you can make informed decisions about whether it's safe to proceed or if you should postpone your trip.
- **Terrain and Accessibility:** Research the terrain and accessibility of your intended rockhounding location. Some sites may require hiking or climbing, while others may be more easily accessible by vehicle. Knowing what to expect can help you plan accordingly and ensure that you have the appropriate gear, such as sturdy footwear, walking sticks, or climbing equipment.
- **Water and Hydration:** When rockhounding, particularly in arid environments like the desert, it is essential to stay hydrated. Be aware of the signs and symptoms of dehydration, which can include thirst, dizziness, confusion, and dark-colored urine. To prevent dehydration, drink plenty of water before and during your trip, and avoid alcohol and caffeine.
- **Heat Exhaustion:** In hot environments, heat exhaustion is a significant concern. Symptoms may include heavy sweating, rapid pulse, dizziness, nausea, and headache. Wear lightweight, breathable clothing to prevent heat exhaustion, apply sunscreen, and take breaks in shaded areas when possible. If you suspect heat exhaustion, rest in a cool place and drink water or sports drinks to replenish electrolytes.

Special Safety Equipment and First Aid Kits

While rockhounding, safety is of the utmost importance, and certain pieces of equipment can assist you in staying safe. First, research the area you're visiting for any potential hazards, like wild animals or a history of unstable ground. If you come across any unexpected hazards, turn around.

These things will keep you safe while rockhounding:
- **A first aid kit:** Accidents can happen when you're out in the field, so always keep a basic first aid kit at hand. Bandages, antiseptics, and pain relievers should all be included. It is best to be prepared for minor mishaps or injuries while working at the collection site.

A first aid kit is necessary when rockhounding.[18]

- **A whistle:** If you get into trouble, a whistle can alert others nearby, who can then come to your aid; make sure it's loud enough for rescuers to hear from a long distance away.

A whistle can alert others to your location if you need help.[19]

- **A small toolkit:** Try and have some basic tools on hand, like a knife or small saw for cutting branches off trees or other plants that obstruct access to areas where rocks can be found.

- **Appropriate clothing and shoes:** Ensure your gear is appropriate for the environment. For example, if you're going to a place with a lot of sand or mud, closed-toe sandals might not be the best choice; instead, go with work boots that provide better protection and grip.

Preparing for Potentially Dangerous Encounters

Safety must always be a top priority when embarking on a rockhounding adventure. Recognizing that you are sharing the wilderness with potentially dangerous wildlife is essential. To best prepare yourself, thoroughly research the area you plan to explore and gather as much information as possible.

Equipping yourself with proper protective gear and specialized tools, such as bear mace if needed, is crucial for ensuring safety. Be prepared for any encounters with potentially hazardous wildlife. Stay vigilant, heed posted signs regarding protected species or dangers in the area, and have an emergency exit strategy in place if necessary.

While exploring, you may encounter snakes, bears, or other animals. Awareness of your surroundings and understanding how to react when encountering wildlife is critical. Avoid startling animals by making noise while walking, alerting them to your presence. If you encounter a bear or another dangerous animal, remain calm and slowly back away, but never turn your back on it.

Should an animal display aggression or threaten your safety, be prepared to flee; never approach a wild animal, regardless of how docile it appears. Finally, respect the environment by adhering to the Leave No Trace principles. Refrain from disturbing plants or animals; leave no litter or debris behind. Preserve the area in its original state, allowing future rockhounds to enjoy it.

Rockhounding offers an enthralling experience of exploration and discovery, but it is essential to remain aware of the potential dangers and risks involved. Utilize proper equipment and safety measures while staying informed on local activities and regulations. If you venture out alone, always inform someone of your plans and expected return time.

Equip yourself with essential rockhounding and specimen-gathering tools to safely and effectively collect rocks, minerals, and fossils from various locations. Always be prepared and exercise caution before setting out.

Chapter 4: Gemstones

As you step into the world of gemstones, you will find yourself in a realm of natural beauty and wonder that has captivated people for centuries - from the sparkling diamonds that have ignited wars and fueled dreams to the velvety emeralds that seem to glow from within or the regal sapphires having adorned the crowns of kings and queens for centuries! The world of gemstones is a glimpse into a mysterious realm filled with dazzling beauty and natural wonder. This chapter will give you a comprehensive look into the world of gemstones; you will learn about their various types, characteristics, and classifications. You'll be amazed at the stories each gemstone holds - from the mystical properties of amethyst to the rich cultural significance of jade. So, prepare yourself to be transported into a world of unparalleled beauty and wonder - a world that is sure to leave you spellbound and inspired!

The World of Gemstones

At its most basic level, a gemstone is a naturally occurring mineral or organic substance valued for its beauty, rarity, and durability. These precious stones are often cut and polished to bring out their natural luster and brilliance and can be found in various colors, shapes, and sizes.

From a scientific perspective, gemstones are formed deep within the Earth's crust through a process of crystallization. This occurs when molten rock or magma cools and solidifies over a long period, allowing the atoms within it to arrange themselves into highly ordered crystal structures. This process creates a wide range of minerals - some are highly prized for their beauty and rarity.

The properties of each gemstone depend on various factors, including its chemical composition, crystal structure, and the conditions under which it was formed. For example, diamonds are made up of carbon atoms arranged in a highly symmetrical crystalline structure, which gives them their characteristic hardness and transparency. In contrast, opals are made up of silica spheres that diffract light to produce a range of colors, creating a unique iridescence.

Gemstones are also highly valued for their cultural, historical, and symbolic significance. Throughout history, they have been used for everything from trade to religious artifacts and healing practices. They have been associated with everything from love and passion to strength and courage and continue to hold a special place in the hearts and minds of people all over the world.

Gemstones can be classified into two categories – precious and semi-precious. Precious gemstones, like the shimmering diamond, radiant ruby, velvety sapphire, and lush green emerald, are revered for their rarity and exceptional quality. These stones have been prized for centuries by royalty, artists, and collectors alike. On the other hand, semi-precious gemstones are just as captivating, each possessing unique properties, colors, and personalities. From the soothing amethyst to the sunny citrine, the fiery garnet to the enchanting peridot, and the dazzling topaz, each gemstone has its own special charm that appeals to the senses and the soul. Whether precious or semi-precious, gemstones are a rare and precious gift from nature that reminds you of the world's beauty, magic, and wonder.

Classification of Gemstones

Gemstones are classified based on various criteria, including chemical composition, crystal structure, and optical properties. The most common classification system used for gemstones is the mineral species system, which groups them by chemical composition. This system divides gemstones into groups based on their primary chemical element, such as corundum for aluminum oxide and beryl for beryllium aluminum cyclosilicate. Another important classification system is based on the crystal structure of gemstones. This system divides gemstones into groups based on their arrangements of atoms and molecules, like the tetrahedral structure of diamond or the trigonal structure of quartz.

Additionally, gemstones are classified based on their optical properties, such as refractive index, luster, and dispersion. This classification system is used to distinguish gemstones based on how they interact with light, like the sparkling fire of a diamond or the bright play of color in opal. Understanding the classification of gemstones is essential for evaluating their quality, rarity, and value.

Chemical Composition

Gemstones can be classified in many ways, one of which is based on their chemical composition. This categorization is based on the minerals' chemical formula and allows gemologists to identify and classify gemstones. These include oxides, silicates, halides, carbonates, and phosphates.

1. Silicates

This group includes gemstones like quartz, garnet, and tourmaline. Silicates are composed of silicon and oxygen atoms, often with additional elements such as aluminum, iron, or magnesium. They are abundant in the Earth's crust and form under a wide range of conditions, which gives rise to a great variety of silicate gemstones. Other examples include aquamarine, emerald, garnet, ruby, sapphire, topaz, turquoise, and zircon.

2. Carbonates

The carbonate group includes gems like calcite, dolomite, and malachite. These minerals are composed of carbonate ions (CO_3) combined with other elements such as calcium, magnesium, or copper. They are typically found in sedimentary rocks and can form through the interaction of carbon dioxide-rich fluids with rocks or organic matter.

3. Oxides

The oxide group includes some of the most prized gemstones, like ruby, sapphire, and diamond. Oxides are composed of oxygen combined with a metal element, such as aluminum, titanium, or chromium. They are formed under high-pressure, high-temperature conditions and are often associated with igneous or metamorphic rocks.

4. Sulfates

The sulfate group includes minerals such as gypsum and barite. These minerals are composed of sulfate ions (SO_4) combined with other elements such as calcium, strontium, or lead. They typically form in evaporite deposits or hydrothermal veins and are often associated with sedimentary rocks.

5. Halides

The halide group includes minerals like fluorite and halite. These minerals are composed of halide ions (such as F- or Cl-) combined with other elements, such as calcium or sodium. They can form through the evaporation of seawater or from hydrothermal fluids.

6. Phosphates

The phosphate group includes gems such as apatite and turquoise. These minerals are composed of phosphate ions combined with other elements such as calcium, fluorine, or copper. They are typically found in pegmatites, hydrothermal veins, or sedimentary rocks.

Crystal Structure

Gemstones can also be classified based on their crystal structure. The crystal structure of a gemstone refers to the arrangement of atoms and molecules within the gemstone. There are six main structures: cubic, hexagonal, trigonal, orthorhombic, monoclinic, and triclinic.

1. Cubic

Gemstones with a cubic structure are symmetrical, with all three axes intersecting at right angles. The length of each axis is equal. As a result, these gemstones seem to be very proportionate geometrically. A diamond is a common gemstone that has a cubic structure. Others include spinel and garnets.

2. Hexagonal

Gemstones with a hexagonal crystal structure have a six-sided prism shape with six angles that measure 120 degrees. These include aquamarine, emerald, and ruby.

3. Trigonal

Gemstones with a trigonal crystal structure have a three-sided prism shape with three angles that measure 60 degrees and one angle that measures 120 degrees. For instance, amethyst, citrine, and quartz.

4. Orthorhombic

Gemstones with an orthorhombic crystal structure have a rectangular prism shape with three axes of unequal length that intersect at right angles. Examples of gemstones with this structure include topaz, peridot, and zircon.

5. Monoclinic

Gemstones with a monoclinic crystal structure have a prism shape with three axes of unequal length, two of which intersect at an oblique angle. Examples of gemstones with this structure include moonstone, orthoclase, and jadeite.

6. Triclinic

Gemstones with a triclinic crystal structure have an asymmetrical shape with three axes of unequal length that intersect at oblique angles. Examples of gemstones with a triclinic structure include labradorite, turquoise, and kyanite.

Gemstone Characteristics

Gemstones possess unique characteristics that set them apart from other minerals. Their beauty is measured by a combination of factors such as color, clarity, cut, and carat weight. Each gemstone's chemical composition and crystal structure determine its physical and optical properties. Understanding these properties is crucial in identifying and valuing gemstones.

1. Diamond

Diamonds are highly sought after.[30]

Diamonds, one of the most highly sought-after gemstones, are prized for their brilliance, durability, and rarity. The four C's - Color, Clarity, Cut, and Carat Weight - are used to determine the quality and value of a diamond. As you may know, colorless diamonds are considered the most precious, while other colors are somewhat valued. The clarity of a gemstone is basically the absence of any external or internal blemish or impurities in its structure. The higher the clarity, the more valuable a diamond is. The cut of a diamond is essential to its brilliance and determines its ability to reflect light. A diamond's carat weight, or size, also plays a significant role in its value.

Chemically speaking, the composition of diamonds is primarily carbon atoms in a lattice system. This unique arrangement of atoms gives diamonds their strength and luster. As mentioned, diamonds have a cubic crystal structure, with a Mohs hardness rating of 10, which is the highest rating, making diamonds the hardest gemstone on earth.

There are various types of diamonds, including natural, synthetic, and treated diamonds. Natural diamonds are formed deep beneath the earth's surface over millions of years, while synthetic diamonds are created in a lab under high pressure and high-temperature conditions. Diamonds that have been somewhat worked upon to improve their clarity, cut, or color are called treated diamonds.

Diamonds are sourced from various locations worldwide, with some of the most famous diamond mines in South Africa, Russia, Canada, and Australia. The history and cultural significance of diamonds and their rarity and beauty have made them one of the most treasured gemstones throughout history.

2. Ruby

Rubies are known for their color.[21]

Rubies are known for their striking red color, which ranges from a vivid pinkish-red to a deep blood red. The color is caused by the presence of chromium, which is also responsible for the gem's fluorescence. Clarity is an important factor in determining the value of a ruby, with fewer inclusions and blemishes indicating a higher quality stone. The cut of the ruby can also greatly affect its value, with a well-cut gemstone exhibiting optimal light reflection and maximizing the intensity of the stone's color. Carat weight is another important factor, as larger rubies are rarer and more valuable.

Chemically, rubies are composed of aluminum oxide with trace amounts of other elements. They have a hexagonal crystal structure and are commonly found in metamorphic rocks such as marbles and schists. Rubies are often sourced from Myanmar, Thailand, Sri Lanka, and other parts of Asia. Synthetic rubies are also available, often used in jewelry as a more affordable alternative to natural stones. Additionally, heat treatment is commonly used to enhance the color and clarity of rubies.

Overall, rubies' unique characteristics and rarity make them a highly sought-after gemstone, prized for their vivid color and brilliance.

3. Sapphire

Sapphires can come in colors such as blue, pink, yellow, and green.[22]

Sapphires are known for their rich and deep blue color, but they also come in various colors, including pink, yellow, and green. Sapphires mostly come with naturally occurring inclusions and impurities, which does reduce their clarity a little. However, some precious sapphire stones have a lower percentage of imperfections. The cut of a sapphire plays a crucial role in how well it reflects light and showcases its color. Regarding carat weight, larger sapphires are rarer and more sought after, making them more valuable.

Sapphires are composed of the mineral corundum, which has a trigonal crystal structure. The chemical composition of sapphires includes aluminum and oxygen, with traces of iron, titanium, and chromium. Natural sapphires are found in various parts of the world, including Australia, Sri Lanka, and Madagascar. They can also be found in Montana, United States, known for its unique sapphires.

Sapphires can be classified into several types based on their color and origin. Blue sapphires are the most well-known and are found in many parts of the world, while pink sapphires are rarer and often come from Madagascar and Sri Lanka. Yellow sapphires are also relatively rare and are found in a few countries, including Sri Lanka and Tanzania. Other types include star sapphires, which have a unique star-shaped pattern, and padparadscha sapphires, which have a pink-orange color and are highly valued for their rarity.

4. Emerald

Emeralds can range from light green to dark green.[28]

Emeralds are breathtaking gemstones that can captivate anyone with their stunning green color. The color of an emerald is the most important characteristic, and it can range from a light, almost translucent green to a deep, dark green that appears almost black. Clarity is also a significant factor in determining the value of an emerald, as well as its cut and carat weight. Emeralds are composed of many different chemical elements but primarily have traces of iron, chromium, and vanadium. They have a hexagonal structure, which gives them a beautiful geometry.

There are various types and sources of emeralds, with the most sought-after coming from Colombia, Zambia, and Brazil. Colombian emeralds are known for their exceptional color and clarity, while Zambian emeralds are admired for their deep green hue. Brazilian emeralds are also well-known for their color but tend to have more inclusions than the Colombian or Zambian variety. Despite their rarity, emeralds have been popular for centuries and remain a favorite gemstone for many jewelry enthusiasts.

5. Amethyst

Amethyst is a stunning purple gemstone.[24]

Amethyst is a stunning purple gemstone that has captivated people's hearts for centuries. Its unique color is a result of trace amounts of iron and aluminum in its chemical composition. The crystal structure of amethyst is made up of silicon dioxide, which forms six-sided prisms with pointed ends.

Amethyst is widely known to be a purple gemstone, ranging from a light lavender tone to shades of deep purple. The most valuable specimens have a rich, saturated color with red and blue flashes. Clarity is also an important characteristic of amethyst, as it should have few visible inclusions or blemishes. Cut is also crucial for maximizing the gemstone's beauty and minimizing flaws. Carat weight is another factor to consider when evaluating amethyst. Larger specimens are rarer and more valuable, but smaller stones can still be quite beautiful.

Amethyst gemstones are mined in many places, including Uruguay, Brazil, and Zambia. Some of the most sought-after specimens are from Siberia, where the deep purple color is particularly intense. In addition to natural amethyst, synthetic versions are produced in laboratories. However, natural amethysts are still highly valued for their rarity and beauty.

6. Garnet

Garnet has a rich history.[25]

Garnet is a magnificent gemstone with a rich history and exceptional qualities. This gemstone is found in various colors, from deep shades of red to shades of green, orange, and purple. Clarity is an important factor in determining the value of garnet, with the finest specimens being transparent or nearly so. Cut can greatly affect the beauty and brilliance of the stone and can vary from faceted to cabochon.

Garnet is a complex mineral with a chemical composition that can vary depending on the specific type. It typically has a crystalline structure, with six main types of garnet distinguished by their crystal structure. Almandine garnet is one of the most common and is known for its deep red color. The pyrope garnet is another famous variety with a rich, dark red hue. Other types include spessartine, grossular, andradite, and uvarovite.

Garnet gemstones are found in the United States, India, Madagascar, and Brazil. It has been used in jewelry for thousands of years, with ancient Egyptians and Greeks valuing the stone for its beauty and perceived protective properties. Today, garnet continues to be a popular choice for fine jewelry, and its enduring appeal is a testament to its timeless beauty and exceptional characteristics.

7. Topaz

Topaz comes in a wide variety of colors.[26]

Topaz is a beautiful gemstone that comes in a variety of colors, from colorless to yellow, pink, blue, and more. The clarity of topaz varies, with some stones being clear and others containing visible inclusions. The cut can significantly impact its appearance, with well-cut stones exhibiting maximum brilliance and fire. Carat weight is also important when selecting a topaz, as larger stones are generally more valuable.

Chemically, topaz is an aluminum silicate mineral that often forms in granitic rocks. Its crystal structure is orthorhombic, meaning it has three axes of different lengths intersecting at right angles. This crystal structure is responsible for the unique optical properties of topaz, such as its double refraction and pleochroism.

Topaz comes in several types, including imperial, blue, and white. Imperial topaz, also known as precious topaz, is the rarest and most sought-after variety, typically orange to reddish-orange. Blue topaz is a popular alternative to aquamarine, with sky blue and Swiss blue being the most common shades. White topaz is often used as a substitute for diamonds because of their similar appearance.

Topaz is found in many locations worldwide, including Brazil, Russia, Sri Lanka, Nigeria, and the United States. Some of the most famous topaz mines include the Ouro Preto mine in Brazil and the Katlang and Shigar Valley mines in Pakistan. Overall, topaz is a beautiful and versatile gemstone that can add a touch of elegance and sophistication to any piece of jewelry.

Gemstones have long been a source of fascination and wonder for humanity, with their exquisite colors, unique characteristics, and historical significance. From the timeless beauty of diamonds to the regal hues of amethysts, each gemstone has its own story to tell. While their value may vary, their allure remains constant. Whether you are a collector, a jewelry lover, or simply someone who appreciates natural wonders, the world of gemstones has something for everyone.

Chapter 5: Minerals and Crystals

As a rockhound, you already know there is nothing like the thrill of discovering a beautiful crystal or rare mineral specimen. While this may seem like just a fun hobby to some, to those who are truly passionate about rockhounding, it is a way of life. This chapter will take you through the intricacies of minerals and crystals. After reading it, you will be better equipped to locate and identify valuable specimens in the field.

Minerals vs. Crystals

Minerals naturally occur on the earth's surface, with a specific chemical composition and a defined crystal structure. This means they are made up of specific types and amounts of atoms arranged in a specific pattern that repeats throughout the crystal structure. Some common examples of minerals include quartz, feldspar, and mica. On the other hand, crystals are solids with a repeating, three-dimensional atomic arrangement that gives them a unique geometric shape. Crystals can be made up of minerals, metals, or other substances and can be found in various shapes and sizes. The repeating atomic structure of crystals gives them unique physical and optical properties, such as the ability to refract light.

A crystalline mineral is a mineral that has a well-defined, repeating atomic structure that forms a crystal. The atoms in a crystalline mineral are arranged in a specific pattern that repeats throughout the crystal, giving it a unique shape and physical properties. Non-crystalline minerals, such as volcanic glass, do not have a repeating atomic structure and do not form crystals.

Physical Properties of Minerals and Crystals

Understanding the physical properties of minerals and crystals is crucial for rockhounds as it will help you identify and distinguish different types of rocks and minerals. The following are the main physical properties of minerals and crystals that rockhounds should be aware of:

1. Color

The color of a mineral or crystal can be one of its most obvious and easily recognizable physical properties. However, color alone is not always a reliable indicator of a mineral's identity. The same mineral can appear in different colors depending on the presence of impurities or other factors. Additionally, some can have a range of colors, making identification based on color alone difficult. Despite these limitations, color can still be a useful tool for rockhounds. For example, certain minerals such as malachite and azurite are known for their distinctive green and blue colors, respectively.

2. Luster

The luster of a mineral, crystal, or gemstone refers to the way light reflects off its surface. Several common types of luster include metallic, vitreous (glassy), and pearly. Luster can be a helpful identification tool for rockhounds, particularly in combination with other physical properties such as color and hardness. For example, pyrite has a metallic luster distinct from quartz's vitreous luster.

3. Hardness

Hardness is a measure of a mineral's resistance to scratching. The Mohs hardness scale, which ranges from 1 (softest) to 10 (hardest), is commonly used to compare the hardness of different minerals. Knowing the hardness of a mineral can be useful in identifying it, as certain minerals are more likely to scratch or be scratched by others. For example, quartz has a hardness of 7 on the Mohs scale, which means it can scratch minerals with a lower hardness (such as calcite) but can be scratched by minerals with a higher hardness (such as topaz).

4. Cleavage and Fracture

Cleavage and fracture refer to how a mineral breaks when subjected to stress. This phenomenon usually occurs along the planes weak in the crystal structure, resulting in flat surfaces. On the other hand, fracture occurs when a mineral or crystal breaks irregularly, which results in uneven surfaces. Both cleavage and fracture can be useful identification tools for rockhounds. For example, the mineral muscovite has a perfect basal cleavage, which means it breaks into thin, flat sheets.

5. Specific Gravity

This is a measure of a mineral or crystal's density compared to water's density. Knowing the specific gravity of a mineral can allow you to distinguish it from other minerals with similar physical properties. For example, gold has a high specific gravity (19.3), which makes it heavier than most other minerals commonly found in rocks and soil.

Other physical properties that can be helpful to rockhounds include streak (the color of a mineral's powder when scraped across a surface), fluorescence (the ability of a mineral to emit visible light when exposed to ultraviolet light), and magnetism (the ability of a mineral to be attracted to a magnet).

Geological Processes behind Mineral and Crystal Formation

Minerals and crystals are stunning to behold and provide important clues about the geological processes that shaped the planet. From the violent volcanic eruptions that produce obsidian and pumice to the slow crystallization of minerals in underground caves, the formation of these natural wonders is a fascinating subject of study. As a rockhound, you get the unique opportunity to witness the geological processes in action and uncover the hidden treasures of the earth.

1. Igneous

The solidification of magma or lava forms igneous rocks. This process takes place both below and above ground. When the magma cools down and solidifies underground, it forms igneous rocks like diorite and granite. When the magma cools and solidifies above ground, extrusive igneous rocks are formed. Their texture and composition depend on various factors, including the rate of cooling, the chemical composition of the magma or lava, and the presence of gas bubbles.

2. Metamorphic

These rocks are created by the transformation of already existing rocks when they're under high pressure, temperature, or both simultaneously. This occurs when rocks are buried deep within the Earth's crust or subjected to tectonic forces. During this process, the minerals within the rocks can change in response to these conditions, resulting in a new texture and composition. Some common metamorphic rocks include schist, gneiss, and marble.

3. Sedimentary

Sedimentary rocks form after the accumulation and compaction of sedimentary materials. After compaction, these materials' cementation takes place, including sand, silt, and other organic matter. This process typically occurs on or near the Earth's surface, in areas like riverbeds, lakes, or oceans. As time passes, these materials automatically become compressed and cement together to form rocks. Sedimentary rocks can contain fossils or other evidence of past environments.

4. Hydrothermal

Hydrothermal processes involve the circulation of hot fluids through rocks, which can dissolve minerals and deposit new ones. These fluids are often derived from magma or from hot groundwater heated by geothermal activity. Hydrothermal processes can form metallic ores like gold, silver, and copper, as well as minerals such as quartz and fluorite. Hydrothermal activity can occur in a variety of environments, including volcanic areas and hot springs.

5. Biological

Biological processes can lead to the formation of rocks such as limestone and coal. For example, accumulating shells, bones, and other organic matter can lead to limestone formation. Over time, these materials become compressed and cemented together to form rock. Coal forms when organic matter, such as plant material, accumulates in a swampy environment and is buried and compressed over millions of years. Biological rocks can provide important information about past life on Earth and the evolution of ecosystems.

Common Minerals and Crystals for Rockhounding

Whether you're a beginner or an experienced rockhound, knowing which minerals and crystals are commonly found is important. Below are some of the most common minerals and crystals you would want to collect.

1. Quartz

Quartz is a popular mineral.[27]

Quartz is a popular mineral among rockhounds due to its abundant occurrence and wide variety of colors. Composed of silicon and oxygen atoms, quartz crystals form in a six-sided prism shape with pointed tips. It can be found in clear, white, pink, purple, green, and brown and can be either transparent or opaque. When searching for quartz crystals, you need to understand their geological origins. Quartz can be found in a variety of settings, including volcanic and hydrothermal areas, sedimentary rocks like sandstone and shale, and metamorphic rocks like gneiss and schist. Some notable regions where quartz can be found include the Ouachita Mountains of Arkansas, the Quartzsite area in Arizona, and the Smoky Mountains in North Carolina.

Once you've found it, you can use several identification techniques to confirm its distinctiveness. Quartz has a hardness of 7 on the Mohs scale, making it relatively hard and able to scratch glass. It also has a distinctive conchoidal fracture, which means it breaks with a curved surface similar to that of broken glass. One popular method for identifying quartz is the streak test. By scratching the mineral against an unglazed porcelain plate, you can see the color of the mineral's powder. Quartz has a white or colorless streak. Another method involves examining the crystal's specific gravity, which can help distinguish it from other minerals. Quartz has a specific gravity of 2.65.

2. Agate

Agate is made up of tiny quartz crystals.

Agate is a beautiful and widely popular mineral for rockhounding enthusiasts. It belongs to the family of chalcedony, a type of mineral made up of tiny quartz crystals. Agates are typically characterized by their colorful bands and patterns formed through the deposition of various minerals in different layers over time. Agate is present in many shades, including back, gray, white, blue, pink, yellow, red, and green. They also exhibit different levels of translucency, from opaque to semi-transparent. The physical properties of agates can vary depending on the specific type and location from which they are sourced.

For those looking to find agates, knowing where to look is important. These minerals are often found in various types of rocks, including volcanic rocks and sedimentary rocks such as limestone and shale. When it comes to identifying agates, a few methods can be used. One of the most common is to examine the banding patterns and colors of the mineral. Another is to conduct a scratch test to determine its hardness. Additionally, some rockhounding enthusiasts use specialized tools such as magnifying lenses and UV lights to identify agates.

3. Feldspar

Feldspar can be found in all types of rocks.[38]

Feldspar is a group of minerals commonly found in igneous, metamorphic, and sedimentary rocks. They are one of the most abundant minerals on Earth and have a range of physical properties that make them a popular choice among rockhounding enthusiasts. Feldspars are found in many colors, like gray, brown, white, and pink. They are characterized by their two cleavage directions, allowing them to break in a smooth, flat manner. This property makes them useful minerals in manufacturing ceramics and glass.

To find feldspar in the wild, looking in specific geological settings is important. They can be found in sedimentary rocks such as sandstone and conglomerate. When identifying feldspar, there are a few characteristics to look for. One is their cleavage, which results in flat surfaces with sharp edges. Another is their hardness, which can be tested with a simple scratch test. Feldspars also have a specific gravity of around 2.5-2.6, which can help differentiate them from other minerals.

4. Citrine

Citrine is associated with positive energy and abundance.[39]

Citrine is a quartz crystal highly valued by rockhounds for its beautiful yellow color and associations with positive energy and abundance. When searching for it, you need to know its physical characteristics, including its color, texture, and hardness. Citrine crystals typically have a yellow to golden-brown color and can be found in clusters or as individual prismatic crystals. They have a vitreous luster and a hardness of 7 on the Mohs scale, which means they are relatively durable and can withstand scratching and wear.

To find citrine, rockhounds often search in areas where quartz crystals are abundant, such as in geodes, cavities, and veins in igneous and metamorphic rocks. It can also be found in sedimentary rocks that have been subjected to weathering and erosion. Once a potential citrine crystal has been found, there are several methods that can be used to confirm its identity. A common method to use is a streak test, which involves the rubbing of crystal against a piece pf porcelain to see what color it leaves behind. Citrine typically leaves a yellow or brownish-yellow streak.

5. Halite

Halite is commonly found in sedimentary rocks.[30]

Halite, also known as rock salt, is a mineral commonly found in sedimentary rocks. It is made up of sodium chloride and is one of the most commonly mined minerals in the world. It is usually colorless or white, but it can also be found in shades of pink, red, yellow, and blue due to impurities in the mineral. Its luster is vitreous, which means it has a glassy appearance. The hardness of halite is relatively low, ranking only 2.5 on the Mohs hardness scale, which means it can be easily scratched by other minerals.

One of the unique properties of halite is its taste. It is one of the very few edible minerals and has a distinctive salty taste. This property has made it an important mineral for the food industry, as it is used in the production of table salt. When rockhounding, halite can be found in sedimentary rocks such as salt domes and evaporite deposits. These deposits are often located in arid or desert areas, such as the Great Salt Lake in Utah or the Salar de Atacama in Chile.

When searching for halite, it is important to take caution and follow safety guidelines, as some deposits can be located in unstable or dangerous areas. Additionally, when handling halite specimens, wear gloves because it can cause skin irritation. Identifying halite is relatively easy due to its distinctive salty taste and cubic crystal structure. These crystals are often transparent or translucent and can be either colorless or have a range of colors due to impurities.

6. Tourmaline

Tourmaline can form in a variety of geological environments.[81]

Tourmaline is a popular crystal among rockhounds due to its various colors and unique properties. It can form in a variety of geological environments, including igneous, metamorphic, and sedimentary rocks. It often occurs in pegmatites, which are coarse-grained igneous rocks that form from the slow cooling of magma.

The crystal's color can vary greatly, from black to brown, red, green, blue, and pink. This is due to variations in the chemical composition of the crystal, with each color representing a different combination of elements.

Pegmatite deposits are a good place to start for rockhounds looking to find tourmaline crystals. Some popular locations for tourmaline hunting include California, Maine, and Brazil. You can perform a streak test to confirm that a specimen is tourmaline. Tourmaline has a white streak, which can help distinguish it from other similarly colored minerals like garnet and ruby.

7. Pyrite

Pyrite is sometimes known as fool's gold.[32]

Pyrite is a common sulfide mineral that has a bright, metallic luster and a brassy yellow color, often resembling gold. It is also known as "fool's gold" due to its resemblance to the precious metal. Pyrite is typically found in metamorphic, sedimentary, and igneous rock formations and is often associated with other minerals such as quartz and calcite. When searching for it, you should look for areas with shale, sandstone, and other sedimentary rocks and areas with hydrothermal activity, such as hot springs and geothermal fields. It can also be found in mineral veins associated with gold deposits.

To identify pyrite, you must look for its characteristic brassy yellow color and metallic luster. It is also quite heavy compared to other minerals of a similar size, with a specific gravity of around 5. Pyrite often forms cube-shaped crystals but can also be found in other forms, such as nodules, grains, and masses. One way to test if a specimen is pyrite is to scratch it against a piece of unglazed porcelain tile. It will leave a greenish-black streak, while gold will leave a yellow streak. It is important to note that pyrite can sometimes be mistaken for gold, so further testing may be necessary to confirm its identity.

As you delve deeper into the world of rockhounding and explore the beauty of minerals and crystals, you'll realize that these natural wonders are more than just shiny objects to collect. They hold vast information about the earth's history, the forces that shape our planet, and the complex chemistry that governs the universe.

As you venture out into the field, keep in mind that safety should always be your top priority. Always wear appropriate clothing and protective gear, and be aware of your surroundings to avoid potential hazards.

Additionally, it's important to respect the environment and property owners' rights. Before setting out on a rockhounding trip, make sure you have any necessary permits and permissions. Leave the area as you found it, taking care not to damage any natural features or disturb any wildlife.

Chapter 6: Rocks

Seeing how there are so many types of rocks, studying them all can be quite confusing at first. In this chapter, you will learn about the three primary types of rocks: igneous, sedimentary, and metamorphic. These three rock types provide essential information about past and present environments, from Earth's history to current landforms. In this chapter, you'll learn the basics behind each type of rock and even pick up some tips on how to find them. You'll become an expert by learning more about these distinct kinds of rocks in no time.

Igneous Rocks

When hot, molten lava cools and hardens, igneous rocks are created. These rocks are either extrusive, meaning they cool and solidify above the Earth's surface from lava, or intrusive, meaning they cool and solidify within the Earth's crust from magma. The chemical composition of igneous rocks depends on the type of magma they originated from, which in turn relies on the minerals that were melted during eruption or intrusion. Quartz, amphibole, pyroxene, olivine, mica, and feldspar are just a few of the many minerals that may be found in igneous rocks, giving them a wide range of colors and patterns.

These rocks originate from deep within the Earth's mantle or along tectonic plate boundaries. As molten rock ascends through fissures in the Earth's crust towards the surface, it cools due to contact with external materials like water or air. This cooling process leads to crystallization, making small crystals visible when the rock is examined under a microscope. The size of these crystals can vary greatly, from microscopic to larger than one centimeter, depending on the rate of cooling.

Igneous rocks are primarily classified based on their formation process into two main types: intrusive and extrusive. Intrusive igneous rocks form deep underground, where high temperatures allow the liquid rock to remain molten for extended periods before eventually solidifying into rocks like granite. Extrusive igneous rocks, on the other hand, cool down and become solid more quickly near the Earth's surface as a result of contact with cooler substances like water or air. Examples of extrusive igneous rocks include basalt and obsidian.

Igneous rocks comprise a significant portion of the Earth's continental and oceanic crust and the majority of mountains. Most mountain ranges consist predominantly of igneous rock formations. In addition to their geological importance, igneous rocks have numerous practical applications for humans, serving as construction materials and decorative stones for buildings, sculptures, and other structures.

Types of Igneous Rocks

1. Granite

Granite rocks are formed when magma and crystallized lava cool in the depths of the Earth's crust. This creates an extremely hard and durable stone with unique characteristics. Granite rocks have a grainy texture due to the individual mineral crystals that make up the composition, which typically includes quartz, mica, and feldspar. They are predominantly gray or pink in color but can also appear white, green, or blue.

Granite is a durable stone.[38]

Identifying granite is relatively easy as its main components create a distinct visual pattern. The quartz in granite has a clear glass-like appearance, while feldspar gives off a white or pink hue, and mica appears as small flakes on the surface, creating sparkles. Granite can be found worldwide in ancient mountain ranges, quarries, and other areas where it has been exposed by erosion.

Mining for granite can be done legally in many places around the globe, such as India, China, the USA, the UK, Norway, and Brazil. It is important to check local regulations regarding collecting rocks before beginning your search, as some areas may require permits for excavation activities.

To collect granite safely, follow these tips:

- Wear protective clothing (gloves and safety glasses) when breaking apart stones
- Bring appropriate tools such as hammers or chisels
- Use caution when operating any power tools
- Always work in pairs so someone is available to help if needed
- Fill any holes you dig to prevent further erosion of the area, and never take more than what you need from any given location.

2. Obsidian

When molten lava rapidly cools, a sort of natural glass is formed, which is known as *obsidian*. It is an igneous rock, which was formed from volcanic activity, and has the chemical composition of silicon dioxide (SiO2). Obsidian can be found in many parts of the world, including North America, Europe, Iceland, Mexico, Ethiopia, and New Zealand.

Obsidian is made up of molten lava.[34]

Due to the high concentrations of iron and magnesium in its chemical makeup, it is typically black or dark green in color. However, other minerals, such as limonite or hematite, can also exhibit streaks or tones of red or brown. In addition to its dark coloring, obsidian often has a smooth texture, making it popular for making jewelry and other decorative items.

Identifying obsidian requires knowing what it looks like and how it feels. It usually has a glossy sheen on the surface when wet. Due to its dense nature, it also tends to be much heavier than other types of rocks. One easy way to recognize obsidian is by looking for conchoidal fractures – these are curved surfaces that form when obsidian breaks apart due to its glass-like structure.

The best places for legal mining for obsidian are areas where volcanic activity once occurred but has cooled significantly, such as areas around volcanoes or lava beds. Special permits are needed in some countries, such as the United States and Canada, before one can mine for obsidian. Other countries may not require any permits at all. However, it's always best to check with local authorities before beginning any mining activity.

When collecting this type of rock, exercise caution since obsidian is a very sharp material when broken into small pieces.

- Wear protective clothing such as gloves, thick shoes, and eyewear if possible while mining in case any large pieces break off and fly towards you.
- Also, note that larger chunks may need special tools such as hammers or chisels to break them apart without shattering.

3. Basalt

Basalt is created when magma rapidly cools very close to the Earth's surface. It has a wide variety of textures and colors since it mostly comprises the minerals olivine, plagioclase, and pyroxene. Basalt is an important source of construction materials such as aggregate, construction aggregate, riprap, asphaltic concrete, and road stone.

Basalt has a wide variety of textures and colors.[85]

Basalt has also been used in many other applications, such as cemetery markers and monuments.

Basalt is found all over the world and can be identified by its dark color (gray to black), grain size (fine-grained to coarse-grained), texture (amorphous to vesicular), and abundance (abundant to rare). It has a

Mohs hardness of 5-6 and a specific gravity between 2.8 - 3.0.

The best mining places are typically where basalt formations are close to the Earth's surface, such as quarries or volcanic regions like the Cascade Range in Oregon or Hawaii. The most common way to identify basalt rocks is by their unique composition with silica content ranging from 45-52% $SiO2$. Other identifying characteristics include their vesicles or pores created during cooling, a mostly uniform grain size, glassy luster or sheen when freshly broken, and a darker color than other types of rocks like granite.

When collecting basalt rocks, it is important to do the following:

- Ensure you are legally allowed access to the area you plan on collecting from.
- Wear appropriate clothing, including boots and gloves, for safety purposes.
- Carry a magnifying glass or hand lens so you can get a closer look at any rock before attempting collection to avoid injury caused by sharp edges.

Sedimentary Rocks

Sedimentary rock is created by the deposition and consolidation of particles, such as mineral grains, shell fragments, organic material, and pieces of other rocks. Sedimentation occurs when materials are transported from their original source through various geological processes and eventually deposited on the Earth's surface. As silt builds up, it is compressed and cemented together to produce strata or solid rock layers.

Depending on how they were created, sedimentary rocks are categorized. Clastic sedimentary rocks comprise bits and pieces of previously existent rocks that have been broken up and reassembled into new parts. These include shale, sandstone, and conglomerate. Minerals such as limestone and dolostone precipitate out of water to produce chemical sedimentary rocks. Coal and oil shale are examples of the leftovers of living organisms that accumulate over time to form organic sedimentary rocks.

Sedimentary rocks provide a record of Earth's past environments because they can contain fossils or traces of organisms that lived in the ancient environment where the sediments were first deposited. For example, evaporites like gypsum often form in shallow marine basins where saltwater has concentrated due to evaporation leaving behind minerals in their wake. Many important resources for humanity can be found within sedimentary deposits, including oil, gas, coal, building stone, metals ore, and clay for pottery manufacture.

Types of Sedimentary Rocks

1. Dolomite

Dolomite is used in agriculture and construction.[36]

Dolomite is a mineral made up of calcium magnesium carbonate and is classified as a sedimentary rock. It can be found in many parts of the world, often formed as a result of sedimentation, dolomitization, or hydrothermal activity. Dolomite rocks are usually white or light gray in color with curved crystal shapes but may also be red or yellow when mixed with other minerals.

Dolomite rocks are widely used in agriculture, construction, and many other industries. In agriculture, it is commonly used to improve the soil and to reduce soil acidity. It is also used for building materials such as concrete blocks, bricks, road base materials, and landscaping stones. Dolomite has been used as an aggregate component in asphalt pavement since the 1950s and continues to be widely utilized today. In addition to its use industrially, it also makes for beautiful ornamental stones for jewelry or carvings due to its attractive crystalline structure.

The best legal mining places for dolomite will vary depending on what part of the world you live in, but some common areas that have sizable deposits include Austria, Germany, China, India, and South Africa. Collecting any type of stone requires permission from landowners unless you are collecting it from a beach or publicly accessible area where collection is permitted. If looking to collect dolomite specifically, you can try identifying potential sites by first determining where there is limestone bedrock, indicating the possible presence of dolomite-rich sedimentary deposits nearby. Additionally, professional geologists can help identify large deposits that could be mined at an industrial scale if needed.

Once a site has been identified, you will need:

- Proper safety gear like gloves and goggles
- Hard hats, helmets, safety boots, and tools like chisels or hammers, depending on how much digging needs to be done to find suitable pieces of dolomite rock
- Other helpful tips include highlighting potential spots with non-permanent marking paints so they can easily be found again if necessary
- Carrying bags, buckets, or boxes to transport collected rock samples safely back home or wherever they need to go next

2. Sandstone

Sandstone is composed of quartz, feldspar, mica, and clay.[87]

Sandstone is a sedimentary rock composed of small grains of quartz and other minerals such as feldspar, mica, calcite, and clay. It forms when sand and silt are deposited on the Earth's surface. Sandstone is usually formed in rivers and tidal zones where there is strong water flow.

These rocks are widely used in construction due to their strength, durability, and resistance to weathering. It is a popular material for constructing buildings, roads, walls, statues, sculptures, monuments, and many more. It can also be used to create mosaics and decorative objects like vases or jewelry boxes.

In terms of identification methods for sandstone rocks, there are several ways to distinguish them from other types of rocks. One way is to examine the stone's texture: Sandstone will feel gritty when rubbed with your finger because it contains layers of very small particles that have been compressed together over time. Color can also be used as a distinguishing factor. Sandstone typically has an earthy hue ranging from tan to yellow-brown or reddish-brown, depending on its composition and location. Additionally, certain minerals may indicate the presence of sandstone. For example, the presence of quartz or feldspar can often signify that rock is composed at least partially of sandstone.

Mining sandstone legally requires obtaining all necessary permits from local government authorities before extraction, as there can be regulations dictating where it can be done and who owns the rights to it (such as private property owners). In some places, it may even require permission from national governments before mining activities take place. The best places for legal mining include public areas such as beaches or quarries owned by the state or local governments that allow visitors to collect stones without any issues.

Tips for collecting sandstones include:

- Wearing protective gear like gloves while handling them since they may have sharp edges
- Using proper tools like hammers and chisels instead of bare hands
- Carrying them safely in bags or baskets
- Avoiding collecting stones from areas where pollution is present (this could lead to potentially hazardous materials being brought home
- Washing them with soap and water before storing them away

- Researching any special storage requirements such as humidity control if required by any stones before putting them away for long-term use

3. Shale

Shale is a type of sedimentary rock formed when deposits of clay, silt, and fine-grained particles are compacted over millions of years. It is composed mostly of clay minerals with minor amounts of other minerals such as quartz, carbonate, and pyrite. Shale has low permeability and is highly impermeable to water. Because it is so dense, it has very low porosity compared to other rocks.

Shale rocks are often found in sedimentary basins worldwide and metamorphic belts. Shale is used in the production of cement, oil and gas exploration, manufacturing bricks, roofing tiles, pottery,

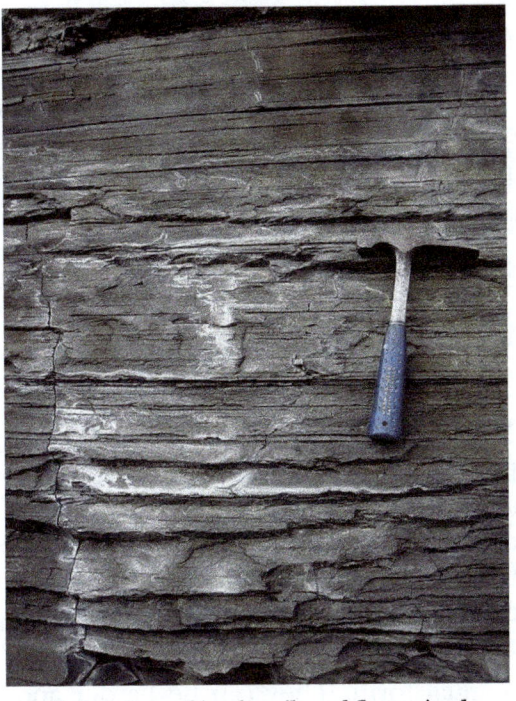

Shale is formed by clay, silt, and fine-grained particles.[88]

and ceramics. It can also be used for construction aggregate or for lining irrigation ditches or pipeline beds. In areas with a significant amount of shale present, it can be mined for use in various industries, such as energy production and construction materials.

The best way to identify them is by observing their composition: they are typically gray to black in color with a fine-grained texture that easily flakes apart when touched. Clay minerals give them an earthy smell when wet or dampened. They may also contain fossils or traces of plant material if they have been compressed over time due to geological processes like heat and pressure.

The best legal mining places for shale depend on the location you live in – check with your local government laws before attempting any sort of collecting activity involving shale rocks, as each country may have specific rules about this particular kind of stone. That being said, some potential places to find shale include quarries, abandoned mines, or even public land areas with outcrops visible on the surface (make sure you have all the necessary permissions before you attempt to collect any).

When collecting shale rocks, it's important to:
- Take safety precautions such as wearing protective equipment like heavy-duty boots, gloves, and eye protection
- Ensure you're aware of hidden hazards like underground shafts or crumbling walls, which could cause injury if not addressed properly beforehand.
- Always remember to respect the environment by taking only what you need and refraining from destroying the area.

Metamorphic Rocks

Metamorphic rocks are created when an existing rock is changed by heat, pressure, or chemical activity. These extreme conditions cause physical and chemical changes within the rock. Metamorphic rocks usually don't melt; they just recrystallize and change shape. This process is known as metamorphism, which can occur at any depth within the Earth's crust or even at the surface where tectonic forces press one rock against another.

Metamorphic rocks have different physical properties than their original form. They can be harder and more durable than their original form due to a higher concentration of minerals and increased crystallization of their grains. In contrast to sedimentary or igneous rocks, which accumulate only in specific environments (such as near volcanoes or in oceans), metamorphic rocks can accumulate anywhere due to tectonic forces pushing and pulling on the Earth's crust in many different directions.

Metamorphic rocks are divided into two categories based on how they form: contact metamorphism and regional metamorphism. Contact metamorphism occurs when a magma source comes into direct contact with an existing rock and creates new minerals through direct heat transfer from the magma source. This process typically occurs close to the surface of the Earth's crust, where temperatures are highest. Regional metamorphism happens further down within Earth's crust over large areas because of immense pressures created by tectonic plates sliding past each other. This process is responsible for creating mountains such as the Himalayas and the Alps.

Types of Metamorphic Rocks

1. Quartzite

Quartzite is used in construction due to its strength.[39]

Quartzite is a metamorphic rock created by subjecting quartz-rich sandstone to severe heat and pressure. It consists primarily of quartz, one of the strongest and most abundant minerals on Earth, and feldspar, mica, chlorite, and other minerals. Quartzite is best known for its incredible strength and durability. It has a higher resistance to pressure than regular sandstone or limestone and is much harder, making it ideal for countertops, flooring, and other uses where strength and hardness are valued.

It is used in many construction projects due to its strength and ability to hold up against wear and tear. Since quartzite has a very low porosity rating compared to other stones like marble or granite, it can be used for kitchen countertops without having to worry about staining or etching. It's also highly resistant to abrasions, impact damage, deep scratches, and chips. Additionally, quartzite is ideal for outdoor applications such as pool coating or patios because it won't fade under UV exposure like other stones would.

To identify natural quartzite, look for its characteristic banding patterns caused by heat and pressure during formation. Quartzites usually have smooth surfaces with no visible grains or crystals unless broken open. The color can range from pinkish-yellow to gray depending on which minerals were originally included in the source sandstone before metamorphism occurred.

The greatest legal mining locations are ones that local governments have licensed because they have met the needed safety laws and requirements. Some examples include:

- Canada's Saskatchewan Learning Mines Program
- India's Bureau of Mines
- Vietnam's Central Highlands Mining Company
- Brazil's Geological Survey Agency (CPRM)
- Australia's Department of Natural Resources and Mines
- South Africa's Department of Mineral Resources
- United States Bureau of Land Management (BLM)
- China's Ministry of Land and Resources
- Russia's Federal Agency for Subsoil Use (Rosnedra) etc.

When collecting this type of stone, it's important to:

- Keep safety in mind. The rocks can be heavy, so you should always wear protective gear, such as gloves, when handling them.
- Note any interesting features you come across along with the coordinates so you can easily locate them if you want.

2. Marble

Marble is composed of recrystallized carbonate minerals. They are most commonly found as calcite or dolomite. It is a sedimentary and igneous rock with a soft texture that makes it easy to carve and polish into stunning sculptures, decorative accents, and more. It is beautiful, incredibly durable, and versatile, making it the perfect material for many projects.

Marble is made of recrystallized carbonate minerals.[40]

Marble is used in various applications, from construction to artwork. In construction, marble can be found in tiles, countertops, flooring, walls, monuments, and other architectural elements. It is also commonly used in artworks such as sculptures and statues. As a natural stone material, it has been treasured for thousands of years as one of the most luxurious building materials available.

The best legal mining places for acquiring marble are usually quarries where the rock has been extracted from the ground through blasting or quarrying techniques. These are often located near cities or large towns where the highest quality marble can be found and purchased at reasonable prices.

When identifying marble rocks, it is important to watch for the distinct grainy structure that sets this type of stone apart from other stones, such as granite or sandstone. The presence of calcium carbonate, along with certain types of iron oxide, gives marble its unique coloration ranging from light gray to pinkish-white hues depending on its mineral content. When examining these rocks with a magnifying glass, you may notice small particles sparkling throughout their surface, indicating their crystalline composition.

When collecting marble:

- Exercise caution to avoid damage during transportation.
- If you plan on using them for artwork or sculpture making, you should look for pieces with straight edges and flat surfaces.

3. Gneisses

Gneisses can be used in landscaping.[41]

Gneisses rocks are formed when shale and granite are subjected to extreme pressure and heat. They are characterized by alternating layers of light and dark minerals, often with a banding pattern that gives them a striped appearance. It primarily comprises mica, quartz, feldspar, and other minerals. It is harder compared to other metamorphic rocks such as slate or schist. This type of rock is found in many parts of the world, but it is most commonly seen in areas where mountain-building forces have acted on sedimentary or igneous rocks.

Gneisses have many uses in construction, including flooring tiles and countertops. It can also be used for landscaping purposes due to its attractive coloring and patterning. It is also used for making railroad ballast, quarry stone products, aggregate for road construction and repair, riprap for shorelines protection and breakwater structures, and as dimension stone for facing buildings or monuments.

Identifying gneisses rocks can be done by looking at their coloration patterns - they typically have bands of light and dark minerals that give them a striped appearance. Gneisses also tend to be harder than other types of metamorphic rocks. You can test this hardness by scratching the surface with another rock or an object like your fingernail or pocket knife blade.

The best places to legally mine gneisses rocks are quarries specializing in mining this type of stone. These quarries will often have permits and safety regulations in place, so you can rest assured that you're mining legally and safely. You can also find gneisses at outcrops - areas where the rock has been exposed to erosion processes such as weathering or glaciation. When collecting from natural deposits or quarries, wear proper safety equipment (such as goggles and gloves) and follow local regulations regarding collecting specimens from public lands or private property owned by someone else.

Chapter 7: Fossils

Fossils are one of the most intriguing aspects of geology. They provide a glimpse into the past to learn about life forms and environments that no longer exist. This chapter will explain what fossils are, explore different types of fossils, look at how they form, discuss identifying them, and provide advice on the best fossil-hunting places. With this information, you can start exploring Earth's fossilized history. From mineralized dinosaur bones to delicate leaf prints preserved in rock, there is something unique and amazing around each corner – you just have to know where and how to look!

What are Fossils?

Fossils are preserved remnants or traces of organisms that once lived on Earth, encapsulated within the planet's crust. They encompass diverse forms, from bone and tooth fragments to impressions of shells, leaves, or even entire preserved bodies. Fossils serve as crucial evidence of past lifeforms and environmental conditions that no longer exist on Earth.

Fossilization, though rare, offers a remarkable window into Earth's history. Generally, fossils form when an organism dies, becomes buried in sediment, and is subsequently preserved over time due to specific conditions such as an oxygen-deprived environment or extreme temperatures. The sediment eventually hardens into rock, creating an airtight seal that safeguards the organism's remains for millions – or even billions – of years.

There are several types of fossils, including mold fossils (impressions left by the original body), cast fossils (created when minerals fill the impression), true-form fossils (unaltered preserved remains), and trace fossils (evidence of activities like burrowing). Moreover, fossils can be classified into two primary categories: body fossils, composed of hard parts like bones and shells, and trace/chemical fossils, formed from organic molecules found in materials like amber or oil shale layers.

Fossils offer scientists a wealth of information about extinct species and can also be used to explore evolutionary relationships among living organisms. They encompass a wide array of forms, such as bones, shells, feathers, leaves, footprints, and even entire fossilized animals. Microfossils, which require a microscope for examination, include minuscule species like bacteria and pollen grains. In contrast, macrofossils, which can be several meters in length or weigh several tons, include petrified trees and dinosaur bones. Fossilization involves the gradual replacement of an organism's organic matter with minerals, a process that occurs over time due to environmental exposure. For fossilization to transpire, the organism must be at least 10,000 years old, with potential origins ranging from the Archaean Eon (nearly 4 billion years ago) to the present-day Holocene Epoch.

Fossils furnish a priceless chronicle of Earth's ancient history, enabling you to comprehend species' evolutionary trajectories and the impact of climate change on these transitions. By examining these age-old remains, humanity can gain valuable insights into the present environment and anticipate potential future developments.

Historical Background of Fossil Study

The study of fossils dates back to when ancient civilizations, such as the Greeks and Chinese, examined physical evidence of past life. In the Middle Ages, European scholars studied fossils to determine the age and origin of geological formations. During the Renaissance period, fossils were widely accepted as a physical record of past life on Earth.

In 1667, English natural philosopher Robert Hooke published one of the first scientific works on fossils, which led to an increased interest in their study by scientists around the world. His research was heavily influenced by his contemporary Nicolaus Steno, who developed the theory that new strata form over old strata following sedimentary deposition. This provided a basis for stratigraphy and allowed scientists to use fossils as markers to measure geologic time.

During the 18th century, increased public interest in natural history led to a surge in fossil collecting, eventually leading to more intensive fossil formation and preservation studies. With developments in 19th-century paleontology, such as William Smith's biostratigraphic correlation tool and Charles Lyell's principle of uniformitarianism, scientists began piecing together what is now called "deep time" or geologic time based on fossil sequences throughout Earth's history.

By the early 20th century, discoveries from radiometric dating techniques such as uranium series dating proved that early estimates from geologists regarding the age of certain species were accurate and further advanced our understanding of deep time. Today's technological advances have enabled researchers and rockhounds to identify many new species that otherwise may have gone unrecorded in Earth's history.

Importance of Fossils

Fossil records play a vital role in understanding evolution and the history of life on Earth. By studying fossils, scientists can uncover a wealth of information about the behavior and anatomy of extinct organisms and their relationships to modern forms. Fossil records are especially important for understanding the evolutionary history of species since they provide direct evidence for past evolutionary changes.

Fossils are the remains or traces of ancient organisms preserved in sedimentary rock. Fossils can include bones, teeth, shells, leaves, pollen, footprints, and even impressions left by soft-bodied organisms such as worms and jellyfish. Their age can be determined by radioactive dating or other methods, which give clues to when and where these

Dinosaur fossils are the most common.[42]

organisms lived in the past. Scientists use these clues to reconstruct the evolutionary history of species – how they changed over time and how they're related to each other.

One of the most significant examples of fossils is dinosaurs. With fossil remains, you can observe how different species evolved over time from small bipedal predators such as Velociraptors to giants like Brachiosaurus as well as the diversity in their habitats. You can also use evidence from fossilized eggs and nests to learn more about dinosaur behavior. Additionally, you can compare fossils from different periods, which helps understand how dinosaurs may have moved across continents over time and adapted to changing climates.

Similarly, fossils of early humans provide insight into human evolution. For example, humans are believed to share a common ancestor with certain species of apes that lived tens or hundreds of thousands of years ago. Scientists can gain insight into human ancestry by studying fossilized remains from those apes – such as teeth, bones, and skulls. For instance, one example is Lucy, an Australopithecus afarensis specimen found in Ethiopia that provides evidence for human ancestor bipedalism some 3 million years ago. Aside from physical characteristics such as reduced canine teeth and a larger brain capacity than other primates, her bones indicate that she was capable of walking upright for long periods of time like modern humans do today.

Fossils show a record of history.[45]

Fossil records are an invaluable source of information about the history of life on Earth. They provide a detailed record of the evolution of species and how they changed over time. They give insight into how organisms interacted with their environment and what adaptations they had to make to survive, giving you a better understanding of how modern species developed. Fossils also provide evidence for the theory of evolution by natural selection and other evolutionary mechanisms such as genetic drift and punctuated equilibrium. For instance, fossilized plants tell what kind of vegetation was present in an area at a particular time in history – such as whether it was grassland or forest – while fossilized fish indicate changes in the ocean's temperature or salinity level over time. This knowledge is important for predicting how environmental changes affect future ecosystems worldwide.

Fossil records provide valuable information about past extinctions – when many species die off at once due to environmental changes or other factors. Studying these mass extinction events helps you learn more about why certain species go extinct and may even give clues about ways to prevent potential future extinctions.

Overall, fossil records are integral for understanding the evolutionary process and uncovering the history of Earth. They provide tangible proof that species continue to evolve over long periods, responding to internal (genetic) and external (environmental) pressures through natural selection. From them, you can learn more about where you come from and how life has changed since it began billions of years ago.

Fossilization and Its Different Types

Fossilization is the process of converting an animal or plant remains into a fossil. This process can take place in numerous ways, with some of the most common types being permineralization, carbonization, and molds and casts. Below is an in-depth description of each type of fossilization process.

Permineralization (also known as petrification) is one of the most well-known processes of fossilization. During this process, minerals such as quartz, calcite, and feldspar are deposited into the pores and spaces within bones or other organic material within sedimentary rocks. Over time, these minerals replace the once-organic material and solidify it into a fossilized form. This type of fossilization requires very specific conditions, including slow sedimentation to provide adequate time for mineral deposits to substitute for the original remains, plenty of moisture to allow these minerals to be transported by groundwater and accumulate in cavities inside organic matter, and an oxygen-free environment so that organisms don't decompose before they can be preserved. Permineralized fossils often contain intricate detail due to their high level of preservation.

Carbonization is another common fossilization type that involves replacing organic material with carbon films on the surface or in cracks within a rock matrix. Carbon films are usually formed during combustion or heating processes related to volcanic eruptions or coal fires. For example, when plants decay at low temperatures, they undergo carbonization rather than decomposition. That leaves behind a distinct black film that can be seen with the naked eye. These films often have a glossy or shiny appearance due to their high concentration of carbon molecules. Carbonized fossils contain less detail than permineralized ones due to their lower levels of preservation but still hold valuable information about ancient life forms and environments that existed long ago.

Molds and casts are also common types of fossils created through sedimentation processes around living organisms prior to burial. Molds form when empty spaces remain after an organism decays away, leaving behind an impression in surrounding sediments that gets filled with new minerals over time, creating an external "mold" resembling the organism's shape when it was alive. Casts occur when new mineral-rich sediments fill up these molds, creating replicas of the organism's structure called "casts" that can sometimes retain details such as mouthparts or antennae that were not visible on molds alone due to their higher levels of preservation.

In addition, trace fossils are also important indicators for studying past life forms even though they don't preserve actual remains like body fossils do; instead, they capture evidence such as footprints, burrows, nests, and feces left behind by ancient animals which exhibit vital information about how creatures behaved millions upon years ago. With that, you can understand more about ancient ecosystems today. Trace fossils offer unique insight because knowledge about these creatures won't come from analyzing their bodies but from understanding how they interacted with their environment during different periods in time. This allows you to see which kinds of animals were part of ancient ecosystems and what they possibly went through.

Overall, many different types of fossilization processes have taken place throughout Earth's history ranging from simple impressions left on rock surfaces all the way up to detailed permineralized specimens containing intricate details; each providing invaluable insight into past lifeforms, environments, and ecosystems.

How to Identify a Fossil

Fossil identification is a process that involves careful examination and analysis of the structure, shape, and features of the fossil to determine its age, origin, and other related characteristics.

The first step is to determine what type of rock it is found in. This can be done by examining the texture, color, grain size, mineral composition, and any patterns or striations that may be present. Depending on the type of rock it is found in, it may indicate where on earth it was formed or how old it is.

Once you have established what type of rock the fossil is embedded in (or if you are dealing with sedimentary deposits), then you can begin to examine the physical features of the fossil itself. This includes looking at its size and shape and any markings or details that may be present on its surface. Pieces of bone may also be visible, depending on how well-preserved the specimen is.

The next step is to analyze its structure more closely by interpreting any apparent patterns or textures. For example, if there are ribs evident on one side of a specimen, then this could indicate that it belonged to an aquatic creature such as a fish or turtle. Other common features include ridges along one side which could suggest they belonged to an arthropod like an insect or crab.

When looking at fossils from plants or trees, there can often be evidence of their leaves imprinted onto them which can help identify them further. These types of fossils usually have distinctive shapes, such as circles for leaves or flat surfaces for bark, and these can offer clues about what type of plant they belong to (oak tree versus maple tree, for example).

The final step before classifying your specimen into a particular species group is to compare your findings with others from similar time periods and geographical areas. Doing this will allow you to narrow down your options until a definitive conclusion has been made about what kind of creature or organism your fossil belongs to.

For those relatively new to fossil identification, many online resources offer detailed descriptions and images that can help novice collectors identify different types of specimens more accurately (especially when presented with unfamiliar fossils). There are also numerous books dedicated to helping people recognize different types of fossils they may encounter while exploring nature's wonders!

Fossil identification can seem daunting at first, but with enough knowledge and practice, anyone can identify most fossils they get their hands on.

Best Fossil Hunting Sites in the World

Fossil hunting is a popular activity enjoyed by many people around the world. Regarding fossils, some places are better than others because they offer abundant remains of ancient plants and animals that can be found with a little effort and some luck.

1. **The United States:** While the U.S. doesn't have a designated fossil-hunting area or park, there are still numerous opportunities to dig for fossils around the country. From Arizona's Petrified Forest National Park to the Badlands of South Dakota and Montana, each state offers its own unique opportunity to explore ancient life forms. For those looking for something easier to access, many local parks may offer up fossils from nearby creeks or rivers. There is also an abundance of fossilized remains available in public land in the western states such as Utah, Wyoming, and Colorado.

2. **Morocco:** One of the best places in the world for fossil hunting is in Morocco. This North African country boasts a wide range of fossils from different geologic periods, ranging from Cambrian to Cretaceous and beyond. Some of the most notable finds include trilobites, ammonites, belemnites, crinoids, bivalves, brachiopods, and even dinosaur bones. Morocco's Sahara desert holds some of the oldest rocks on Earth, with ages estimated to be up to 600 million years old. Much of this rugged terrain is sparsely populated and unexplored; this makes it an ideal place to hunt for fossils. Fossil hunters should focus on areas around rivers or oases where sedimentary rocks are exposed by erosion.

3. **United Kingdom:** The United Kingdom is another great place to find fossils. It may not be as glamorous as other locations, but there are still plenty of exciting discoveries waiting to be

made here. The British Isles have seen numerous geological changes over the millennia due to its location at the intersection between tectonic plates and glaciers. As a result, there is a wealth of ancient marine life well-preserved in sedimentary rocks within England, Scotland, Wales, and Northern Ireland. While trilobites are perhaps the most popular finds in these regions (due to their abundance), other fossilized remains such as sea urchins, crinoids, and brachiopods can also be found in certain areas - especially around Jurassic Coast World Heritage Sites like Lyme Regis or Charmouth beach in Dorset County on southern England's coastline.

4. **South Africa:** South Africa offers some great opportunities for fossil hunters due to its vast array of diverse landscapes and ecosystems - making it an ideal spot for uncovering fossils dating back more than 500 million years ago! The Karoo Basin area contains world-famous fossil beds that have yielded remarkable specimens such as dinosaurs and primitive mammal species like Euskelosaurus Browni - one of the earliest known four-legged animals that lived during the Early Triassic period (approximately 250 million years ago). Other parts of South Africa have likewise yielded fascinating fossils from marine creatures such as shellfish, starfish, and crinoids; these ancient remains can be uncovered at sites such as Natal Drakensberg Park or Blombos Cave near Cape Town.

5. **Australia:** Australia also has an impressive geological history, making it an excellent destination for fossil-hunting enthusiasts. Numerous ancient sites across the continent provide abundant evidence of past life forms - some even going back over 600 million years. Many of these prized specimens were uncovered by amateur paleontologists - who often took advantage of Australia's dry climate, which facilitates easier excavations compared to humid environments like rainforests or wetlands (where most large-scale excavations take place). Some famous spots include Lightning Ridge in New South Wales, which is home to opalized fossils from extinct animals such as kangaroo-like marsupials, or Murgon Fossil Site near Brisbane, which yields large numbers of marine invertebrates like corals and shells, among others.

6. **Argentina:** Argentina is another amazing destination for fossil hunting – especially if you want to find dinosaur bones! This South American country has been home to many prehistoric creatures dating back millions upon millions of years – some even surviving until today (like Giant Armadillos). There are multiple industrial sites located throughout Argentina that offer paleontological expeditions specifically dedicated to discovering dinosaur remains – these include sites like Talampaya National Park located just outside San Juan province, where researchers have found various species, including Argentinosaurus Huinculensis – one of the largest known land dinosaurs ever discovered! Additionally, local museums like Egidio Feruglio (also situated near San Juan) house thousands upon thousands more specimens which makes them essential stops when visiting Argentina with hopes of uncovering fossils.

7. **China:** With more than 500 million years of documented geological history, China has emerged as one of the top destinations for fossil hunters looking for ancient life forms preserved in limestone deposits. Of particular interest are Yunnan Province's fossil beds which have yielded specimens dating back hundreds of millions of years ago. Collecting fossils on public land requires permission from local authorities, so it's important to check before you dig!

8. **Canada:** Canada is home to an abundance of well-preserved fossil beds spanning millions of years into prehistory. That makes it another great destination for budding paleontologists around the globe. Alberta's Dinosaur Provincial Park offers visitors a chance to get up close and personal with dinosaurs that roamed this region during prehistory, while British Columbia's Burgess Shale Fossil Beds provides an opportunity to view one-of-a-kind preserved soft tissue creatures from 500 million years ago!

9. **Ethiopia:** Ethiopia has been known as a hotspot for undiscovered paleontological treasures since 1974 when well-preserved hominid bones were first uncovered at Hadar – the site now famously linked with "Lucy" – the 3 million-year-old hominid skeleton found here! Notable discoveries include primitive antelopes dating back 5 million years ago near Gona

Afar Triangle and numerous other mammal teeth unearthed along Ethiopia's Red Sea coastline thanks largely due to its rich mineral deposits, which have helped preserve these treasures from eons past!

10. **Germany**: Germany boasts some impressive finds dating back more than 350 million years, including species such as spiders, snails, and shark remains found among sedimentary rocks deposited here during the Carboniferous period. This treasure trove can be explored through various field trips organized by universities in Germany or through various research expeditions abroad offered by international universities seeking out these valuable finds!

No matter where you choose to go on your next adventure, each destination offers different experiences and rewards when searching for valuable fossils – so why not embark on one today?

Chapter 8: Specimen Cleaning and Care

Mineral specimen cleaning and care is an important step in the mineral collecting process and, unfortunately, one that can often cause confusion. This chapter considers the importance of cleaning minerals and the versatile tools required, outlines general guidelines for several kinds of mineral cleaning, and even identifies some of the easier-to-clean specimens. Whether you're a novice or an experienced collector, this chapter will provide valuable insight into properly caring for your mineral specimens so you can mount, display, and enjoy them for years.

The Importance of Mineral Cleaning

1. Preserves Delicate and Fragile Specimen

Proper mineral cleaning is essential for preserving delicate and fragile specimens, as scrubbing and scraping can cause irreversible damage. For instance, some fragile minerals like calcite or gypsum may be scratched or cracked when cleaned with processes like rubbing or scraping. In addition, harsh substances like hydrochloric acid should never be used to clean minerals because they can dissolve the crystal lattices of even the toughest minerals. On the other hand, gentler techniques, such as using a soft brush or a toothbrush to remove dust and debris, are ideal for cleaning delicate specimens. Furthermore, some gentle chemical solutions like an ammonium carbonate solution can also be used to help remove any oil or grease on the surface of many minerals. When cleaning delicate and fragile specimens, it is important to always use extreme caution and patience to avoid any unnecessary damage; this will ensure that the specimen remains in its best condition for years to come.

2. Preserves Beauty and Luster

Proper mineral cleaning can maintain the natural beauty and luster of specimens by removing dirt, dust, and other particles that have accumulated over time. Mineral cleaning helps preserve the physical integrity of specimens, ensuring they look as close to their natural state as possible.

For example, a quartz crystal could accumulate dirt and debris from its surroundings, which can make it look dull or even discolored. By carefully cleaning the specimen with a soft brush, water, or an organic solvent, grinding away any excess soil or debris, and then polishing it with a cloth or soft brush, one can bring back its original shine and clarity. This kind of treatment also protects the specimen's integrity since it is not subjected to harsh chemicals that could damage or alter its appearance or structure.

Mineral cleaning is important in preserving geological specimens for future generations because it helps ensure their aesthetic charm and scientific accuracy remain intact. It also allows us to appreciate the beauty and intricacies hidden beneath layers of dust and grime that have built up over centuries – showcasing these remarkable pieces in all their glory for everyone to enjoy!

3. Aids in Proper Identification

Proper mineral cleaning is essential for the proper identification of minerals. Minerals are identified by their physical and optical properties, including color, luster, hardness, streak, and crystal habit. To properly observe these characteristics, however, it is important to have a mineral specimen free from dirt or debris that could obscure the true properties of the mineral. Proper cleaning techniques can vary depending on the type of mineral being cleaned but generally involve using a soft brush, such as a paintbrush or toothbrush, along with warm water and mild detergent if necessary. Mechanical abrasion may also be used in certain cases.

For example, sedimentary rocks like sandstone are best cleaned using warm water and a soft brush to remove surface dirt without damaging delicate fossils which may otherwise be obscured. In contrast, igneous rocks such as basalt may require mechanical abrasion through tumbling in abrasive material like cornmeal or crushed walnut shells to remove weathered surfaces that obscure their true texture and color.

Mineral identification is an important part of geology and the science of mineralogy; knowing each specimen's unique physical and optical properties can help geologists identify potential resources and understand processes at work within the Earth's crust. Therefore, specimens must be cleaned before attempting any identification process so that accurate observations can be made about each mineral.

4. Prepares the Specimen for Further Study

Proper mineral cleaning is an effective way to prepare a specimen for further study. It generally involves using specialized tools, such as a soft brush, to remove dirt and debris from the surface of the mineral. This allows for more accurate observation and examination of the specimen under magnification or different light sources, such as ultraviolet light.

For example, when examining a meteorite under magnification, it is important to clean off any surface dust that may be obscuring its features to get a clearer view of its structure. Similarly, some minerals can only be examined for specific characteristics under UV light if they are properly cleaned first. In this case, the act of cleaning removes impurities that would otherwise prevent the process of fluorescence from taking place.

In addition to brushing away dirt and debris, proper mineral cleaning also includes soaking specimens in distilled water or other solvents, such as dilute acids or alcohols, in order to remove any embedded dirt or oils that have adhered to the surface. This allows scientists and geologists to get a better look at the specimen's features without obstruction or interference from these substances.

5. Checks for Fractures

Proper mineral cleaning can make all the difference in identifying a mineral's true form and potential surprises. During this process, the dirt and debris that can often obscure the real features of a mineral are removed. This can be done with a variety of methods, such as brushing them off with a soft brush or even using an ultrasonic bath with a detergent to get rid of any grime. Once they are clean, it is then easier to tell if they contain additional crystal faces or fractures that may not have been visible when still covered in dirt.

For example, during the process of cleaning quartz crystals, you may find that what looks like one single crystal face is actually two separate faces on either side of a hidden fracture line. Take pyrite, for instance, which typically appears just like a regular rock unless it is cleaned well enough to reveal its glittery gold shine. While certain minerals need more intense cleaning than others, properly cleaning them will make assessing their true form and potential characteristics easier.

The type of method used for proper mineral cleaning also depends on the mineral being handled. For softer minerals like calcite or malachite, hand-brushing may do the trick, whereas harder minerals such as quartz or amethyst will require mechanical tools such as dental picks and brushes to get into crevices and remove stubborn bits of debris. With proper technique and patience, even delicate fossils can be uncovered from their surrounding matrix with careful brushing or light acid bath treatment. No matter what type of mineral you are dealing with, each requires its unique approach to proper cleaning to bring out all its hidden treasures.

Mineral Cleaning Guidelines

A few general rules should be followed when cleaning any kind of mineral. First and foremost, always use lukewarm water when cleaning your minerals. Hot water can cause damage to some sensitive minerals, so you should avoid using it unless absolutely necessary. Also, never use soap on minerals, as it can cause damage and discoloration. In addition, always use soft brushes when scrubbing away dirt and debris from minerals; metal brushes can scratch surfaces and cause permanent damage. Finally, never try to scrub off encrustations or coatings yourself; these will require special chemical cleaners or other treatments that should only be done by an experienced collector.

Mineral-Specific Cleaning Methods

The best way to clean your specific type of mineral will depend on its composition, structure, and surface texture. For example, some soft minerals such as calcite may need nothing more than just brushing with a soft-bristled brush to remove dirt and debris, whereas more hardy materials such as quartz require more aggressive techniques (such as hot water treatment) to get them really clean. Here's a quick overview of how you should clean different kinds of minerals:

- **Soft Minerals:** These should be rinsed with lukewarm water and lightly brushed with a soft-bristled brush. Do not use abrasives or harsh chemicals on these types of minerals, as they can easily be damaged by them.
- **Hard Minerals:** These are usually tougher materials that require more aggressive cleaning methods. Hot water treatment is often

used for hard granular crystals like quartz; however, this method may not work on all kinds of hard crystals since some may have delicate interiors that could become damaged if the temperature gets too high during the process. It's best to start with milder methods, like brushing with warm water, before trying anything else if you aren't sure how your particular crystal might react to heat treatments.

- **Precious Metals:** These require special chemical cleaners to remove dirt particles without damaging the surface finish or coloration/luster present in many precious metals (such as gold). Do not attempt to clean these yourself unless you know what specific chemicals are safe for use on each individual kind of metal; otherwise, it is best left up to experts who know exactly what each metal needs in order to stay looking its best without becoming damaged by improper cleaning agents or techniques.

Cleaning minerals properly is an important part of caring for your collection in terms of aesthetics and preservation. So, make sure you take your time and do adequate research before attempting any kind of treatment on your specimens!

Tools and Devices for Mineral Cleaning

Mineral cleaning is a process in which minerals are made more aesthetically pleasing or valuable. It is important that the right tools and devices are used when cleaning minerals because damage can occur to the specimen if the wrong tool is used. Beginners may not know what to use, so here is a list of some of the most common mineral cleaning tools and devices that can be used.

1. **Toothbrush:**

A toothbrush is a useful tool for mineral cleaning because its bristles are firm enough to remove dirt and debris but gentle enough not to cause any damage while doing so. It's also great if you need to reach areas that are difficult to access with

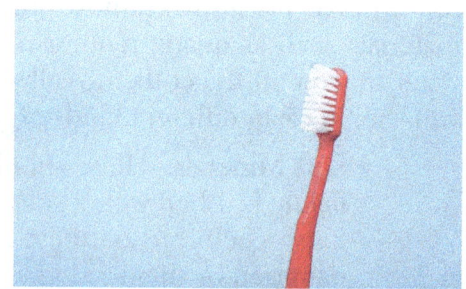

Toothbrushes clean effectively without causing damage."

cotton swabs or Q-tips, like tight corners or narrow edges of a specimen. Remember to use a soft-bristled toothbrush instead of a hard one so as not to scratch or damage your specimens.

2. **Soft Cloth:** For larger specimens, a soft cloth can be used to clean away dirt and debris from the surface of the mineral. Natural fibers such as cotton are best for this purpose, as they do not scratch or damage delicate specimens like synthetic fibers might.

A soft cloth can be used to clean away dirt."

Dry brushes are common when cleaning minerals."

3. **Dry Brush:** A dry brush is one of the most commonly used tools for cleaning minerals. It consists of a stiff-bristled brush that can be used to remove dirt, dust, and debris from the mineral surface. This tool is great for removing light surface contaminants and can be used on both large and small specimens. Dry brushing should always be done gently and with care to avoid scratching or damaging the mineral's delicate structure.

4. **Cotton Swabs or Q-Tips:** These are ideal for cleaning minerals in hard-to-reach places, such as crevices, grooves, and other tight spaces. They come in handy when you want to get rid of stubborn particles that cannot be removed by simply dry brushing them away. In addition, cotton swabs are usually made from soft material, which makes them perfect for polishing delicate mineral surfaces without causing any damage. Dip a cotton swab in a mild detergent solution to

clean tough spots before using it on the specimen surface.

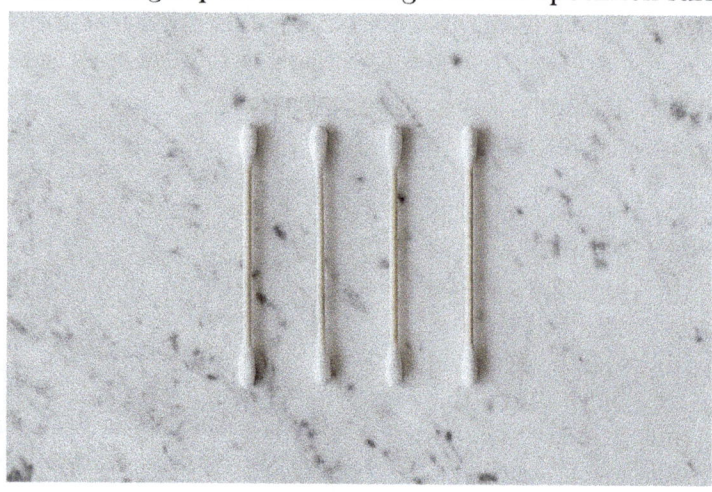

Cotton swabs are ideal for cleaning hard-to-reach places.[47]

5. **Tweezers**: Tweezers are extremely helpful when handling small minerals, such as gemstones, and larger ones with intricate designs or shapes that require careful handling during the cleaning process. For example, tweezers can help you maneuver around tight spaces better than other tools due to their slender tips; this allows you to easily grip the specimen without crushing it or causing any damage whatsoever! Make sure that the ones you use have blunt tips since sharp tips can cause puncture marks in your specimens.

Tweezers make it easier to handle small minerals.[48]

6. **Air Abrasives:** Air abrasives are devices that create an air stream filled with abrasive material (usually sand) at extremely high speeds, which allows you to safely remove stubborn dirt/debris buildup on minerals without causing any harm or damage to them whatsoever due to their gentle nature despite their high-speed capabilities. This type of device is excellent for removing larger chunks of dirt/debris buildup quickly and efficiently while still preserving delicate surfaces on your mineral specimens all at once!

7. **Ultrasonic Cleaner:** This device is designed specifically for deep-cleaning minerals at microscopic levels without damaging them, making it perfect for those who want their specimens to look as close to perfect as possible! This machine uses sound waves combined with special liquid solutions (detergents), which create bubbles and cavitation forces powerful enough to remove even the most stubborn particles without damaging the delicate structure of your minerals!

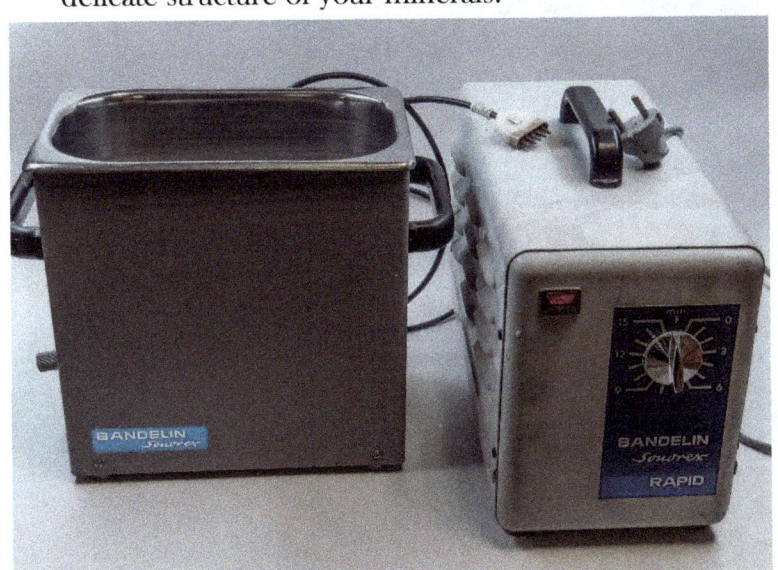

An ultrasonic cleaner cleans minerals at microscopic levels.[49]

8. **Vacuum Cleaner:** Finally, Vacuum cleaners are often used by professional collectors who need an efficient way of removing all traces of dirt from specimen surfaces quickly and effectively without having to resort to scrubbing manually or using harsh chemicals that could potentially harm their valuable pieces!

These work by sucking up dust particles into a filter bag where they can be disposed of safely without ever coming into contact with your specimens again, making them ideal for keeping collections looking neat and pristine!

Vacuum cleaners are essential for removing traces of dirt.[50]

9. **Magnifying glass:** Finally, although it isn't considered a cleaning, it can be useful for examining small details on your specimen so you can better observe any imperfections before attempting to clean them off.

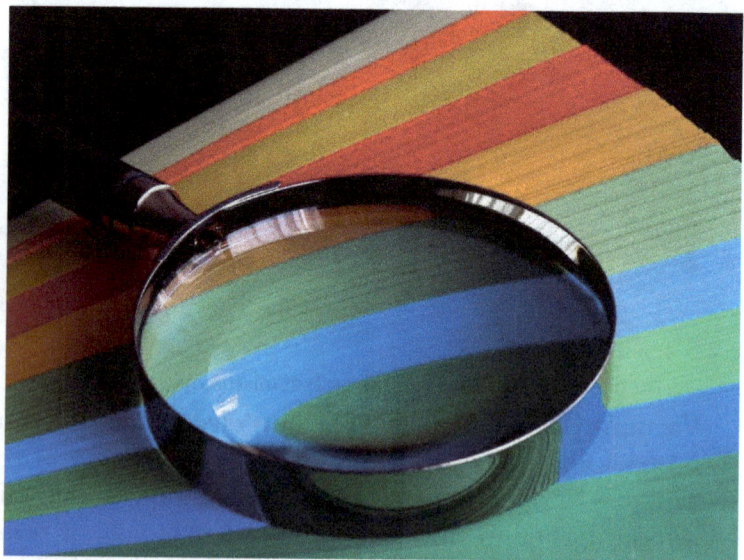

A magnifying glass can help you see small details on your specimen.[51]

With these tools and devices, you should have no issue keeping your mineral collection as beautiful as possible!

Easy to Clean Minerals

1. **Quartz** – Quartz is one of Earth's most common and versatile minerals. It is composed of two main components: silicon dioxide (SiO_2) and oxygen (O_2). The SiO_2 gives quartz its hardness, which is why it is often used for making jewelry and other items. It also has an incredibly smooth surface that makes it easy to clean without damaging the mineral itself. To clean quartz, use a soft cloth or brush with warm water and mild soap or detergent. Avoid using any corrosive chemicals or abrasives that could scratch the surface of the quartz.

2. **Feldspar** – Feldspar is a silicate mineral composed primarily of aluminum silicate ($Al_2Si_3O_8$). It can be found in igneous rocks like granite and basalt and, depending on its composition, can range in color from white to pink. Sometimes feldspar can contain small amounts of iron oxide, which can give it a reddish hue. It is very durable yet still relatively easy to clean; simply use a soft cloth dipped in warm water with some mild soap or detergent to remove any dirt or debris from its surface.

3. **Hematite** – Hematite is an iron oxide mineral with a metallic grayish-black coloration due to the presence of iron within its chemical structure (Fe_2O_3). Its name comes from the Greek word "*haima*," meaning "blood," because hematite sometimes has streaks of red due to the presence of rust on its surface. It has very low cleavage, but because it contains iron, it should only be cleaned regularly with water and mild detergents. Avoid using any corrosive chemicals or abrasives on the surface of the mineral.

4. **Talc** – Talc is another silicate mineral composed primarily of magnesium silicate ($Mg_3Si_4O_{10}(OH)_2$). It typically forms during metamorphic processes when heat causes existing rock structures containing talcose rocks to recrystallize into new shapes; this process makes talc much softer than other types of minerals like feldspar or quartz, which have harder surfaces due to their higher levels of crystallization over time. To clean

talc, use warm water and either soap or mild detergent, then gently scrub with a soft-bristled brush; avoid using any type of acidic cleaner which could damage the delicate surface structure of talc over time.

5. **Pyrite** – Pyrite is an iron sulfide (FeS_2) mineral that has a metallic gold/yellow look due to its high sulfur content giving off a distinct brassy smell when rubbed between fingers as well as giving off sparks if struck hard enough against metal objects like steel tools or coins. Pyrite requires special care when cleaning because not only does it have cleavage along certain planes, making it more prone to breakage, but also because some acidic cleaners might corrode away at its surface over time if used too often, damaging its appearance permanently. For the best results, use warm water mixed with mild soap/detergent, followed by gently scrubbing pyrite's surfaces with a soft-bristled brush and avoiding contact with acids.

6. **Calcite** – Calcite is calcium carbonate ($CaCO_3$) in crystal form, typically ranging from white through light yellowish-brown colors making this carbonate mineral one of the most commonly found forms on Earth's crust. Its name derives from the Latin word "calx," meaning lime, referring back to the calcium component in the calcite's chemical formula mentioned above. Calcite needs specialized care during cleaning; warm water combined with mild detergents followed by gentle brushing across the calcite's surfaces should do just fine, avoiding contact with anything acidic whatsoever.

7. **Gypsum** – Gypsum is another carbonate mineral composed of calcium sulfate dihydrate formula ($CaSO_4 \cdot 2H_2O$). Gypsum usually appears whitish with yellow shades. However, other shades might occur depending upon impurities included within gypsum's chemical structure. To clean it, use warm water mixed with mild detergents and a gentle brushing session. Be careful of possible damage caused by dryness inside the gypsum's structure, especially along fracture lines.

Chapter 9: Your First Rockhounding Trip

Have you ever felt the thrill of finding newly unearthed rocks and stones? If not, it's time to plan your first rockhounding adventure! But with so much to consider before setting out, it can often be a confusing and intriguing task. This chapter will provide you with tips on navigation tools, safety guidelines, and a blueprint of the trip ahead to ensure that it is as smooth and stress-free as possible. Whether you're an experienced hounder or a complete beginner, after reading this chapter, you'll have everything you need to plan a perfect rock-hunting excursion!

Tips to Plan a Rockhounding Trip

Rockhounding is an incredibly rewarding activity that requires careful planning and preparation to maximize your chances of success. It involves searching for rocks, minerals, gems, fossils, or other geological specimens. While there is no one-size-fits-all approach to rockhounding, this guide will provide a basic outline of how to plan a

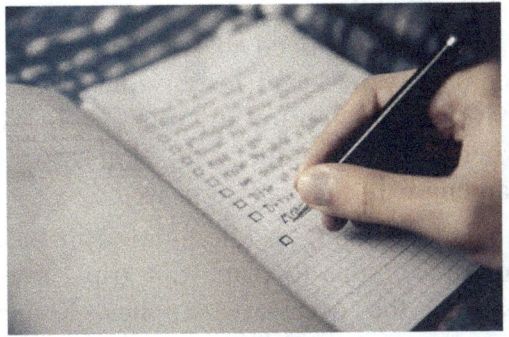

Planning your rockhounding trip will help give you a clear sense of direction.[53]

successful rockhounding trip.

First, you must research the area you plan on visiting. There are several factors to take into consideration when deciding on a location – including accessibility, facilities available (such as shops or restrooms), local regulations regarding collecting activities, and any potential hazards that may exist in the area. Make sure you understand the local geology well, including which minerals and fossils can be found in the area. Additionally, it's important to familiarize yourself with the laws and regulations that govern rockhounding activities in your chosen destination.

Once you've done your research, it's time to start planning out the details. Determine how long you want to spend – whether it's a day or a full weekend – and make sure you factor in any additional travel time if necessary. If you plan on bringing children along with you, pack snacks, water, and other supplies they may need during their outing.

When it comes to the specific tools you'll need for rockhounding, there are several options available. A geologist's hammer and chisel are ideal for removing larger samples of rocks or fossils from a site. If you search for smaller specimens, a handheld magnifier or loupe will help you examine small details. Finally, make sure you bring a durable bag or backpack to transport whatever you find back home safely.

While out on a rockhounding adventure, always practice safety and be aware of any potentially hazardous conditions, especially if you're exploring large boulder fields or dig sites. Rockhounding also requires physical exertion, so wear protective clothing and footwear suitable for the terrain. Also, don't forget to bring plenty of water – especially during the hot summer months – as dehydration can be a very real risk in these environments.

Finally, you need to remember that rockhounding is an activity that requires respect and responsibility when it comes to nature. Before you leave any site, return any rocks or fossils you don't want to take back to where you found them. By doing so, future generations of rockhounds can enjoy those locations as well.

If done right, rockhounding can be a fun and rewarding experience. Just make sure to plan your trip carefully by researching the area and packing the necessary supplies. Remember to always practice safety, respect nature and leave any sites you visit exactly how you found them. With proper preparation, your next rockhounding trip is sure to be a success!

Safety Equipment

When it comes to rockhounding trips, safety should always be a priority. Many types of safety equipment can help you stay safe while on your trip. Here are some tips on what kind of safety equipment you should have with you when going rockhounding:

1. **Protective Clothing and Gear:** Wearing protective clothing and gear is essential for any outdoor activity, but especially for rockhounding trips. Wear long-sleeved shirts, pants, or jeans that cover your legs and closed-toe shoes that provide good traction. A good pair of work gloves will protect your hands from sharp rocks and other debris and offer protection from the sun's rays. A hard hat or headlamp is important to ensure you don't hit your head on rocks while digging.

2. **First Aid Kit:** When going rockhounding, having a first-aid kit with you is important in case of any unexpected injuries. Ensure the kit contains basic items like bandages, antiseptic cream, pain relief medication, and an ice pack. It's also wise to include a snakebite kit if you plan on exploring areas where snakes may be present.

3. **Water and Snacks:** You should always bring plenty of water when embarking on any outdoor activities, as dehydration can occur quickly in hot climates. Additionally, bringing some snacks with you can keep your energy levels up.

4. **Communication Device:** It's important to bring some kind of communication device with you when going rockhounding. This can be either a cellular phone or a two-way radio. This will allow you to call for help in case of an emergency.

5. **GPS/Compass:** If you are exploring an unfamiliar area, it is important to have a good sense of direction and know where you are at all times. A GPS or compass will ensure you don't get lost and can find your way back to the car or campground should the need arise.

6. **Safety Ruler:** Using a safety ruler when rockhounding is essential for your own protection and the environment around you. A good quality safety ruler provides an extra layer of protection from any sharp edges or hazards that may be present in areas where you are exploring.

7. **Flashlight/Headlamp:** Having a flashlight or headlamp with you is important for safety and convenience. This will allow you to explore even after dark.
8. **Backpack:** A sturdy backpack is an excellent way to store all necessary gear while on the trails. Make sure to choose a bag that has plenty of room and is comfortable to carry, as well as one that will protect your items from the elements.

Rockhounding trips can be a great way to explore nature and discover hidden gems, but safety should always come first. By following these tips on safety equipment, you can ensure that you have the best possible experience while out rockhounding!

Tips on Mining Equipment for Rock Hounding Trip

Rockhounding trips can be a great way to explore the outdoors and find precious gems, minerals, and fossils. To make these trips successful, you must have the right equipment. Here is a list of essential mining equipment that every rockhound should consider carrying on their next trip:

1. **Rock Hammer:** A rock hammer is one of the most essential tools for any type of rockhounding trip. It will allow you to chip away at rocks and break them apart to examine them more closely. Many different types of hammers are available, so make sure you choose one that fits your hand comfortably and has enough weight to do the job.
2. **Chisels:** Chisels are another essential mining tool for rockhounding. They can be used to carve into rocks and break them apart, as well as to shape the edges of a specimen so that it looks more aesthetically pleasing. When choosing chisels, make sure they are made from high-density steel and have comfortable handles.
3. **Safety Goggles:** When breaking apart rocks, there is always the chance of chips or fragments flying in all directions. To protect your eyes, wear safety goggles. Make sure you also choose a pair with UV protection since many gemstones will emit ultraviolet light when exposed to sunlight.

4. **Dust Mask:** Since a lot of dust will likely be created when breaking apart rocks, it is important to wear a dust mask to protect your lungs from airborne particles. Choose a dust mask that fits snugly on your face and has several layers of protection.
5. **Collecting Bags:** When out rockhounding, you will need something to put all your finds in to stay organized and not get lost or damaged. Invest in collecting bags with multiple compartments which can easily fit into a backpack. This way, you can keep all of your specimens contained and safe while still having plenty of room for other essential items.
6. **Magnifying Glass:** A magnifying glass is an invaluable tool when examining specimens closely. Look for one with multiple magnification levels so that you can get a better view of smaller details.
7. **Geologist's Hammer:** A geologist's hammer has two different ends, one pointed and the other flat. The pointed side is used for chipping away at rocks and breaking them apart, while the flat end allows you to examine specimens more closely without damaging them. Choose one with a comfortable handle, as this tool will be used frequently during your rockhounding trip.

With the right equipment, rockhounding trips can be fun and successful. Remember that safety should always be your priority when heading out into the wilderness. With the proper tools and knowledge, you can have an enjoyable time while also keeping yourself safe from harm.

Tips on Navigation Tools

Navigation tools are the most important pieces of equipment to bring when going rockhounding. When searching for rocks in unfamiliar places, navigation tools help you find your way back and make sure you don't get lost while exploring. Here is a list of items that can help you stay on track during your next rockhounding trip:

1. **Field Guides:** A field guide is essential for identifying rocks and minerals in the field. It provides detailed information on how to recognize different geological features, types of rocks, and common formations. It also offers helpful advice on where to search for certain minerals or stones in specific locations. It

is lightweight, compact, inexpensive, and can be easily carried in a pocket or bag.

2. **Site Map**: A site map is a detailed topographical map of the region where you will be rockhounding. It provides information about local landforms, terrain features, roads, and vegetation which can help you plan your route and locate areas of interest. The map also contains symbols indicating mining claims, restricted areas, and other data useful for rockhounding.

3. **GPS Receiver:** A Global Positioning System (GPS) receiver is another essential tool for rockhounding trips. This device uses satellites to accurately pinpoint your location so you don't get lost while exploring unfamiliar territory. Most modern-day GPS receivers are equipped with a detailed map of the region and other useful features like waypoints, track logs, and route planning.

4. **Compass**: A compass is an old-fashioned but still essential navigation tool for rockhounds. While GPS receivers provide more precise information about your location, compasses are more reliable regarding directions because they don't rely on satellites or electricity to function. Compasses also come in handy when navigating through dense vegetation where satellite signals may be blocked or distorted.

5. **Binoculars:** Binoculars can help you spot potential sites from a distance before heading out into the field. This is especially helpful for those who are searching for precious stones that sparkle in the sunlight, such as diamonds or rubies. Binoculars are lightweight, compact, and relatively inexpensive compared to other navigation tools.

6. **Whistle:** A whistle is an important item to bring along when rockhounding in remote areas, just in case something goes wrong and you need help. It can be heard from far away and used to signal distress, if necessary, which could potentially save your life.

These are some of the most important navigation tools that should be brought on every rockhounding trip. While they may all seem like small items, they can make a huge difference when it comes to finding valuable rocks, staying safe, and getting back home in one piece.

Rockhounding Techniques

Rock-hunting is an enjoyable and educational activity for both adults and children. It can teach kids about the natural world around them while also providing a pleasant escape from everyday life. However, some safety considerations should be taken into account before embarking on a rock-hunting trip.

Before heading out on any rock-hunting excursion, research the area you intend to visit and become familiar with local laws and regulations regarding collecting rocks or minerals. Some parks may have restrictions in place banning the removal of any materials, so it is best to check ahead of time to avoid any potential legal issues. Additionally, it is important to check the weather before embarking on a rock-hunting expedition; extreme temperatures or inclement weather can put you at risk of heat stroke or hypothermia if you don't take the proper precautions.

Pack appropriate clothing and equipment for the environment when setting out for a rock-hunting trip. Wear sturdy boots with good grip and traction to ensure your safety and protect from slipping on wet surfaces. Bring layers, such as a waterproof jacket, to stay warm in cold conditions. Depending on the location, you may also want to bring some sunscreen, sunglasses, insect repellent, and a hat for protection from the sun's rays and any potential biting insects.

Bringing along a basic toolkit is also essential for any rock-hunting trip. A hammer and chisel are necessary to break apart rocks that may be too large or heavy to carry in their entirety. Handheld magnifying glasses help identify small pieces of minerals, while a couple of brushes can come in handy for dusting off dirt or debris from the surface of rocks. You may also want to bring some safety equipment such as gloves, goggles, and kneepads – especially if you plan on looking under larger boulders or into crevices that have sharp objects.

When out on a rock-hunting trip, take your time and pay attention to your surroundings. Be aware of any potential hazards and keep a lookout for snakes, spiders, and other critters that may be lurking in the rocks and crevices. Additionally, do not damage any of the natural resources you encounter while searching; try to leave as little evidence of your activity as possible.

Finally, when returning home from a rock-hunting trip, inspect each rock and mineral before packing them away in your collection boxes or bags. This will prevent any unwanted pests from coming into contact with your valuable finds. Remember to label each specimen with its location information, so you can easily refer back to it when needed.

Rock-hunting can be an exciting and rewarding experience for adults and children. By following these tips and preparing ahead of time, you can ensure a safe and successful rock-hunting excursion. With the right precautions, this activity can be educational and enjoyable, with lifelong memories. So, get out there and start collecting! Happy hunting!

Chapter 10: Legal Considerations

Rockhounding is a thrilling pastime that involves the search and collection of rocks, minerals, and fossils. However, you must be aware of the legal considerations associated with this pursuit. In this chapter, we will delve into the legal aspects of rockhounding that you need to consider, such as ethical guidelines, private property regulations, and area-specific restrictions and prohibitions.

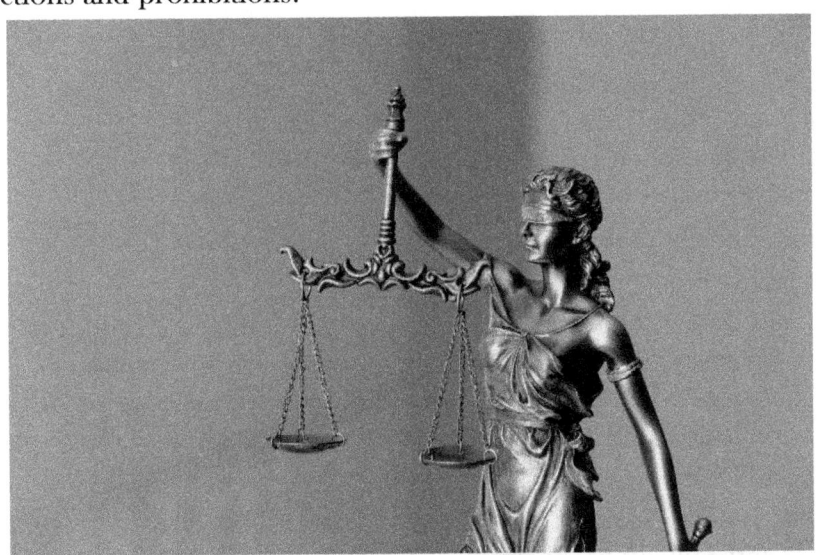

It is important to know the laws and regulations before rockhounding.[53]

When you engage in rockhounding, you need to adhere to the established principles of conduct that govern this activity. By being a responsible rockhound and demonstrating respect for the environment, others' property, and geological formations, as well as properly disposing of waste, you contribute to the preservation of this hobby for future generations to appreciate.

It is also vital for you to consider the legal implications of private property when rockhounding. In most cases, you will need to seek permission from landowners before searching for rocks on their land. Trespassing on private property can result in penalties such as fines and imprisonment, among other consequences. Therefore, familiarizing yourself with private property rules and laws is essential before you embark on a rockhounding adventure.

Furthermore, various locations have distinct regulations regarding what is permissible and prohibited during rockhounding expeditions. Some areas may impose restrictions on your collection of specific rocks or minerals or limit the quantity you can gather. You may be required to obtain permits to collect specimens in certain places, or additional rules may apply.

Knowledge of and adhering to these guidelines and restrictions is paramount in preserving the natural beauty and geological significance of the areas you explore.

Rockhound's Code of Ethics

Rockhounds, as individuals and as teams within clubs, take great satisfaction in their polite behavior when out in the field. They understand the importance of preserving their good name if they want to continue receiving favorable treatment at collection sites.

The following code of ethics is widely accepted throughout the rock-collecting community:

- **"I will not trespass on private and public properties and get permission before taking anything from privately owned grounds."** - This shows how important it is to ask someone's permission before going onto their property to collect rocks or minerals.
- **"I will be knowledgeable about and follow all laws, regulations, and guidelines governing collection on private properties."** It is important to follow the rules, laws, and regulations that apply to rock hunting on private property to stay out of trouble with the law.

- **"To the best of my abilities, I will determine the property boundary lines on which I want to collect."** To avoid unintentional trespassing and property damage, be careful of the boundaries of the area where you plan to collect.

- **"I will not use any weapons or explosive materials in rock hunting areas."** No weapons or explosives should be used while rockhounding to protect the environment and not hurt yourself or others.

- **"I will not deliberately damage any property, including fences, signs, and buildings."** You must respect properties like fences, signs, and buildings by not destroying them on purpose. Doing otherwise could get you in trouble with the law and hurt the good name of the rock-hunting community.

- **"I will not make any changes to the gates of the collecting grounds."** This reminds you not to change or damage the gates of the collecting grounds, whether they are private or public. Respect the property owner's wishes to keep getting access to their property.

- **"I will only start fires in approved areas and make sure to put them out before I leave."** You should only build a fire in places that are specifically marked, and before leaving, you must put it out.

- **"I will not throw out any burning items, like matches or cigarettes."** You must be careful and use good judgment when smoking or using matches. Don't throw away anything that could catch fire without considering the possible risks.

- **"I will plug any holes I dug."** You must fill in any holes or places you dug that could hurt people, cattle, and other living things in the area.

- **"I will not pollute wells, streams, or other water sources."** You must be careful about what you do near water sources. You should not do anything that could pollute wells, streams, or other bodies of water.

- **"I will only take what I have the need for."** You must show that you greatly appreciate the specimens you find. Be careful not to damage the specimens you find and not take too many of them. This principle shows how important it is to respect and value the environment and the natural resources it provides.

- **"I will value and safeguard natural assets."** This promise to protect the wealth of natural resources should come from a deep respect for the environment and the living things it supports. By showing that you know about and follow important rules, you hope to encourage responsible rock hunting and protect the environment for future generations.

Those are consistent throughout every rockhounding community. Other principles include the following:

- I will help the Rockhound Project H.E.L.P. (Help Eliminate Litter Please) by leaving all collecting areas litter-free, no matter how I find them.
- I agree to follow the instructions of the fieldwork leaders and other authorized personnel at all times while collecting specimens.
- If I find any fossilized wood or other materials on government land that should be preserved for the benefit of coming generations and national scientific and educational reasons, I will notify the leaders of my society or the union to which I belong, the Bureau of Land Management, the National Park Service, or other appropriate authorities.
- I shall follow the "Golden Rule," utilize Good Outdoor Manners, and always behave in a way that will enhance the status and reputation of rockhounds worldwide.

Rules of Using Public Land

The following are guidelines that protect public properties.

- Using motor vehicles and ATVs is restricted to existing or recognized routes. In rainy weather, avoid driving on unpaved roads. In addition to the danger of being stuck, extensive rutting is likely to develop, degrading the road's condition for other visitors.
- Leave no trace by properly disposing of garbage (pack it out and bury it 6-9 inches underground) and by using already primitive sites instead of making new ones.

- Several popular rockhounding locations on public lands are close to protected wilderness areas. These are wilderness areas that are being studied. In these areas, motorized traffic is confined to approved routes. No motorized or mechanical conveyances are allowed in wilderness areas. Bicycles are not exempt from this rule.
- Cutting down living or dead fauna is not acceptable.
- Surface collecting is the only kind of rockhounding permitted. You are not allowed to dig until you are cleared to do so.

The Reason behind Rules and Restrictions

The main reason there are rockhounding restrictions is to protect the environment, which is frequently hurt by the activity. Excavating and digging for minerals can have very bad effects on the environment. If rockhounding is done without care, it can upset fragile ecosystems and put rare or endangered species at risk of extinction.

Cultural and historical places are typically the homes of priceless cultural treasures, including petroglyphs, antiquities, and ancient houses; there are restrictions to safeguard these locations. If you go to these places to look for rocks and minerals, you might accidentally damage or destroy them.

Another reason there are limits and bans on rock hunting is that it uses natural resources. Some places are known for having a lot of valuable minerals and rocks, but too much rock hunting can cause these resources to run out.

Mining and rock-hunting rules exist in some parts of the United States, including California, Colorado, and Oregon. For example, in California, the Department of Conservation oversees how minerals and rocks are taken from public lands. In Colorado, the Division of Reclamation, Mining, and Safety ensures that mining rules are followed to protect the environment and people's health. The Department of Geology and Mineral Industries regulates mining and mineral exploration on public land in Oregon. This includes making sure that rules about protecting the environment, cleaning up after mining, and keeping the public safe are followed.

By following the rules that are in place and being responsible when rockhounding, people can enjoy this exciting hobby while helping to protect the environment and cultural heritage.

The federal agencies in charge of public property determine the legality of collecting rocks, minerals, and fossils from it. Gathering rocks, gemstones, and fossils is often prohibited, but there are some collection permits with specific restrictions.

The first step in determining if rock gathering is permitted is deciding what public property you are on and which public authority controls it. Research each kind of public property, the rules and regulations governing whether rockhounding is permitted, and the limits that apply if so.

You should get expert legal assistance when ownership is unknown or when you're in doubt. Even though it can appear to be a lot of work, figuring out what is and isn't legal before a trip can make a big difference.

Bonus: Grow Your Own Crystals

Isn't it amazing that you can grow some of these beautiful and expensive crystals? Growing crystals yourself can be much easier than you think, especially when items like Epsom salt, alum, and sugar are available in your home. The step-by-step instructions on making each crystal are so easy that children can grow them for fun.

You might have questions like; what type of crystals can be grown at home? How to begin the process? How safe are growing crystals at home? How long does it take to grow a crystal successfully? The answers to these questions and more will be made clear in this chapter.

What Crystals Can You Grow at Home?

There are a lot of crystals that can be grown at home. Here are some of the most popular ones.

- **Sugar Crystals**

Sugar crystals, also known as rock candy. They are obtained from cane sugar; you can get them from your local markets.

- **Salt Crystals**

To grow salt crystals, you only need salt- the table salt (sodium chloride) you use for cooking. The shape of salt crystals is cubic.

- **Alum Crystals**

Many individuals tend to utilize alum as a seasoning in their soup recipes. In addition to its culinary uses, it is also frequently employed as a water purifier. It can be readily obtained from nearby markets or supermarkets. To cultivate alum crystals within your residence, a handy fishing line is necessary.

- **Epsom Salt Crystals**

Epsom salt is a salt from a naturally occurring magnesium sulfate. It is also called Epsomite, and it is popular for its ability to relieve muscle pains. As a result, aside from your local markets, you can also get Epsom salt in drug stores. This is the fastest crystal to grow at home.

- **Borax Crystals**

Borax is a whitening agent for clothes. It is a powder usually added to washing detergents to make clothes whiter. Borax is very easy to get. You only need to walk to the detergent aisle at your local supermarket or order it online.

- **Sulfur Crystals**

The sulfur powder used to make these can be purchased online from local markets and pharmacies. The process of making sulfur crystals is by melting. Seeing how sulfur is quite flammable, an adult should supervise the kids if they're the ones making sulfur crystals.

- **Lead Crystals**

Many people confuse lead crystals with glass composed of a large amount of lead. A glass with a large amount of lead is called flint glass or lead crystal glass. Whereas the "lead crystal" is one obtained from lead acetate. Saturn was known to be the alchemical name for lead, which is why lead crystals are called the tree of Saturn.

- **Copper Sulphate Crystals**

Copper sulfate crystals are blue diamond-shaped crystals, and they are obtained from copper sulfate. This sulfate is originally used in its anhydrous form as a drying agent. It is also used as an animal nutritional supplement, an additive when making foods and fertilizers, and for several industrial applications like wood, paint, textiles, ink, leather, batteries, and even petroleum.

- **Bismuth Crystals**

They are simple grayish blocks that become stair-shaped crystals with iridescent colors after melting. Those pretty colors you see when something melts are caused by light playing around with a special film on the crystals that form when they cool down. You can get bismuth blocks from supermarkets or online stores.

Methods of Growing Crystals at Home

There are different methods of growing crystals at home, but they depend on the solubility of crystals in water or other solvents, their volatility, and other properties. However, the basic ones are:

1. Growth by Melting

The process of melting growth is the most popular method of growing crystals. It works for almost all crystals and is effective in growing bulk crystals. This particular method requires melting and then solidifying the substance to form crystals. The substance can also be made into crystals by allowing the liquid to cool below its freezing point and solidify. Another good thing about this technique is that the rate of growth of crystals is higher than in other methods. However, with this technique, your crystals are prone to contamination either from the atmosphere or the vessel you use.

This method can further be broken down into:

• Bridgman Method

This involves growing single crystal boules. To get a single crystal material from your polycrystalline material, you need to heat it up in a container until it melts. Then, let it cool slowly from one end while keeping a seed crystal nearby. As you cool it down, the single crystal material will start forming along the container's length. You can do this method either horizontally or vertically.

Some of the advantages of this method include the following:

- It is cost-friendly.
- It is simple and easy to implement, requiring minimal attention and maintenance.
- Crystals can be formed in a sealed ampule.
- Dislocations are produced from reduced thermal stresses.

• Zone Melting Method

When using zone melting, a tiny bit of material is melted in a bigger piece of solid to make a liquid area.

The advantages of this technique include the following:

- The chance to manipulate the distribution of soluble impurities through a solid.

- Impurities are usually concentrated in one spot. That makes removing them easy.
- It can be useful in purifying semiconductor crystals like Gallium and Silicon.

- **Skull Melting**

If you're growing materials that don't melt easily, then it's a good idea to go with this method. For example, cubic Zirconium and other imitations of a diamond can be produced using the radio-frequency skull system, which is a super-hot melt process. For this reason, the materials involved have to have high melting points.

- **Vernuil Method**

A very clean and smooth substance made by combining oxygen and hydrogen is sprinkled onto the end of a specially chosen, perfectly shaped crystal. This crystal seed must be fixed to a lowering mechanism. The formation of crystals results from the coordination of the consumption of Oxygen and Hydrogen with the rate of decline.

The good thing about using this method is that your crystals are saved from container contamination as no containers are involved. Single crystals of sapphire and ruby can be grown with this method, and their growth can be observed.

- **Kyropoulos Method**

The growth of crystals using this technique is simply the result of the cooling of a seed crystal. While heat is dissipated, the temperature of the furnace must be controlled. This is so that the temperature does not exceed the material's melting point. Crystals grown with this method are grown in large-diameter spaces, allowing for the formation of optical components like prisms.

2. Growth from Vapor

This is mostly used to grow large crystals and thin coatings. This method can also grow crystals of gas compounds and even diamonds. The process of growth from vapor is divided into two:

- The physical transport method involves moving things from a really hot place to a cold place by changing them from solid to gas or liquid to gas. The diffusion or evaporation of materials leads to deposits in the form of single crystals.

- The chemical transport method involves transporting materials in the form of chemical compounds. The growth of crystals here highly depends on the type of reaction in the growth area.

3. Growth from Solution

This is the method of growing crystals from aqueous solutions. This thing happens when it gets really hot and super pressurized. The watery mixtures that are a part of it are usually alkaline. It supports the growth of materials or alumina and calcite, amongst others. It is divided into three types:

- **High-Temperature Solution Growth**

This growth method uses solvents that are effective at above-room temperatures. The materials to be crystalized are dissolved in these solvents. As the solution becomes highly supersaturated, crystals are formed.

- **Low-Temperature Solution Growth**

The solvents usually used in this technique include water, acetone, and ethyl alcohol. There are three methods under this technique, and they include:

a. Slow Cooling method

Large volumes of saturated solution are required for this technique, however, at a reduced temperature range, higher than room temperature. This solution is then poured into a crystallizer and sealed. It happens when things are really hot and squished together. The watery mixtures involved are usually kind of alkaline. Crystals start to form after a small crystal is put into the liquid and the container it's in is cooled down with water.

b. Solvent Evaporation Method

Here, an excess amount of the solute is used, and this is based on the principle that the rate of evaporation of solvent and solute are different. The volume of the solution decreases as the solution loses particles weakly bound to themselves as vapor forms. Although, in many cases, people prefer to use a solvent with a higher vapor pressure so that when the solvent evaporates, the solution becomes supersaturated.

c. Temperature Gradient Method

For this method to work, you would have to transfer the material involved from a hot region containing the material's source to be grown to a cooler region with a supersaturated solution – the smaller the temperature variation, the larger the growth rate.

- **Gel Growth Method**

All that is required here is the combination of the two appropriate compounds to give rise to the crystal required. The crystal is formed due to the chemical reaction between the two compounds. The gel obtained by chemical processes like hydrolysis is called chemical gel (for example, silica), while that obtained from a physical process like cooling is called physical gel (for example, clay and gelatin).

This method of growing crystals is important for the following reasons:
1. A high-quality output.
2. It can be applied to studying how crystals are formed.
3. The degree of convection is reduced with this method.

Of all the methods listed above, the solution method is the best method for growing crystals at home.

Growing Crystals, Yourself
Sugar Crystals

Ingredients:
- 2-3 cups of sugar
- 1 cup of water
- A glass jar
- A string, wool or cotton
- A pencil
- Paper towels
- Food coloring (optional)

Instructions:
1. Bring water to a boil in a small kettle or saucepan.
2. Remove the heat and then slowly stir in the sugar. You can put in one teaspoonful or tablespoonful at a time.
3. Put enough sugar in the water until the water can't take in any more sugar

4. In case you want the sugar crystal to have a particular color, a few drops of food coloring can be added to the solution
5. By using a separation method called decantation, the solution should be properly poured into a jar without adding undissolved sugar
6. Take a pencil and tie a string in the middle of it
7. Place the pencil on the rim of the jar and make sure the string is close to the jar's bottom but not touching the sides or the bottom of the jar
8. Cover the top of the jar using a few paper towels and keep it in a secure environment.
9. Within 24 hours, the crystals will start to grow on the string. You can remove and dry them after a day or wait until the crystals become as large as you want.

Salt Crystals

Ingredients:
- Table salt (preferably un-iodized salt)
- A glass jar
- 1 cup of boiling water (preferably distilled water)
- A string
- A butter knife or pencil

Instructions:
1. Pour your boiling water into a saucepan
2. Slowly stir your table salt into the water until the solution becomes saturated and the salt can no longer dissolve in the water.
3. Pour the mixture into the container, being careful not to let any remaining salt particles into the container.
4. Then, tie a piece of string to the center of a butter knife or pencil.
5. Position the knife on the outer edge of the jar and let the string hang loosely into the solution without making contact with the inner walls or base of the jar.
6. Once that's done, cover the jar with several layers of paper towels
7. Like the sugar crystal, the salt crystal will start growing within a day.

Alum Crystals

Ingredients:

- 2 tablespoons of alum
- About 1/2 a cup of hot tap water
- Two glass jars
- One nylon fishing line (the fishing line has to be nylon because alum does not stick to nylon)
- A butter knife or pencil

Instructions:

1. Take one of the jars and fill it up with hot water from the tap.
2. Next, add in the alum until it stops dissolving.
3. After that, leave the jar alone in a safe spot overnight.
4. The following day, pour the alum into the second jar, making sure to keep an eye out for any seed crystals that may have formed.
5. Once you spot a good-sized or well-formed crystal, use a piece of nylon fishing line to tie it up.
6. Attach the other end of the line to the middle of either a butter knife or pencil.
7. Allow the fishing line to dangle near the bottom of your jar while your knife rests on the rim. Make sure that the crystal is fully immersed.
8. Cover the jar with a paper towel.

Epsom Salt Crystals

Ingredients

- ½ cup of hot tap water
- A measuring cup
- ½ cup of Epsom salt
- Food coloring (optional)

Instructions

1. Put the hot tap water in the measuring cup. It should be about ½ cup.
2. Add half a cup of Epsom to the water and stir.

3. To make your crystals colorful, just add a bit of food dye!
4. Then, pop the cup into the fridge until everything cools down.
5. You should see the crystals the moment you remove them from the refrigerator.
6. Decant the solution and allow the crystals to dry.

Borax Crystals

Ingredients:
- 4 tablespoons of Borax powder
- Pipe cleaners
- A thread
- One cup of boiling water
- A pencil or butter knife
- A glass jar

Instructions:
1. Collect a vast amount of fuzzy, bendy wires and bend them into whatever form you desire.
2. Fasten a string to each wire to keep them secure.
3. Attach the opposite end of the strings to the center of a writing instrument or table knife.
4. Gently pour a cup or more of hot water into the jar and slowly add four tablespoons of borax powder for each cup of water.
5. Vigorously stir the concoction continuously until little borax settles at the bottom of the jar.
6. Position the pencil or knife on the border of the jar. Let the curly pipe cleaners hang close to the bottom without making contact with the foundation or the edges of the jar.
7. Cover with a paper towel and allow it to sit overnight so the borax crystals will grow in the twisted pipe cleaners.
8. Take out the pipe cleaners and lay them on a new paper towel to dry.
9. You can now remove your crystals.

Sulfur Crystals

Ingredients:
- Sulfur
- A saucepan

Instructions:
1. Place the sulfur in the saucepan and place over medium heat.
2. Slowly and carefully melt the sulfur to avoid starting a fire.
3. Once it has fully melted, remove the heat, and allow it to cool. As the sulfur cools, the crystals will begin to form.

Lead Crystals

Ingredients:
- Lead acetate (about 10 grams)
- A brass nut
- 100 ml of water
- Zinc strip

Instructions:
1. Dissolve the lead acetate in 100 ml of water to form a solution.
2. Put the zinc strip into the solution. You can add or leave out the brass nut because brass has zinc in it.
3. The lead acetate will react with the zinc to form black lead crystals and zinc acetate. The formation of crystals will resemble an inverted tree.
4. Take out the crystals from the mixture so that lead sulfate forms a white or gray coating on their surfaces.

Copper Sulfate Crystals

Ingredients:
- Copper sulfate
- A cup of boiling water
- A glass jar
- A saucepan

- A butter knife
- Small plate

Instructions:
1. Mix the copper sulfate in the water by slowly stirring until the water can no longer dissolve it.
2. Then, pour a small amount of the mixture onto a plate and save the rest for later use.
3. As the mixture on the plate begins to evaporate, tiny seed crystals will be left behind.
4. To retrieve the best crystals, use a butter knife to scrape them off the plate and put them in the saved mixture in a jar.
5. Make sure the crystals do not touch each other in the jar.
6. Store the jar in a secure place, allowing the crystals to grow to the desired size.
7. When ready, use a butter knife to remove the crystals from the jar, then stash them in an airtight container or plastic bag until they turn greenish-gray after evaporation.

Note: Do not use your bare hands to touch the crystals or the solution.

Bismuth Crystals

Ingredients:
- Bismuth
- A fork
- 2 saucepans (preferably stainless steel)

Instructions:
1. Put the bismuth in one of the pans and heat it up until it's liquid.
2. Once it's melted, you'll see a gray film on top of it that keeps it from turning into crystals.
3. Use a fork to gently remove this gray layer.
4. Heat up the other pan and transfer the melted bismuth to it.
5. Then, slowly cool down the pan to promote crystal formation.
6. This process should take a short time, approximately 30 seconds.
7. Pour away any liquid bismuth that appears as soon as the bismuth begins to form.

8. Once it has fully cooled, remove the crystals.

Note: The saucepans used to heat the bismuth should not be used for cooking again because it is a heavy metal and quite toxic.

Some Fun Facts about Crystals

- Crystals you make at home can be great gifts
- Crystals like bismuth can make beautiful jewelry.
- They can be used to decorate trees.

The growth of crystals depends on the nature of the material from which the crystals would be borne, the temperature, the solubility, and how prepared you are to make the crystals and duly follow instructions. Growing crystals can be challenging, but like many other experiments, it is a fun activity for you and your kids. Making crystals yourself is a great way to get them without going rockhounding. You should try any one of the methods above in your spare time and see for yourself how fun and rewarding it can be.

Conclusion

Embrace rock collecting as the enjoyable pastime it really is! Although it may seem daunting initially, you can easily begin with a few basic tools by following this book's guidance. Be sure to tap into all available resources, including expert insights and advice from seasoned rock collectors.

As you embark on more adventures and amass a diverse collection of rocks and minerals, you'll grow more confident with the tools and techniques used in the hobby. Additionally, your ability to identify a wide range of rocks and precious minerals will improve.

Rock hunting offers more than just the pleasure of admiring beautiful specimens; it's a gateway to learning about geology, geography, history, and other science-related disciplines. Each rock or mineral has a unique story about its origins and formation, allowing you to better understand the world around you as you uncover these natural treasures.

It's essential to collect rocks responsibly, ensuring that you're in a legal area and taking care of the environment. Refrain from collecting rocks or minerals from protected areas, such as national or state parks.

As you expand your knowledge and experience in rock hunting, consider joining a group or attending rock and mineral shows. These events provide an excellent opportunity to connect with fellow collectors and deepen your understanding of the hobby.

Typically, these short events have a reasonable entrance fee and showcase a wide variety of extraordinary specimens. While vendors are the primary focus, you'll also find demonstrations, exhibits, and displays. You may even have the chance to trade or purchase specimens to grow your collection.

Stores that sell gemstones, rocks, and minerals are good places to meet people who share your interests and to see good examples of the things you've been learning about. The people who work there might know about good clubs and places to go to find rocks in the area. Tourist stores might have some rocks from the local area, but they may not have employees who know as much as the people who work in specialty stores.

Rockhounding is an enjoyable activity for people of all ages, providing endless opportunities for discovery, whether you're a teenager starting your journey or an adult seeking a new hobby.

Keep in mind that finding museum-quality specimens is rare. With some luck, you'll discover pieces that are perfect for your personal collection. Uncovering those specimens requires dedication and effort, and even seasoned experts occasionally come up empty-handed. The key is to venture out and relish the experience!

Part 2: Rocks, Gems, and Minerals

What You Need to Know about Crystals, Gemstones, Agates, and Other Rocks

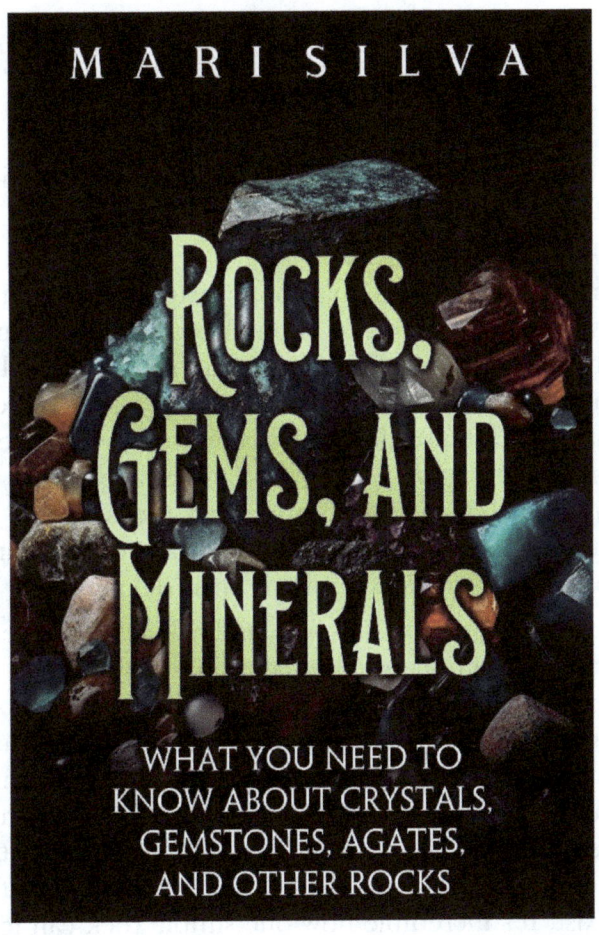

Introduction

Do you have a passion for rocks and gems? Are you looking to build a collection or turn your interest into a business? This guide will cover all these topics and more.

Rocks, gems, and minerals may appear to be mundane objects to some, but they contain a wealth of knowledge about our planet. Taking a closer look at these earthly wonders reveals some incredible facts. For example, many types of gemstones are formed under extreme pressure and temperatures so intense that our bodies cannot survive them. They also exist in a dizzying variety of colors and shapes, each with its own unique composition. Uncovering more about rocks, gems, and minerals can provide an exciting window into the natural world around us. It's an opportunity for exploration that is sure to bring delight!

Rocks have the power to transport us back across time, as many as millions of years ago. Though inanimate, they nevertheless tell tales that span multiple eras. These geological stories can help us further understand our planet's history and present conditions. On the other side of the geological spectrum lie gems and minerals. While gems are prized for their beautiful shimmer – and what is deemed rare beauty – minerals are more valued for their practical use in construction projects. From walls to roads, minerals comprise the basic building blocks that allow larger structures to exist. It's incredible how one simple rock can tell a story that spans millennia, offers unconditional beauty, and can simultaneously be used in crucial engineering endeavors.

Learning about these wonders of nature helps us connect with our Earth's origins and appreciate them in our everyday lives. This guide will explore each type of rock and mineral, teaching you their individual characteristics and helping you identify them. This guide will show you how to use them in a variety of ways, from creating jewelry to collecting specimens. From ore to crystals, this guide will provide you with the essential knowledge you need to make the most of your rocks and gems.

This comprehensive guide is ready to take you on a journey through the fascinating world of rocks, gems, and minerals. By the end, you'll have the tools to become a rock and mineral expert like never before. The simple and easy-to-understand layout makes it a great resource for novice and experienced enthusiasts alike. So read on to discover what these fantastic objects can teach you!

Chapter 1: The Basics of Rocks, Gems, Crystals, and Minerals

Do you know what makes up the Earth's crust? When we look at a landscape or stepping stones leading to our front door, we look at rocks. When we admire a diamond or an opal, we look at gemstones. And when we hold a rose quartz crystal or a piece of pyrite, we look at minerals. Rocks, gems, and minerals each have characteristics that make them distinct.

This chapter explores the scientific definitions of rocks, gems, and minerals. It will discuss how they are formed and uncover the different types of each. It will also introduce some fun facts about them that you may have never heard before!

Rocks

Rocks are fascinating geological objects which help us understand our environment. They come in all shapes and sizes, from tiny stones to mammoth boulders, and each one offers a better glimpse into the world of science. Rocks are composed of minerals or pieces from previously existing rocks and are created naturally through geologic processes. Rocks form when sediment is compressed and heated by tectonic forces, allowing them to take on specific characteristics depending on their environment. Rocks play an integral role in our understanding of the universe around us.

The study of rocks gives us insight into many mysteries of our planet and how it was formed over the ages.[54]

Rock Formations

Nothing beats a great adventure outdoors to appreciate rock formations' incredible beauty. Not only are they mesmerizing for their sheer size, but many areas have different types of rock formations that boast dazzling colors from crushed minerals and even fossils from other life forms. Exploring those smaller details can be especially rewarding when paired with spectacular views composed of ancient mountains eroded over time. The awe-inspiring grandeur of some unusual rock formations can make for an unforgettable experience.

Types of Rocks

From the Grand Canyon to Mount Everest and even the roads we drive on, rocks are the foundation of the Earth. The Earth's crust comprises millions of different kinds of rocks, but do you know that there are only three types? These three types have specific characteristics and are formed through different processes.

1. Igneous Rocks

Igneous rocks are the most commonly found on the Earth's surface. These rocks form when molten rock material, magma, cools and solidifies. Depending on where they form, igneous rocks can be categorized as extrusive or intrusive.

When magma cools and hardens gradually *beneath the earth's surface*, intrusive igneous rocks are created. On the other hand, extrusive igneous rocks are created *on the earth's surface* as magma rapidly solidifies and cools. Some examples of igneous rocks include basalt, granite, and pumice.

2. Sedimentary Rocks

Sedimentary rocks are formed when weathering and erosion break down rocks into small fragments that get transported to a new place by water or wind. These pieces –referred to as sediment – are deposited and compacted in the new place. Sedimentary rock is the end product. Clastic, chemical, and organic sedimentary rocks can be further divided into categories. The collection of grains and rock pieces results in clastic rocks. Shale and sandstone are two examples. Chemical rocks form from the precipitation of minerals from water. An example of this is limestone. Organic rocks, such as coal and fossils, are composed of the remains of plants and animals.

3. Metamorphic Rocks

Metamorphic rocks are formed when existing rocks get transformed by immense heat and pressure. They are often found at the site of mountain-building processes, where tectonic plates collide, creating high temperatures and pressures. Foliated and non-foliated metamorphic rocks can be distinguished based on the source rock. Due to the arrangement of minerals under intense pressure, foliated metamorphic rocks appear layered or banded. Slate and Gneisss are two examples. The surface of non-foliated metamorphic rocks is uniform and rough. Quartzite and marble are two examples.

Every rock on Earth falls into igneous, sedimentary, or metamorphic. The type of rock and its characteristics reveal valuable information about its history and the processes that occurred to create it. Understanding each rock type's properties is essential in geology, mining, and environmental conservation. So, the next time you come across rocks on your walks, remember these simple entities are more than just pebbles. They are a fundamental piece of the Earth's history.

Interesting Facts about Rocks

Rocks are one of the most fascinating subjects that everyone can appreciate. Even though they might not seem like much, they possess a range of interesting facts that people might not be aware of. From precious stones to ordinary gravel, rocks play an essential role in our daily lives. Here are some interesting facts about rocks that will surely spark your curiosity.

- The moon is made up of rocks called lunar rocks, and scientists have been studying them since 1969 when Apollo 11 landed on the moon.
- Did you know that the world's largest rock is in Australia? It's called Uluru, also known as Ayers Rock. This sandstone rock stands nearly 348 meters high and measures 9.4 kilometers in circumference.
- Did you know that some rocks can float? Pumice is a type of volcanic rock that is filled with gas bubbles. This unique structure makes it light enough to float on water.
- Did you know how old rocks can be? Some rocks, such as granite, can be as old as 3 billion years! Some of the rocks you see in your backyard could have formed within the very first days of Earth's history.
- Did you know that there is a special type of rock called Tektites? Tektites are formed when meteors impact the Earth's surface and melt the rocks around it. These melted rocks are then forced into the atmosphere and eventually fall back to Earth as Tektites.

Rocks hold a valuable history of the Earth's past, and studying their composition can provide essential clues about past geological activities. It's like a time capsule with secrets about the early Earth's environment, conditions, and the organisms that once roamed it.

Gems

Humans have always been fascinated with shiny, rare objects that can be worn as jewelry. And there's no object more precious than a gemstone. Gems are more than just objects of beauty. They are minerals formed deep beneath the Earth's surface that take millions of years to develop. The mysteries of their journey from the Earth's crust to our jewelry boxes are enchanting. Let's dive deeper into the world of precious stones to satisfy your curiosity.

Definition

In the simplest form, gems are rocks valued for their rarity, beauty, and durability. They are formed deep within the Earth's mantle, under extreme pressure and heat. Geological activities such as volcanic eruptions and earthquakes cause gems to rise to the Earth's surface, where they are discovered by humans. Though diamonds are the most sought-after gemstone, many other precious and semi-precious gems such as rubies, emeralds, sapphires, topaz, and more exist.

How They Are Formed

There are various ways in which gems can be formed, depending on the minerals that have been subjected to heat and intense pressure beneath the Earth's mantle. For example, diamonds are formed when carbon goes through extreme pressure and temperature, typically found deep within the Earth, up to 150 to 200 km deep. Alternatively, some gems may also be formed through geological processes like volcanic activity, erosion, or mining. These processes can take millions of years, which is why gems are considered rare and valuable.

Setting the Value

Apart from their formation, the beauty of the gemstones also depends on their color, cut, and clarity. While formed under high pressure, different minerals cause color variations, commonly called the "chroma." Some gems require specialized treatment to enhance their natural color and transparency, while others can be used in their raw form. The gem's cut refers to the proportions and symmetry of the facets or flat surfaces. Through cutting, gems are fashioned into different shapes, such as round, oval, or princess, multiplying their worth in turn.

Gemstones are easy to purchase, and their value largely depends on the "four Cs" carat, cut, color, and clarity. The carat refers to the weight of the stone, whereas color is an important aspect of higher-priced gems. Clarity is the lack of inclusions, the naturally occurring imperfections, and the cut refers to the facets' number, position, and angles.

Types of Gemstones

Gems have always been as charming as the mystery of their origin. They have been serving mankind as a sign of luxury and prosperity since time immemorial. Let's take a deeper look at different types of gemstones:

1. Precious Stones

The term "precious" indicates scarcity, high quality, and cost. The four precious stones are diamonds, rubies, emeralds, and sapphires. Diamond is the epitome of all precious stones. It is the hardest mineral on Earth, looks stunning in its colorless form, and its luster is enhanced if colored. Ruby is the iconic red gemstone that signifies love, courage, and protection. Emerald is a green gemstone that symbolizes beauty, elegance, and rebirth. Sapphire is a blue gemstone that represents sincerity, loyalty, and peace. Precious stones have been used in royal jewelry and engagement rings for centuries due to their rarity and durability.

2. Semi-Precious Stones

The term "semi-precious" indicates abundance, lower cost, and lower hardness. Semi-precious stones encompass a broad range of mineral specimens. Some popular examples are amethyst, garnet, peridot, topaz, and turquoise. Amethyst is a purple gemstone that represents wisdom, peace, and intuition. Garnet is a red gemstone that symbolizes protection, strength, and confidence. Peridot is a green gemstone that signifies healing, balance, and growth. Topaz is a yellow gemstone representing good fortune, success, and creativity. Turquoise is a blue-green gemstone that symbolizes friendship, communication, and protection. Semi-precious stones are an affordable choice for everyday jewelry and offer a diverse selection of colors and designs.

Main Differences

The main differences between precious and semi-precious stones are their costs, hardness, rarity, and symbolism. Precious stones are more expensive than semi-precious stones due to their scarcity, quality, and origin. Semi-precious stones are cheaper but still offer a vibrant range of colors and shapes. Precious gems have a higher score on the Mohs hardness scale, which means they are more resistant to scratches and damage. Semi-precious stones are softer and require more precautions to maintain their luster over time. Precious gemstones are rarer and have a more significant meaning in the world of jewelry because of their tradition and value. Semi-precious gemstones have more cultural diversity and offer a broader range of possible symbols and purposes.

Interesting Facts about Gemstones

There is no denying that gems are more than just jewelry. They are natural treasures with remarkable stories to tell. From their formation to their journey to our jewelry boxes, the precious stones have an awe-inspiring journey that makes them extremely valuable. Here are some interesting facts about gemstones:

- Did you know that more than 4,000 different mineral species exist on Earth?
- Opal is the only gemstone to display all of the rainbow's colors simultaneously.
- The world's oldest diamond is estimated to be 3.2 billion years old!
- Rubies are one of the few gems that can be found in the same color as they were when first mined.
- Emeralds are the rarest of all precious stones, and some can cost hundreds of thousands of dollars!
- Amethysts are believed to have healing and spiritual qualities.

The rarity, beauty, and durability of gems make them a perfect symbol of love and friendship and an ideal collection to pass down to the next generation. Don't underestimate the gemstones' allure and ability to transform your outfit and mood. As the saying goes, "Diamonds are forever," and so is the enduring beauty of all other gems. So, choose the gemstone that speaks to you, and cherish it for life.

Minerals

Regarding natural resources, minerals have always been a fascinating subject of study. Revered for their beauty, value, and industrial applications, minerals can be found on every continent and across every ocean. This section will take a closer look at the world of minerals, defining what they are, their properties, and how they're formed. Whether you're a collector, student, or simply curious about the subject, this information will enrich your understanding of the beauty and complexity of minerals.

Minerals occur naturally in our world and have a crystalline structure with a defined chemical composition. A substance must be naturally formed without human intervention and have a unique crystal structure to be considered a mineral. Some of the most common minerals include quartz, feldspar, calcite, and olivine. Each mineral is unique and can be distinguished by its structure, color, hardness, and other factors.

Mineral Properties

Minerals have a range of physical properties that distinguish them from one another. These properties include luster, cleavage, and hardness.

- **Luster:** the way minerals reflect light
- **Hardness:** the resistance of a mineral to scratching
- **Cleavage:** the way any mineral splits along clean planes

These properties can be used to identify a mineral, along with its color and other characteristics. Some minerals, like diamonds, are known for their extreme hardness, while others, like sulfur, are prized for their vivid colors.

Mineral Formations

Minerals are formed in various ways, often through the slow cooling and crystallization of magma or the mineral deposit left from evaporating bodies of water. In some cases, minerals grow over long periods in rock cavities, forming unique and intricate crystal structures. Other minerals, like gold and silver, are formed deep within the Earth and are mined for their value. Some minerals can even form through biological processes, such as the formation of shells and bones. Understanding the different ways in which minerals are formed can give us insight into the history and geology of the Earth.

Types of Minerals

Geologists classify minerals as inorganic, naturally occurring compounds with a particular chemical makeup and crystal structure. These rocks and minerals are vital in various facets of our daily lives, including technology, agriculture, construction, and medicine. Let's take a closer look at the different types of minerals and their uses and discover their role in our day-to-day activities.

1. Native Elements

Native elements are minerals that are composed of single elements. They are relatively rare, but some of them, such as gold (Au), copper (Cu), and silver (Ag), are very coveted for their beauty and value. Gold, for example, has been used for millennia as a form of currency, jewelry, and even dental fillings. On the other hand, copper is instrumental in conducting electricity and is used in various electronic devices like smartphones and laptops.

2. Silicates

The largest group of minerals is silicates which comprise nearly 90% of the Earth's crust. This group includes feldspar, mica, quartz, and clay. Silicates are useful in the production of ceramics, construction materials, and electronic components. For example, quartz is an essential component of watches and electronic components. The right balance of quartz ensures that they keep accurate time.

3. Oxides and Hydroxides

Oxides and hydroxides contain oxygen and hydrogen atoms but different numbers of cations. Hematite is one of the most common oxides and is used in pigments, jewelry, and the production of iron. Bauxite, another oxide, is used in the production of aluminum. Hydroxides, on the other hand, are important components of soil chemistry and are used in wastewater treatment plants.

4. Sulfates and Carbonates

Sulfates and carbonates are minerals that play a significant role in construction, agriculture, and medicine. Sulfates are components of gypsum and are used in the production of wallboard, cement, and fertilizer. Carbonates include minerals like calcite, dolomite, and aragonite – essential components of limestone and marble. They are used in the production of cement and other construction materials.

5. Halides

Halides are minerals that contain halogen atoms, such as chlorine, fluorine, bromine, or iodine. Fluorite, for example, is used in producing hydrofluoric acid, which is used in the semiconductor industry. Halides are also used as salt in various food products, while iodine is used in producing X-ray contrast agents and iodized salt.

These five major groups of minerals are just a few of the many types found within the Earth's crust. Each type's unique properties and characteristics make them invaluable in various industries and applications. As science advances, we are sure to uncover more uses for rocks and minerals.

Interesting Facts about Minerals

While it may seem like minerals are just rocks and stones, they have a variety of properties that make them truly fascinating. Here are some interesting facts about minerals:

- The world's oldest known mineral is zircon, which was discovered in rocks dating back over 4 billion years old!
- The diamond is the hardest mineral, with a hardness of 10 on the Mohs scale.

- Some minerals are fluorescent, meaning they glow when exposed to certain types of light.
- Aquamarine, the official birthstone for March, is a blue-green variety of beryl.
- "Mineral" comes from the Latin word for "to lead," referring to the idea that minerals could be melted and molded into shapes.
- Some minerals, such as opal, contain water trapped in their structure.
- Calcite is the most common sedimentary mineral and is formed by the precipitation of calcium carbonate from water.
- The largest crystal ever found was a giant selenite weighing 55 tons and measuring 11 meters long!

Exploring the world of minerals can be a fascinating and enriching experience. From their definition to their unique properties and formations, minerals offer a glimpse into the natural world and the complexity of the Earth. Whether you're a passionate collector or simply interested in learning more, understanding the world of minerals can help us appreciate the natural world in new and exciting ways.

Rocks, gems, and minerals are integral to the Earth's makeup and essential materials for our daily lives. Rocks are aggregates of minerals that form when minerals cool and solidify. Gemstones are minerals cut and polished to create beautiful jewelry pieces. By understanding the different types available in nature, we can appreciate their integral role in our day-to-day lives. These natural wonders remain essential to the modern world, from simple construction materials to precious gems.

Chapter 2: Igneous Rocks

Have you ever been amazed by the natural beauty around you? From stunning landscapes to intriguing rock formations, the natural world has its way of leaving us in awe. Igneous rocks are a fascinating aspect of the natural world that hold valuable information about the Earth's history. From the slow-cooling granite to the rapid-cooling obsidian, each igneous rock has a particular story to tell. The significance of igneous rocks lies in their place in geology.

This chapter will explore the nature of igneous rocks, their formation process, and how to identify them. Firstly, the four categories of igneous rocks (felsic, intermediate, mafic, and ultramafic) will be examined, and examples of each type will be provided. Finally, some tips for identifying these types of rocks in their natural environment will be discussed. By the end, you'll better understand them and their significance in geology.

Overview of Igneous Rocks

One of the most awe-inspiring sights in nature is a volcano erupting. The lava flows, the pyroclastic explosions, and the fiery flares of molten rock are a spectacle to behold. But have you ever wondered what happens to all that magma once it has cooled and hardened? The answer is igneous rocks. The world of igneous rocks is fascinating, from their formation to their different types and unique features.

What Are Igneous Rocks?

Igneous rocks are formed from solidified magma or lava that has cooled and crystallized. The word igneous comes from the Latin word *ignis*, meaning fire. These rocks are created underground or above the Earth's surface during volcanic activity. Igneous rocks are among the most common types of rocks on the planet, and they can be found in various locations, from volcanic islands to mountain ranges and even in the depths of the ocean.

How Are Igneous Rocks Formed?

As mentioned before, igneous rocks are formed by solidifying molten rock material, whether above or below the Earth's surface. Intrusive or plutonic igneous rocks include granite, while an example of extrusive or volcanic igneous rocks includes basalt. Volcanic eruptions can also cause pyroclastic flows, forming tuff, ash, and other igneous rocks.

Types of Igneous Rocks

Igneous rocks can be classified into two major categories, intrusive and extrusive. Extrusive igneous rocks have a fine-grained texture due to their rapid cooling and lack of visible crystals, like obsidian or basalt. Intrusive igneous rocks are characterized by visible crystals on their surface and have a coarse-grained texture, like granite or diorite.

Igneous rocks can also be classified based on their mineral composition. Mafic (or basaltic) rocks are high in iron and magnesium and have a dark color. On the other hand, Felsic (or granitic) rocks are high in silicon and aluminum and are usually lighter in color. Intermediate rocks have a mineral composition in between mafic and felsic rocks. These rocks are fascinating and beautiful natural formations. Their unique features and formation process make them essential in our understanding of Earth's geology. The next time you come across a rocky outcrop or a volcanic landscape, you'll be able to identify the type of rock formation and appreciate the beauty and wonder of igneous rocks.

Felsic Rocks

When it comes to understanding the Earth's crust, rocks are a crucial component that tells us a lot about the geological history of our planet. The Earth's crust comprises different types of rocks, including igneous rocks. Felsic rocks are one of these fascinating igneous rocks with very particular compositions and characteristics. The term felsic comes from the words feldspar and silica, which are two of its primary components.

Examples of Felsic Rocks

Felsic rocks are light in color and rich in silicon, aluminum, potassium, calcium, sodium, and oxygen. Some of the most common types of felsic rocks include granite, rhyolite, and pumice. Granite is a coarse-grained rock and the most prevalent type of felsic rock. On the other hand, Rhyolite is a fine-grained volcanic rock, rich in silicon, making it resistant to weathering. Pumice is a type of volcanic rock that floats in water, and it appears in different shapes, including volcanic glass with bubbles.

Granite is an example of a popular felsic rock.[55]

Characteristics of Felsic Rocks

One of the critical features of felsic rocks is their composition, which consists of high levels of silica and alkali metal oxides such as potassium and sodium. These minerals give felsic rocks their light color and resistance to weathering. Felsic rocks also have a higher viscosity than mafic rocks, which implies that they resist flowing as quickly as mafic rocks. Besides, felsic rocks often have visible crystals, which give them a distinctive appearance. This type of rock is also associated with explosive volcanic eruptions.

Tips to Find Felsic Rocks

If you're trying to find felsic rocks, one of the best places to start is in mountain ranges, particularly in regions with a lot of volcanic activity. Another way to find felsic rocks is to search for exposed rocks with visible crystals. Granite, for example, is an excellent place to find felsic rocks since the visible crystals can be seen with the naked eye. Finally, you can look for areas of the landscape with different colored rocks, particularly those with red or pink tones.

Uses of Felsic Rocks

Felsic rocks, or igneous rocks rich in the elements of feldspar and quartz, are fascinating creations of the natural world and have many uses. From roofing tiles to applications in geothermal energy, these versatile rocks have been a boon to humanity and industry. Felsic rocks can also act as aquifers for water storage, and their formations often include valuable minerals like quartz and gold. They have even been used to fill lake and ocean beds for land reclamation. Felsic rocks can also be seen in some of the most stunning landscapes on Earth. From towering ash clouds billowing at volcanoes to glimmering lava flows coating hillsides, they truly do make up some of nature's most beautiful artwork.

These rocks are a fascinating component of the Earth's crust. Their composition and characteristics make them easily distinguishable from other types of igneous rocks. From their rich colors to their unique mineral makeup, felsic rocks are a fascinating topic for both geologists and rock enthusiasts. These rocks were formed by magma that was rich in silica, resulting in a distinctive texture and appearance. Looking closely, you may even spot some feldspar or quartz minerals embedded within the rock. Felsic rocks are a testament to the intricate and complex nature of our planet's geology, a reminder of the fascinating forces that continue to shape our world today.

Intermediate Rocks

Are you passionate about rock collecting and want to take your hobby to the next level? Intermediate rocks could be a fascinating new challenge for you. These rocks are more complex than basic rocks yet less intense than advanced-level rocks. Intermediate rocks offer a variety of unique colors and patterns that will keep you engaged for hours. This section will discuss the characteristics and examples of intermediate rocks and provide you with some tips on how to find them.

Examples of Intermediate Rocks

Intermediate rocks are mainly classified based on their chemical composition. These rocks have a silica content ranging from 52% to 66%. Some popular examples of intermediate rocks are andesite, diorite, and trachyte.

Andesite is an example of an intermediate rock.[56]

- **Andesite** rocks have a medium-gray color tone and are usually identified by their fine-grained structure. You will often find black, white, or brown mineral deposits in andesite rocks.
- **Diorite** is a coarse-grained rock with a salt and pepper-like appearance that comes from the mingling of dark and light minerals. Mica and amphibole minerals are to be found in this rock type.
- **Trachyte** rocks are often identified by their dull gray color and fine-grained structure. These rocks are composed of alkali feldspar, plagioclase feldspar, and small amounts of biotite, hornblende, and other minerals.

Characteristics of Intermediate Rocks

Intermediate rocks are distinguished by their unique features. They are often dark gray or light green, with spots or streaks of black, white, or brown minerals. The grains within these rocks are neither too fine nor too large and can be seen with the naked eye. Intermediate rocks are also denser than basic rocks, which makes them harder and more resistant to erosion. These rocks often have a more complex internal structure with layers and bands of different minerals. The mineral composition determines its strength, durability, and resistance. These rocks often contain a mix of feldspar, quartz, and mica minerals.

Tips to Find Intermediate Rocks

Intermediate rocks can be found in a variety of locations. If you are looking for diorite, search for outcrops around granite, volcanic rocks, or mountain-building zones. Andesite rocks can often be found in areas with recent volcanic activity or the areas of the Pacific Basin. Trachyte rocks are found in locations that were once sea floors but now make up dry land. Look for exposed rocky outcrops with white, gray, or pale green shades around these areas. When searching for intermediate rocks, keep an eye out for the distinctive patterns and textures that characterize these rocks. Try to look for rocks along riverbeds, streams, or dry lakebeds. You could also check where rocks have been recently exposed within road cuts or construction sites.

Uses of Intermediate Rocks

From forming the foundation of roads and sidewalks to providing a protective barrier around buildings, intermediate rocks are essential for residential and commercial projects. They also play a key role in creating bridges and large-scale structures, making it possible to build spans that can support a tremendous amount of weight. Quite impressive, don't you think? The uses of intermediate rocks extend far beyond these practical purposes as well. They have been featured in architectural works of art such as sculptures and monuments, adding structural stability without compromising aesthetics. From utilitarian to stylish, intermediate rocks always deliver remarkable results!

Rock collecting can be an enriching and fascinating hobby. With intermediate rocks, you can explore an even more complex area of rock collecting, discover unusual colors and patterns, and grow your knowledge about these interesting rocks.

Mafic Rocks

Have you ever heard of mafic rocks? Well, if you haven't, then you're in for a treat because we're going to explore the wonders of these amazing rocks. Mafic rocks are some of the most common in the world and can be found almost everywhere. They may not be as well-known as their cousin, granite, but they are just as important. So, let's dive into the world of mafic rocks and learn all about their examples, characteristics, and tips to find them.

Examples of Mafic Rocks

Mafic rocks are also known as basaltic rocks, and one of the best-known is basalt. Basalt is a volcanic rock often found near the surface of the Earth. It is usually a dark color with a fine-grained texture, known for its durability and resistance to weathering. Another example of a mafic rock is gabbro, an intrusive rock usually found deeper in the Earth's crust. It is often used as a construction material due to its strength and durability.

Gabbro is an example of a mafic rock.[57]

Characteristics of Mafic Rocks

Mafic rocks are characterized by their high levels of magnesium and iron. They are high in density, dark in color, and have a low silica content. Mafic rocks are also known for their ability to conduct heat and electricity, making them useful in various industrial applications. They can be formed below and above the Earth's surface and come in a range of textures, from fine-grained to coarse-grained.

Tips to Find Mafic Rocks

Mafic rocks can be found in various environments, including volcanic regions, oceanic crust, and even some mountain ranges. One of the best ways to find them is to look for areas with volcanic activity. The lava flows that come from volcanoes are often made up of mafic rocks like basalt. Another way to find mafic rocks is to look for areas of exposed bedrock, especially where erosion occurs. Look for dark-colored rocks with a coarse texture; these are often signs of mafic rocks.

Uses of Mafic Rocks

Mafic rocks have many uses, including construction, roadwork, and industrial applications. Basalt, for example, is often used as a building material for both residential and commercial structures. It is also used in constructing roads and bridges due to its durability and strength. Gabbro is used in countertops, flooring, gravestones, and markers due to its resistance to wear and tear. Mafic rocks are also used in steel production, as they can be added to the molten metal to increase its strength.

Mafic rocks may not have the same popularity as their cousin, granite, but they are just as crucial. The high levels of magnesium and iron in mafic rocks make them useful in various applications, from construction to industrial uses. So, the next time you come across a dark, dense rock, take a closer look, and you might be looking at a magnificent mafic rock.

Ultramafic Rocks

Nature is full of surprises, and exploring rocks and minerals is one of the best ways to discover what our planet offers. Ultramafic rocks are a particular type of rock that is fascinating to study due to their unique characteristics. If you love geology and are curious about ultramafic rocks, then read on and learn all about these incredible rocks.

Examples of Ultramafic Rocks

Ultramafic rocks are a group of igneous and metamorphic rocks which are composed predominantly of minerals with a high magnesium and iron content. Some common examples of ultramafic rocks are peridotite, dunite, pyroxenite, and serpentinite. Peridotite is the most abundant type of ultramafic rock and is commonly found in the Earth's mantle. Dunite is a type of peridotite that is almost entirely made up of olivine. Pyroxenite is composed mainly of pyroxene minerals like augite and enstatite, while serpentinite is formed by the alteration of ultramafic rocks under the influence of water.

Peridotite is an example of ultramafic rocks.[58]

Characteristics of Ultramafic Rocks

Ultramafic rocks have several characteristics which distinguish them from other rock types. Firstly, they are rich in magnesium and iron, which give them a characteristic dark green to black color. They also have a high density, making them heavier than most other types of rock. Ultramafic rocks are also known for their resistance to weathering, erosion, and chemical breakdown, due to the high stability of their mineral content. This is why they are often found as exposed outcrops and are sometimes used in construction as durable building materials.

Tips to Find Ultramafic Rocks

One of the best ways to find ultramafic rocks is to look for them in areas with geologically active tectonic processes. Specifically, areas with mantle upwellings or areas of past geological activity like ophiolite complexes can be ideal locations for finding ultramafic rocks. These rocks are usually closer to the Earth's surface along fault lines and fractures, so searching for areas where rocks are exposed or accessible can be helpful. Ultramafic rocks are also valuable sources of minerals like chromite and nickel, making them of interest to mining companies. Thus, taking a mining tour can also provide an opportunity to see ultramafic rocks up close.

Uses of Ultramafic Rocks

Ultramafic rocks are rich in raw materials and can be used for various purposes. They make up the thickest section of the Earth's mantle and hold valuable iron, magnesium, chromium, gold, and platinum deposits. Ultramafic rocks are ideal for manufacturing essential items like cellular phones and television sets because they contain both ferromagnesian silicate minerals with large amounts of magnesium and iron.

Ultramafic rocks are also an excellent source of refractory metals such as titanium, tungsten, chromium, molybdenum, cobalt, and beryllium, which help protect sensitive equipment when exposed to extreme temperatures or conditions. In addition to their industrial uses, ultramafic rocks play a significant role in environmental science because they contain minerals that absorb pollutants from runoff water or forest fires. Truly invaluable natural resources!

Ultramafic rocks are fascinating geological marvels worth exploring if you are interested in geology. With their unique characteristics, they provide a glimpse into the inner workings of our planet and offer insights into how our world came to be. By taking some time to study and explore them, you can gain a better understanding and appreciation of the natural world around us.

Identifying Igneous Rocks

With their interesting textures and vibrant colors, igneous rocks are truly a sight to behold. From silky smooth obsidian to grainy granite, each igneous rock is a product of its own unique formation process. While identifying these rocks may seem daunting at first, once you start to notice the subtle differences in texture and appearance, you'll begin to understand the fascinating stories they have to reveal. Here are some tips to help you identify and classify igneous rocks.

- **Mineral Content:** Igneous rocks are made up of different minerals, each type having its own distinct mineral compositions. For example, felsic rocks typically comprise quartz, feldspar, mica, and other silicate components. Mafic rocks, on the other hand, contain more dark minerals such as olivine and pyroxene.

- **Texture:** Igneous rocks come in various textures, from smooth and glossy to coarse and grainy. Obsidian is an example of smooth and glossy igneous rock, while granite has a coarse, grainy texture.

- **Color:** Igneous rocks come in a variety of colors, from dark gray to yellow and pink. Pay attention to the overall hue of the rock and any variations in the color.

- **Visible Crystalline Structures:** Most igneous rocks contain at least some large crystalline structures that can be seen with the naked eye. Observe any patterns or shapes in these crystals to help identify the type of rock.

When it comes to identifying igneous rocks, practice makes perfect. The more you handle and observe these rocks, the more familiar you will become with their unique properties and characteristics. Additionally, don't be afraid to seek resources such as books, online guides, or fellow rock enthusiasts who can help you.

Igneous rocks are classified into extrusive or volcanic and intrusive or plutonic. Extrusive rocks cool down quickly on or near the Earth's surface, while intrusive rocks cool down slowly deep in the Earth's crust. Igneous rocks are also classified based on their mineral composition and texture and can range widely from fine-grained basalt to coarse-grained granite.

In conclusion, igneous rocks are an essential part of the Earth's geology, and understanding their properties and characteristics is crucial in fields such as geology, mining, and construction. While this chapter has only scratched the surface of what we know about igneous rocks, hopefully, it has sparked your interest and curiosity about the natural world. Geology is an exciting and ever-evolving field, so keep exploring and discovering, and who knows what amazing things you might find.

Chapter 3: Sedimentary Rocks

Have you ever wondered about the rocks which make up our planet's land surface? It may surprise you that most of these are called sedimentary rocks. From sandstone to shale and limestone, sedimentary rocks have been around for millions of years. They're more than just stunning geological formations. They also contain vital clues about the geologic history of our planet. Studying these remarkable rocks can open your eyes to untold stories of our Earth's evolution.

This chapter will explain the basics of sedimentary rocks, including their composition and characteristics. Also discussed will be the three categories of sedimentary rocks, clastic, organic, and chemical. After learning about these categories, specific types of sedimentary rocks, such as limestone, sandstone, siltstone, and shale, will be discussed. This chapter will end with a summary and the benefits of knowing about sedimentary rocks.

Introduction to Sedimentary Rocks

Sedimentary rocks are often taken for granted, mostly because they appear so common and plain and are seen everywhere. However, these rocks are not only abundant, but they also hold an extensive record of Earth's history. This is what makes sedimentary rocks fascinating to study. Let's uncover the stunning splendor that resides within sedimentary rocks as we delve deeper into their captivating world.

Formation of Sedimentary Rocks

Sedimentary rocks form when tiny particles and organic matter gather and amalgamate. These materials are then compressed and cemented together to form a solid rock. There are three main sedimentary rock types: clastic, chemical, and organic. Clastic sedimentary rocks are made when small pieces of rocks and minerals combine together. Chemical sedimentary rocks are formed from the precipitation of minerals from a solution. Organic sedimentary rocks are formed from the accumulation of shells, bones, and plant remains.

Layers and Formation

Sedimentary rocks are formed in layers, and each layer tells us a story about the past. Each layer's thickness, composition, and color give us clues about how the rock was formed and how the environment changed over time. The oldest layer is found at the bottom, while the most recent layer is at the top. The layers also reveal how the landscape has changed, including the presence of rivers, oceans, and deserts during different periods. We can learn about the history of climate, geography, and life on Earth through sedimentary rocks.

Common Sedimentary Rocks

Sandstone, limestone, and shale are some of the most common sedimentary rocks. Each of these rocks has unique properties and uses. Sandstone is made of sand grains cemented into solid rock. It is often used as a building material. Limestone is made of calcium carbonate, often deposited by shells and the remains of marine organisms. It is a popular building material and is also used in agriculture and industry. Shale is made of clay and often contains fossils. It is used as a source of oil and natural gas.

Uses of Sedimentary Rocks

Sedimentary rocks have a wide range of uses. They are used as building materials, such as sandstone, limestone, and slate. They are also used in agriculture. For example, limestone is used to raise the pH of acidic soils. Sedimentary rocks are also used in industry. For example, shale rock is used as a source of oil and natural gas. Furthermore, these rocks also have great value in geology as they provide insights into the history of our planet and how it has changed over time.

Clastic Sedimentary Rocks

Have you ever wondered how the Rocky Mountains and other canyons were formed? Or how volcanoes produce their distinctive rocks? Well, the answer probably lies in the world of sedimentary rocks. Of the three main types of rocks, sedimentary rocks make up most of the Earth's crust. Among the sub-classifications of sedimentary rocks are clastic rocks. Understanding clastic rocks can give you an understanding of the history of the Earth and how it evolved over millions of years.

Formation of Clastic Rocks

Clastic rocks are formed from the accumulation of rock or mineral particles or other small fragments, such as shells or fossils, that are transported and then deposited by water, ice, or wind. The name *clastic* comes from the Greek word *klastos*, which means "broken." There are numerous types of clastic rocks depending on their composition and the size of the particles. One common example is sandstone, formed by the accumulation of sand-sized grains cemented together. Shale, siltstone, and conglomerate rocks are other examples of clastic rocks that form through the compaction and cementation of sedimentary grains or clasts.

Siltstone.[59]

Characteristics of Clastic Rocks

This type of rock shares some common characteristics, like layers or bedding, which develop due to the sedimentation process. They are also porous and permeable, meaning they can hold and transmit fluids. Their color can vary from light to dark depending on their origin and composition. Clastic rocks can be hard or soft, depending on the degree of cementation, and they can be weathered or eroded easily. Some clastic rocks contain fossils, which provide clues about the past environment, climate, and formation of the rock.

Tips for Identifying Clastic Rocks

Identifying clastic rocks can be challenging, but with a few tips, you can start differentiating them from other types. One of the most noticeable features is the presence of different grain sizes or textures, which can be seen with the naked eye or with a magnifying glass. Another clue is their density and weight. Clastic rocks tend to be lighter compared to other rocks like igneous or metamorphic rocks. You can also test their hardness by scratching their surface with a knife or a nail. If the surface is easily scratched, it's probably a softer clastic rock like shale.

Understanding the world of clastic sedimentary rocks can provide a wealth of knowledge about the Earth's geology and history. By knowing their characteristics and identifying features, you can start to recognize them in different geological settings. Clastic rocks provide a window into the geological past, from the sandstone formations in Utah's national parks to the shale layers exposed in the Grand Canyon walls. So next time you take a hike or visit a natural wonder, remember to look for clues in the rocks around you and discover the amazing world of clastic sedimentary rocks.

Organic Sedimentary Rocks

Sedimentary rocks are truly amazing creations formed over millions of years under different geological conditions. One of the categories of this type of rock is organic sedimentary rock, which is formed through the accumulation of organic remains. These rocks are full of beauty and intrigue, and this section will explore the different types of organic sedimentary rocks, their characteristics, and how to identify them.

Examples of Organic Rocks

Organic sedimentary rocks are formed from the accumulation of organic matter, including coal, limestone, and chert. Coal is formed from the remains of ancient vegetation subjected to pressure and heat over millions of years. Limestone is formed from the accumulation of small shells and skeletons of marine organisms in seawater. Chert is formed from the accumulation of the hard remains of ancient sponges and sea squirts.

Chert.[60]

Characteristics of Organic Rocks

Organic sedimentary rocks exhibit characteristics that distinguish them from other sedimentary rocks. They are composed of organic matter, which gives them a dark color and an earthy odor. They also contain fossils and other organic remains often visible to the naked eye. When analyzed under a microscope, organic rocks have a granular or crystalline texture due to their organic composition.

Tips for Identifying Organic Rocks

The identification of organic rocks requires some knowledge of geology and paleontology. To identify an organic rock, it is crucial to examine its color, texture, and odor. Organic rocks are usually dark in color and have a distinctive earthy odor due to their organic composition. Their texture can be granular, crystalline, or nodular, depending on the type of organic matter that has been accumulated. You can also identify organic rocks by looking for fossils or other organic remains, such as shells or skeletons.

Another helpful tip is to examine the environment in which the rock was found. For example, limestone is often found near the ocean, while coal is found in land areas where ancient vegetation used to grow. This can provide clues as to the type of organic rock that you are dealing with.

Sedimentary organic rocks are a fascinating category of rocks that tells a story about the ancient environment in which they were formed. The accumulation of organic matter over millions of years can create a beautiful and unique rock full of surprises. By examining their color, texture, and environment of origin, you can identify and appreciate the beauty of organic rocks.

Chemical Sedimentary Rocks

Have you ever taken a stroll down a beach or along a rocky shoreline and noticed how varied the rock formations can be? No two rock formations are ever the same. Some are soft and crumbly, while others are hard and unyielding. Some are formed from layers of sand and silt, while others have been shaped by the sheer force of nature, like wind and water. But did you know some rocks are formed by chemical reactions right beneath our feet? Chemical sedimentary rocks may not be as glamorous as their igneous and metamorphic counterparts, but they are no less fascinating!

Examples of Chemical Rocks

Some common types of chemical sedimentary rocks include limestone, dolomite, rock salt, and chert. Limestone is probably the most commonly known and used. It is mainly made up of calcite, a mineral composed of calcium carbonate. Dolomite is similar to limestone but has a higher magnesium content. Rock salt, as the name implies, is composed mainly of halite, a mineral that forms from the evaporation of seawater. On the other hand, Chert is a hard, dense rock that forms from the accumulation of microscopic fossils and shells.

Dolomite.[61]

Characteristics of Chemical Rocks

So, what sets chemical sedimentary rocks apart from other types of rocks? For one, they're formed by chemical processes rather than by erosion or melting. This means that they're usually formed in places like shallow lakes or oceans with high concentrations of dissolved minerals. They are also usually crystalline, meaning that they have a distinct structure and composition. Finally, chemical rocks are often characterized by layers or bands of different colors and textures, reflecting the varying conditions under which they were formed.

Tips for Identifying Chemical Rocks

If you're curious about these rocks and want to know how to identify them, there are a few things to look for. For starters, chemical rocks are usually quite hard and dense, with a crystalline or granular appearance. They are also often composed of relatively easy-to-recognize minerals like calcite, halite, or gypsum. Additionally, chemical rocks often have distinct layers or bands that reflect changes in the chemical makeup or environmental conditions from one period to another.

Chemical sedimentary rocks are an often overlooked but fascinating part of the geological landscape. From the sparkling crystals of halite to the dense layers of chert, these rocks represent the complex interplay of chemical and environmental factors that shape our world. Whether you're a professional geologist or just an amateur rock enthusiast, exploring and understanding these unique formations can help deepen your appreciation for the natural world around us!

Limestone

Limestone is an extremely popular sedimentary rock for its versatility, beauty, and durability. It has been used for various purposes for thousands of years and is still extensively used to this day. From construction to ornamental pieces, limestone is a hugely important natural resource.

Definition of Limestone

Limestone is formed from the mineral calcium carbonate. It comprises shells, coral, and other marine debris that have settled on the ocean floor and have been compacted and cemented over time. Limestone can vary in color and texture, from white to gray to tan, and may have different patterns and markings depending on the minerals present in the sediment that make up the rock.

Structure of Limestone

Limestone has a unique structure characterized by its porosity and permeability. It is a soft rock that can easily be carved and shaped but is also durable enough to withstand weathering and erosion. Limestone can comprise various layers or beds, which may have different compositions, thicknesses, and orientations. Some limestone deposits may contain fossils, which can provide valuable insights into the history of life and the environment.

Limestone.[69]

Uses of Limestone

Limestone has been used for a wide range of purposes, from construction to agriculture to art. It is a popular material for building and landscaping, as it is easy to work with, can be polished or textured, and has a classic, elegant look. Limestone is also used for making cement, as it contains high levels of calcium and magnesium. Additionally, limestone is a common ingredient in fertilizer, as it is rich in essential plant nutrients.

Tips for Identifying Limestone

If you are interested in identifying limestone, there are several things to look for. First, limestone is typically light in color, although it can come in various shades. It may be white, gray, or tan and have natural markings and patterns unique to each deposit. Limestone is also somewhat soft and can be scratched with a knife or nail. Finally, limestone is often found in areas that were once covered by shallow seas, such as beaches, cliffs, or quarries.

Limestone is an intriguing and versatile rock that has been used for centuries for a variety of purposes. Its unique structure and characteristics make it a popular resource for construction, agriculture, art, and more. Whether you are a geology enthusiast, a builder, a sculptor, or just curious about the world around you, learning about limestone can be a valuable and rewarding experience. With these tips for identifying limestone, you can explore the wonders of this beautiful rock and discover its many uses and applications.

Sandstone

When it comes to rocks and minerals, sandstone stands out for its beautiful colors, textures, and durability. This sedimentary rock has been used for centuries in construction, art, and various practical purposes. To better understand sandstone, let's explore its distinct structure, several of its various uses, and tricks to recognize it.

Definition of Sandstone

Sandstone is a type of rock comprising small grains of sand and minerals like feldspar or quartz. The grains are compacted and cemented together, forming a solid and hard rock. Sandstone is found in various colors, ranging from light beige and yellow to darker browns, reds, and even green.

Sandstone.[63]

Structure of Sandstone

Sandstone has a unique structure which makes it different from other sedimentary rocks. It comprises small grains of sand visible to the naked eye. These grains vary in size and can be angular, rounded, or even partially melted due to extreme heat and pressure. The cement that binds these grains together can comprise silica, carbonate, or clay minerals. Some sandstones have layering or bedding planes, which are visible lines that separate the different layers formed over time.

Uses of Sandstone

Sandstone has been used for centuries in construction due to its durability and attractive appearance. Many historical buildings and monuments, such as The Taj Mahal, Petra, and The Grand Canyon, are made of sandstone. It is also used as a decorative stone, as it can be carved and sculpted into various shapes and designs. Sandstone is used in landscaping and garden design due to its natural and rustic look. It is also used as a material for paving, wall cladding, and flooring.

Tips for Identifying Sandstone

One of the best ways to identify sandstone is by its texture. Sandstone has a rough, grainy surface due to the visible grains of sand. Due to its density, it is also heavier than other rocks of the same size. You can also identify sandstone by its appearance. It has a visibly layered texture, and many sandstones have a rusty appearance due to the iron content in the minerals. Finally, you can confirm that you have found sandstone by doing a simple acid test. If the rock fizzes when you drop a few drops of vinegar, it is likely sandstone.

Sandstone is a rock that stands out due to its unique structure, beautiful colors, and durability. It has been used for centuries in construction, art, and practical purposes and continues to be popular today. If you come across a rock with a rough surface, visible grains of sand, and a layered appearance, it might be sandstone. So, the next time you see an old building made of sandstone or a natural sandstone formation, take a moment to appreciate this rock that stands the test of time.

Siltstone

Have you ever heard of siltstone? This sedimentary rock may not be as well-known as some of the most popular rock types, but it plays an important role in our everyday lives. Siltstone is a versatile rock with various uses, from construction materials to decorative purposes.

Definition of Siltstone

Siltstone is a sedimentary rock composed of silt-sized particles, smaller than sand and larger than clay. This type of rock is formed through sediment accumulation, particularly fine-grained particles such as silt and clay. Siltstone is often found in layers and can have a range of colors, including gray, green, brown, and red.

Structure of Siltstone

Siltstone has a fine-grained structure with closely packed layers of silt-sized particles. The rock has a smooth texture and can have a platey or blocky appearance, depending on how it was formed. Siltstone is not very porous and has a relatively low permeability, meaning it does not allow water to pass through easily. Due to these characteristics, siltstone is often used as a building material for structures that require strong, stable foundations.

Uses of Siltstone

Siltstone has a range of uses in construction, decorative, and industrial applications. It is often used as a building material for walls, floors, and foundations. Siltstone is also used in landscaping and as decorative stones in gardens and outdoor spaces. In industry, rock is used as a raw material for the production of cement and other building materials. Additionally, siltstone can be crushed and used as a soil amendment to improve drainage and aeration in garden beds.

Tips for Identifying Siltstone

If you want to identify siltstone, there are a few key characteristics to look for. Siltstone has a medium to fine-grained texture and often has visible layers or laminations. The rock is dense and hard, with a smooth surface that can be scratched with a knife or nail. Siltstone often has a gray or brown color but can also be green, red, or other shades. In the field, siltstone can be identified by its blocky or platey appearance, and it often breaks into flat, smooth fragments.

Siltstone may not be the most well-known type of rock, but it is an important one with various uses in construction, decorative, and industrial applications. Its fine-grained structure and dense, hard texture make it a strong and stable building material for structures that require a solid foundation. Whether you're a geology enthusiast or just curious about the rocks around you, siltstone is a fascinating type of rock to learn about and appreciate.

Shale

Chances are, if you've heard the word "shale" before, it was probably about the controversial natural gas- and oil-extraction process known as fracking. But shale isn't just a source of fuel. It's a sedimentary rock with a complex structure and a wide range of potential uses. This section will look at the different aspects of shale, from its definition and structure to its various applications and tips for identifying it in the field.

Definition of Shale

Shale is a fine-grained sedimentary rock composed of clay minerals and other inorganic and organic minerals such as quartz, calcite, feldspar, and mica. It forms through the compaction and cementation of clay, silt, and other fine-grained rocks. This process can occur on land (terrestrial shale) and underwater (marine shale). Shale is typically very thin, with a thickness of fewer than two inches, and it can be found in layers within larger formations of rock.

Shale.[64]

Structure of Shale

Shale is a layered rock characterized by its fiscality, or ability to split neatly along parallel planes. This distinctive feature results from the clay minerals that make up the bulk of the rock. These minerals tend to align in thin, flat plates that can easily slide past each other. The shale layers can also exhibit a range of other features, such as ripple marks, fossilized marine organisms, and small cracks and faults. These characteristics are key for understanding the depositional environment of the shale and its potential uses.

Uses of Shale

Shale has a variety of applications in industries ranging from construction to energy production to agriculture. Shale is often used as a raw material for manufacturing bricks, tiles, and other ceramic products in the construction industry. It is also used for road construction and as a filler material in concrete. Shale can also be a valuable natural gas and oil source, as mentioned earlier. In agriculture, shale is used as a soil conditioner, as it helps to improve soil drainage and aeration.

Tips for Identifying Shale

Identifying shale in the field can be challenging because it often appears similar to other fine-grained sedimentary rocks like siltstone, mudstone, and shale's cousin, slate. However, some key characteristics can help you differentiate shale from these other rocks. One way to identify shale is to look for its distinctive fiscality. If a rock splits neatly along parallel planes, it's likely shale. Another way to identify shale is to perform a scratch test with a knife. Shale is typically softer than slate and will leave a mark when scratched. In addition, shale often has a dull, flat appearance compared to the shiny, reflective surface of slate.

Shale may have gained notoriety as a source of natural gas and oil through the contentious process of fracking, but its complex structure and diverse applications make it an intriguing and valuable rock for a range of industries. From its fine-grained composition to its distinctive fiscality, shale offers unique opportunities for exploration and exploitation. Whether you're a geologist, a builder, or just a casual rockhound, understanding shale and its many facets can deepen your appreciation for the intricate and ever-evolving world of rocks and minerals.

Sedimentary rocks are a diverse group of rocks formed through the compaction and cementation of loose sediment. These rocks can be divided into clastic, organic, and chemical. Clastic sedimentary rocks are composed of particles of broken-down material from preexisting rocks. Examples of these types of sedimentary rocks include sandstone, conglomerate, shale, and limestone. Organic sedimentary rocks are composed of organic material from living organisms, such as coal and limestone.

Chemical sedimentary rocks form through the precipitation of minerals dissolved in water and can include evaporites like halite and gypsum. The unique characteristics of sedimentary rocks, such as their fiscality and depositional environment, make them incredibly valuable in various industries. As you explore the world of rocks and minerals, take the time to appreciate and understand all of the different types of sedimentary rocks. From sandstone to shale, these remarkable rocks are a testament to the power of nature and its ability to shape our planet.

Chapter 4: Metamorphic Rocks

Did you know that some rocks are transformed from one type to another? This transformation is called metamorphism, and the result of this process is known as a metamorphic rock!

Metamorphic rocks are some of the most interesting and beautiful formations on Earth. From quartzite to marble, schist to gneiss, these rocks have significantly transformed from their original igneous, sedimentary, or even earlier metamorphic form. This chapter will explore more about what metamorphic rocks are and how they form. The two main types of metamorphic rocks and some other notable examples will also be discussed. By the end of this chapter, you should have a good understanding of metamorphic rocks and how to identify them.

What Are Metamorphic Rocks?

The Earth's crust is a fascinating labyrinth filled with an array of minerals, rocks, and sediments that have been formed due to various geological processes over millions of years. Metamorphic rocks are one such type of rock and can be described as any rock that has been substantially changed from its original igneous, sedimentary, or earlier metamorphic form. From marble to quartzite, phyllite to schist, and gneiss to slate, each of these rocks has a unique origin story that is characterized by intense pressure and/or heat.

Definition of Metamorphic Rocks

Metamorphic rocks have been transformed from their original state through heat, pressure, and chemical reactions while still in a solid state.

These rocks are formed from preexisting rocks (known as parent rocks or protoliths) subjected to intense pressure and heat from the proximity of magma or another heat source. The extreme temperature and pressure conditions alter the rock's mineral composition, chemical properties, and physical appearance to form metamorphic rocks.

Structure of Metamorphic Rocks

Metamorphic rocks come in different compositions and structures depending on the intensity of the conditions of their formation. They have distinct banding, layering, or a combination of both and can have a variety of mineral orientations. Their texture ranges from coarse to fine, depending on the degree of strain and recrystallization. In some cases, metamorphic rocks preserve the characteristics of the parent rock, such as its fossils, but in most cases, they have a completely different look and feel.

Formation of Metamorphic Rocks

Metamorphic rocks are formed through two processes: regional metamorphism and contact metamorphism. Regional metamorphism happens when rocks are subjected to high pressure and temperature caused by the collision of tectonic plates or when deep-seated rocks are exposed to the Earth's surface. Contact metamorphism occurs when rocks come into contact with magma or any other heat source, causing them to crystallize, recrystallize, and form new minerals. The type of metamorphic rock formed depends on the composition of the parent rock, the duration and intensity of heat and pressure, and the presence of fluids that contribute to the alteration of the minerals.

Metamorphic rocks show the remarkable effects of the enormous forces of heat and pressure on geological materials. They are a fascinating piece of Earth's history and have significant value in a range of areas, including architecture, construction, and sculptures. Understanding the formation and structure of metamorphic rocks offers valuable insights into how the Earth's crust has evolved, the role of tectonic plates in shaping the Earth's surface, and the potential for discoveries. By exploring the world of metamorphic rocks, we get a new appreciation for the planet we inhabit and the forces that created it and are still at work creating it.

Foliated Metamorphic Rocks

If you're a geology enthusiast, you've probably heard of foliated metamorphic rocks. These rocks have unique features that distinguish them from other rock types. But what are they, and what makes them special? This section will explore foliated metamorphic rocks, their characteristics, their different types, and tips for identifying them.

Definition

Foliated rocks are metamorphic rocks with a layered or banded appearance created by high pressure and heat exposure. These rocks share a property called foliation. Foliation is the arrangement of minerals in a metamorphic rock, which creates parallel layers or sheets. These rocks are formed through the process of metamorphism, which occurs when rocks are subjected to high temperatures and pressures caused by tectonic activities like mountain building, contact metamorphism, and regional metamorphism.

Characteristics of Foliated Metamorphic Rocks

One characteristic of foliated metamorphic rocks is the presence of cleavage. Cleavage refers to the ability of a rock to break along flat and parallel surfaces. For example, a schist can easily be broken into thin flat sheets along its cleavage. Other characteristics include the arrangement of specific minerals like mica, chlorite, and hornblende in a layer-like structure that creates a banded appearance. The more intense the pressure and heat, the more pronounced the banding becomes. The grains in these rocks also tend to be elongated or flattened, making them look stretched out.

Types of Foliated Metamorphic Rocks

There are various types of foliated metamorphic rocks, and all differ in their composition and texture. Slate is one such type, which has a fine-grained texture signified by microscopic clay minerals. Phyllite is another type with a shiny appearance with a texture between slate and schist. Schist is the most common type and is characterized by large grains

Phyllite.[65]

of mica, which gives it a shiny appearance. Gneiss has a coarse texture and is more coarse-grained than schist. Lastly, migmatite is a rare type that forms when a rock undergoes partial melting.

Tips for Identifying Foliated Metamorphic Rocks

While identifying foliated metamorphic rocks may seem challenging, there are certain indicators to look out for. One way to identify them is to look for parallel lines or banding in the rock. Other factors to consider include the type of minerals present, the texture of the rock, and the presence of cleavage. Some rocks may also have a shiny or reflective appearance, indicating the presence of mica or other minerals.

Foliated metamorphic rocks offer a fascinating glimpse into the geological history of our planet. These rocks' unique features and composition are a testament to the powerful forces that have shaped our world. By understanding the characteristics, types, and identifying factors of foliated metamorphic rocks, we can appreciate the beauty and complexity of our planet's geology. So, the next time you come across a foliated rock, take a moment to marvel at the natural wonder of it all!

Non-Foliated Metamorphic Rocks

Rocks are some of the oldest materials on our planet Earth. They've been shaped and reshaped over time due to various geological forces. Metamorphic rocks transform form and composition over time due to heat, pressure, and other factors. Non-foliated metamorphic rocks are those rocks that lack a visible alignment of minerals. In simpler terms, they don't have layers. This particular type of metamorphic rock has several characteristics, types, and tips for identifying them.

Definition

Non-foliated metamorphic rocks are rocks that have transformed without producing a layered or banded texture. This means that they have a uniform composition throughout the rock. They typically crystallize under conditions of high pressure and low temperature. Due to their uniform composition, they are often used for building and construction purposes.

Characteristics of Non-Foliated Metamorphic Rocks

Non-foliated metamorphic rocks have several characteristics which set them apart from other forms. For one, these rocks tend to have a lack of visible layers or bands of minerals. They are also generally hard and durable, making them ideal for construction use. Some examples of non-foliated metamorphic rocks include marble, quartzite, and hornfels.

Types of Non-Foliated Metamorphic Rocks

There are several types of non-foliated metamorphic rocks, each with unique composition and characteristics. Marble, for instance, is a non-foliated metamorphic rock composed almost entirely of calcite, a mineral that makes it slightly harder than limestone. On the other hand, quartzite is a metamorphic rock composed almost entirely of quartz grains. And hornfels is a fine-grained metamorphosed rock composed of several different minerals, including quartz, feldspar, and mica.

Quartzite.[66]

Tips for Identifying Non-Foliated Metamorphic Rocks

There are a few things to look out for to identify non-foliated metamorphic rocks. One of the most notable things about these rocks is that, unlike foliated metamorphic rocks, they do not have a visible layering or banding of minerals. They also are usually quite hard and durable, which makes them useful for construction. Finally, there is often a uniform texture throughout the rock.

Non-foliated metamorphic rocks are an essential part of our geological history that has shaped our planet. These rocks are incredibly hard and durable, thanks to the transformation they undergo. They don't have layered minerals, offering a uniform texture throughout the rock. This makes them useful for construction and building purposes. Knowing the characteristics, types, and tips to identify them can be helpful to geologists, construction workers, or anyone interested in the Earth's geological history.

Notable Examples of Metamorphic Rocks

Metamorphic rocks provide a unique glimpse into the planet's geologic past, as their original identity has been partially or completely altered. Notable examples of metamorphic rocks include slate, schist, marble, quartzite, and gneiss. All of these metamorphic rocks possess incredible strength due to the changes they undergo during their formation. These rocks' hard, durable qualities make them ideal for various construction and building purposes. They are also popular among collectors and can be found in many homes, offices, and museums.

Marble

Marble is a beautiful and versatile stone widely used for architectural, sculptural, and decorative purposes. The unique characteristics of marble make it a popular choice for homeowners, designers, and builders worldwide. This metamorphic rock is formed by transforming limestone or dolomite through heat and pressure. Stone made from limestone or dolomite has tiny crystals of calcite. It looks different based on what the original rock was made of.

History

Marble has been used since ancient times to symbolize wealth, power, and beauty. The ancient Greeks and Romans built magnificent temples, statues, and buildings with marble, and their art and architecture legacy is still visible today. The world-renowned marble quarries of Carrara, Italy,

Marble.[67]

have operated since Roman times and provided the precious material for masterpieces like Michelangelo's David and the Pantheon in Rome. Today, marble is still quarried in many countries like Italy, Spain, Greece, Turkey, Brazil, and the USA. The rich variety of colors, textures, and marble patterns makes it a favorite among designers and architects.

Properties

The properties of marble make it an excellent choice for many applications. Marble is a durable, heat-resistant stone that can withstand high traffic in areas like bathrooms, kitchens, and floors. Its smooth surface makes it easy to clean and maintain and does not attract bacteria or allergens. Marble is also a popular option for countertops, vanities, and backsplashes because of its resistance to stains and scratches. It can last for decades and improve with age, developing a natural patina that adds to its beauty if cared for properly.

Uses

One of the main attractions of marble is its uniqueness. No two pieces of marble are alike, and the variations in color, pattern, and veining give each slab its character. From the classic white and gray marbles to the exotic green, red, and pink varieties, marble can add elegance and refinement to any space. The popularity of marble has also led to the development of new finishes and treatments that enhance its versatility. Honed or matte finishes are great for a subtle and sophisticated look, while polished or glossy finishes give an irresistible shine.

Care

Caring for marble is essential to maintain its beauty and longevity. Marble is susceptible to etching caused by acidic substances like vinegar, lemon juice, or wine, so avoiding contact with these liquids is essential. It is recommended to clean marble with a pH-neutral cleaner and a soft cloth or sponge. Avoid using abrasive cleaners or scourers that can scratch the stone's surface. Sealing marble is also recommended to prevent stains and water damage. If you notice any cracks or chips in the marble, it is essential to address them promptly to avoid further damage.

Marble is a stunning and fascinating material that has stood the test of time. From ancient origins to modern applications, marble symbolizes beauty, luxury, and elegance. Its unique properties, versatility, and variety make it a favorite among architects, designers, and homeowners worldwide. Caring for marble is essential to ensure its durability and beauty for years to come. Whether you choose classic white marble or exotic green marble, there is no denying that marble is a timeless and exquisite choice.

Quartzite

When it comes to rocks that people know and love, quartzite is not usually the first that comes to mind. Most people have never even heard of it. However, this metamorphic rock deserves some attention for its hidden beauty and unique characteristics.

What Is Quartzite, Exactly?

Quartzite is a metamorphic rock formed when quartz sandstone is exposed to high heat and pressure deep within the Earth's crust. This process causes the sand particles in the rock to recrystallize and fuse, creating a denser and harder rock than the original sandstone. Quartzite is often mistaken for marble or granite because of its glossy surface and vibrant colors.

Characteristics

One of the most notable characteristics of quartzite is its durability. Quartzite is incredibly resistant to wear and tear, unlike other natural stones that can be vulnerable to scratching, staining, and etching. This makes it ideal for kitchen countertops, flooring, and outdoor paving. It is also heat-resistant, so you can place hot pots and pans directly on the surface without fear of damage. With proper care and maintenance, quartzite can last a lifetime.

Advantages

Quartzite is highly sought after for its impressive range of colors and patterns, providing endless design possibilities. Because of the variety of minerals that can be present in the original sandstone, quartzite can come in an array of colors, such as white, gray, pink, and yellow. Some even have unexpected colors like blue and green. The patterns found within the rock can range from subtle grains to bold swirls and veining. This means quartzite can be used in any design style, from traditional to modern.

Despite its many benefits, quartzite is often overlooked in favor of more well-known natural stones like granite and marble. The main reason is the misconception that quartzite is difficult to work with. Quartzite requires some skill and expertise to fabricate and install, but with the help of a professional stone supplier, it can be an easy and stress-free process.

Overall, quartzite is a unique metamorphic rock that deserves more attention in the world of natural stone. With its durability, color range, and hidden beauty, quartzite is a great option for any home renovation project.

Don't be afraid to explore this hidden gem and discover how it can enhance your living space.

Phyllite

Nature never ceases to amaze us with its spectacular output. The evolution of rocks is a living example of how every inch of our planet has a unique story to tell. One such rock is phyllite, making its mark among the metamorphic rocks. Found in various parts of the world, phyllite is a rock that has undergone a remarkable transformation from sedimentary or igneous rock to its metamorphic form.

Formation

Phyllite is a metamorphic rock formed from the continual pressure and heat metamorphosing slate, one of the many sedimentary rocks. The process of metamorphosis of phyllite has gone through various phases, resulting in its distinct texture and beautiful appearance. One can experience the beauty of phyllite by examining it closely, touching its smooth surface, and peering into its mica crystals. The mica crystals are responsible for the sheen and shine, while chlorite crystals lend it its beautiful green color.

Characteristics

Phyllite rocks' unique texture lies in their appearance, which resembles closely stacked fan-like shapes formed due to their frequent layers. These layers result from the repeated compression and flattening of the sedimentary rock when metamorphosing into phyllite. Owing to its texture, it has become an excellent building material in countries such as Germany, where it has found its application in renowned structures.

Phyllite rock plays a crucial role in Earth's ancient history's chemical, physical, and geological studies. It contains essential minerals like garnet, staurolite, and biotite, which help when studying the Earth's past. Scientists can determine which group of rocks was present during the formation of Phyllite, which can provide insight into the time several rocks in that region were created.

Uses

Phyllite's durability and hardness make it an excellent building and flooring material, primarily when it is present in layers. Apart from building materials, it is also used in electrical engineering, synthetic diamond manufacturing, and cosmetic products manufacturing.

Phyllite's beauty speaks for itself and its significance in Earth's natural history. It is a product of nature's magic and evolution. Phyllite's unique texture and composition make it an excellent choice for various applications, from decorative tiles to scientific research. Its charm and relevance continue to amaze geologists, archaeologists, and common folk alike. So, the next time you stumble upon a phyllite rock, take a moment to acknowledge its magic and wonder.

Schist

Schist.[68]

Nature is a masterful artist, and some of its finest masterpieces come in the form of metamorphic rocks. Schist is one such rock that has piqued the interest of geologists, collectors, and enthusiasts alike. Schist rocks are some of the most beautiful geological specimens with their sparkling appearance and intricate patterns.

Formation

Schist is a metamorphic rock that forms from preexisting rocks due to heat and pressure. As the rocks are subjected to high pressure and high temperature, the minerals inside them start to recrystallize and align themselves along parallel planes. This process leads to the formation of the distinct banding and foliation characteristic of Schist. The heat and pressure levels required for schist to form are higher than that required to form slate but lower than that required for gneiss.

Types

Schist comes in various types, depending on the rock from which it is formed and the minerals that are present in it. The most common types of Schist are mica-schist, garnet-schist, and talc-schist. Mica-schist is the most recognizable due to its distinctive shiny appearance caused by the presence of mica minerals. Garnet-schist is another type that is recognizable due to the presence of garnet, which gives it a reddish color.

Talc-schist, on the other hand, is created from the metamorphism of ultramafic rocks, and it has a greasy texture due to the high presence of talc.

Uses

Schist is a sought-after rock for collectors and enthusiasts because of its beauty and rarity. Its varied types and patterns make it a visual delight as well as a collector's dream. Furthermore, schist is also used for several practical applications. The rock's banded and foliated structure makes it a popular choice for decorative stones, while its high resistance to wear and tear makes it ideal for use in flooring, countertops, and roofing.

Schist is a stunning and versatile rock that can be appreciated for its aesthetic and practical features. Its glittering appearance and formations illustrate the extraordinary abilities of our planet's natural processes. Schist's usefulness and beauty have made it an object of human fascination for centuries, and its allure continues to enchant people today. So, the next time you admire a schist formation, you can marvel at the fascinating geological processes that shaped and gave birth to these stunning jewels of the Earth.

Gneiss

Rocks have been around us for millions of years, and metamorphic rocks, in particular, are fascinating because they are formed through the transformation of rocks. One such type of rock that deserves attention is gneiss. Gneiss is a metamorphic rock with a layered structure composed of different minerals.

Gneiss.[69]

What Is Gneiss?

Gneiss is a metamorphic rock formed through the process of metamorphism. It is a combination of different minerals compressed together during high-pressure and high-temperature conditions, which change the rock's original structure. Gneiss's strong foliation or layering makes it distinguishable from other metamorphic rocks.

How Is Gneiss Formed?

Gneiss is formed through metamorphism, where rocks undergo immense heat and pressure. The parent rocks of gneiss are usually igneous or sedimentary rocks subjected to metamorphic processes. These processes include regional and contact metamorphisms, where rocks experience high temperatures and pressure due to movements in the Earth's crust. This causes the minerals within the rock to change and combine to form gneiss.

Different Types of Gneiss

Gneiss is a complex rock, which means it has different types based on the minerals present. The most common type is biotite gneiss, which has a layer of biotite mineral sandwiched between two layers of feldspar. Another type is granitic gneiss, composed of granite minerals such as quartz, feldspar, and mica. Similarly, mafic gneiss is composed of dark minerals like hornblende and pyroxene.

Uses of Gneiss

Gneiss has many uses because of its unique properties. It is often used in construction as a decorative stone because of its different colors and patterns. Gneiss can be polished to a high luster, making it attractive as a building material. In addition, gneiss is used as a dimension stone, making it ideal for cut and design purposes. Given its durability and strength, Gneiss can also be used to create beautiful countertops, flooring tiles, and walls. Gneiss is commonly used for walkways, outdoor sculptures, and garden beds in landscaping. Additionally, this rock can be crushed and used as ballast, concrete aggregate, or railroad track materials.

Gneiss is a fascinating metamorphic rock with a unique structure and diverse uses. Its composition and properties make it a valuable rock in various industries, and its beauty makes it a choice building material for construction purposes. With its durability and decorative properties, gneiss is not just a rock but a work of art that time and pressure have created.

Metamorphic rocks are a very visible reminder of the power of nature and the Earth's ability to transform what was once thought to be nothing into something beautiful and valuable. The types of metamorphic rocks discussed in this chapter have become a staple in many industries as people have found ways to utilize their unique properties. From construction to landscaping, these rocks deserve recognition and admiration. With their incredible strength and beauty, it's no wonder that metamorphic rocks have become so popular.

Chapter 5: Minerals and Crystal Systems

Minerals are remarkable substances that can form into many shapes and sizes. What's even more amazing is their underlying structure, which scientists have long studied in detail by scientists. Minerals follow organized patterns known as crystal systems, each with unique characteristics. For example, the cubic system has equal lengths on each side to form a perfect cube, while other systems feature less perfect shapes, such as hexagons and prisms.

Whether you are just beginning to learn or already adept at identifying them, minerals offer something for everyone to explore through crystal systems. This chapter will cover how minerals are classified, the different types, and their associated crystal systems. Some of the properties of minerals and how to use them for identification will also be touched upon. By the end, you'll be able to look at a mineral specimen and identify its crystal system.

Minerals and Crystals

Regarding geology and mineralogy, minerals and crystals are the building blocks of everything we see around us. They are the natural components that make up the Earth's crust and form the bedrock of geological processes. Minerals exhibit a variety of structures and physical properties, and their importance in various fields, including industrial applications, medicine, and nanotechnology, cannot be overstated. This section will explore the world of minerals and crystals and understand their significance in geology and mineralogy.

Minerals and Their Formation

Minerals are naturally occurring inorganic solids with a defined chemical composition and a distinct crystal structure. They are formed through various geological processes, such as crystal precipitation from molten lava or groundwater solutions, a chemical reaction between different minerals, and metamorphic changes resulting from heat and pressure. Key properties of minerals include color, hardness, cleavage, and luster, which help geologists identify and classify minerals.

Types of Crystals and Their Properties

Crystals are the repeating structure of atoms in a mineral, giving it its distinctive shape and properties. Different types of crystals exhibit varying levels of symmetry and complexity. The seven crystal systems, including cubic, tetragonal, orthorhombic, monoclinic, triclinic, hexagonal, and rhombohedral, are based on the axial length and angle of the crystal structure. Each system has its particular characteristics, such as optical, magnetic properties, and piezoelectricity.

Significance of Minerals

Minerals have a wide range of industrial applications, from manufacturing materials like ceramics, glass, and cement to electronic devices like transistors, batteries, and superconductors. They are also essential for advanced technologies like solar panels, wind turbines, and electric vehicle batteries. Some minerals like gold, iron, and copper have been used as currency and traded for thousands of years.

Mineral Exploration and Mining

Mineral exploration involves finding and identifying mineral deposits in the Earth's crust. Geologists use various techniques such as geological mapping, geochemical analysis, and remote sensing to locate minerals. Once mineral deposits are discovered, they can be mined, which involves the extraction of ore from the ground and processing it to extract the mineral of interest. Mining can have significant environmental impacts, and sustainable mining practices are essential to minimize these impacts.

Importance of Conservation and Sustainability

Given the finite nature of mineral resources, sustainable mining practices are becoming increasingly essential to minimize the impact of mining on the environment and the surrounding communities. However, conservation practices are equally crucial, as they help preserve the Earth's natural resources and ensure their availability for future generations.

Minerals and crystals are the foundation of geology and mineralogy, and their importance in various fields cannot be overstated. Understanding their properties and structures is essential for their identification, classification, and use in a wide range of applications while ensuring sustainable mining practices and conservation efforts will help in preserving these natural resources for the future.

Types of Minerals

Minerals are essential elements in our planet's crust, formed over millions of years by different geological processes. They play a crucial role in the formation of rocks, soils, and natural resources, as well as being vital for our health and well-being. With over 5,000 identified minerals, we have compiled the eight main types of minerals that are commonly found on Earth. Join us in discovering each mineral's unique features and importance in our daily lives.

1. **Silicates:** This type of mineral is the most abundant and flexible of all minerals, with silicon and oxygen being the most prominent components. Silicates comprise over 90% of the Earth's crust, with quartz being the most common mineral. They are used in a wide range of applications like construction, electronics, and silicon chips and are essential for human health.

2. **Oxides:** Oxides combine oxygen with metals like iron, copper, and aluminum to create valuable resources like iron ore and aluminum ore. These minerals are crucial in industries like construction and manufacturing. The most common oxide is corundum, the base mineral for rubies and sapphires. In nature, it is often found in the form of dust or sand.

3. **Sulfates:** Sulfates are minerals that contain sulfur, water, and metals like copper, zinc, and iron. Gypsum is an example of a sulfate mineral and is commonly used in the construction industry to create plaster and drywall. Sulfate minerals also play an important role in forming soil and water quality. The most common sulfate mineral is barite, which can be found in large deposits worldwide. In addition, it is used in a wide range of industrial applications.

4. **Sulfides**: Sulfides are minerals that contain sulfur and metals like lead, gold, silver, and copper. These minerals are the primary source of many metal ores, like zinc ore and copper ore, and have significant economic value. While sulfides are essential for extracting valuable metals, they can also be toxic and hazardous to our environment. The most commonly found sulfide mineral is pyrite, which is also known as fool's gold.

5. **Halides**: Halides are minerals formed when halogen elements like chlorine, fluorine, and iodine combine with metals like sodium, potassium, and calcium. Halite or rock salt is a common halide mineral used in the food industry and can be found in natural salt deposits. Its high chlorine content is also used in industrial processes like water treatment and wastewater management. The most common halide mineral is fluorite, a valuable fluoride source for dental health.

6. **Carbonates:** Carbonates contain carbon and oxygen, with minerals like calcite and dolomite being the most common. These minerals are significant in the formation of natural habitats like caves and coral reefs, as well as being an essential ingredient in concrete and cement. The most common carbonate mineral is calcite, which is composed of calcium and magnesium. With its high calcium content, it is often used as a dietary supplement in the form of limestone. The mineral is also used in the production of marble and glass.

7. **Phosphates**: Phosphates are minerals containing phosphate and oxygen, with apatite being the most common example. Phosphate fertilizers are widely used in agriculture to enhance plant growth, and phosphate minerals also play a crucial role in human bone formation. Phosphate is also used in laundry detergents and toothpaste to help remove food stains. The most common phosphate mineral is monazite, which contains rare Earth elements and is used in electronics production.

8. **Native Elements:** Native elements are minerals that naturally exist without combining with other elements, like gold, platinum, and silver. These minerals have significant economic value in the jewelry industry and have been used extensively throughout history as a form of currency. Some native

elements, like silver and gold, are also used in electronics and dentistry. The most common native element is quartz, composed of silicon and oxygen. Quartz is often used in clocks, watches, and microchips.

The world of minerals is fascinating and diverse, and they play an essential role in our daily lives. The eight primary mineral types offer crucial resources that have shaped our civilization, from building materials to food ingredients and electronics to jewelry. Understanding the importance of minerals and their uses can help us appreciate their value and encourage their sustainable use. With discoveries of new minerals being made every day, we can expect to learn more about the unique features and importance of these valuable resources.

Crystal Systems

Crystals are fascinating to look at and hold. From their exquisite beauty to their unique properties, crystals have been used for decorative and spiritual purposes for centuries. One thing that makes crystals so intriguing is the different ways they can grow and form. This section will explore the six different types of crystal systems, including isometric, tetragonal, orthorhombic, hexagonal, monoclinic, and triclinic. Let's dive in!

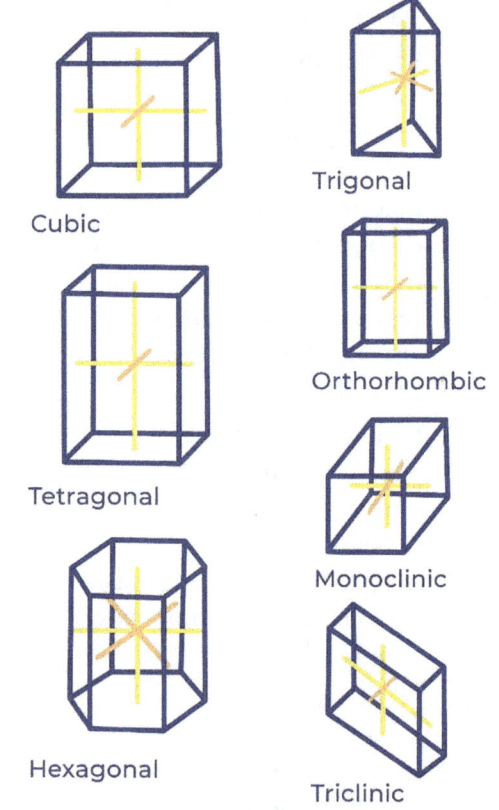

The 6 main crystal systems.

1. Isometric System

The isometric system, also known as the cubic system, is characterized by crystals with three axes intersecting at 90 degrees, equal length, and perpendicular to each other. The most common example of this system is the diamond. Other examples include galena, pyrite, fluorite, and garnet. The working of this system is based on the fact that all faces and angles are equal. You will see an identical pattern regardless of which direction you look at the crystal.

2. Tetragonal System

This system resembles the isometric system, except that one axis is longer or shorter than the other two. Crystals in the tetragonal system are characterized by three axes, two of which are perpendicular while one is inclined. Examples of this system are zircon, cassiterite, and chalcopyrite. Characterized by elongation in one direction, the tetragonal system is asymmetrical. This means that the faces of a crystal in this system are not all equal in size.

3. Orthorhombic System

Crystals in the orthorhombic system are characterized by three axes of different lengths that are all at right angles to each other. They are not equal in length, with one axis being shorter and the other two being longer. Examples of this system are topaz, barite, and aragonite. This system is also characterized by a lack of symmetry. You will see different faces and angles when looking at a crystal from this system.

4. Hexagonal System

Crystals that belong to the hexagonal system have four axes that define their structure. Out of these, three are of equal length and at 120 degrees to each other, and a fourth axis is perpendicular to the other three. Examples of this system include quartz, beryl, and tourmaline. Due to the presence of four axes, crystals in this system have a hexagonal shape. This system is also characterized by symmetry, which means that when looking at the crystal, you will see identical faces and angles regardless of which direction you are looking at it.

5. Monoclinic System

This system has three axes of different lengths, two of which intersect at an oblique angle, while the third is perpendicular to both. Crystals in this system often have a distinguishing incline, making them easily identifiable. Examples of this system include gypsum, azurite, and epidote. This system has the distinctive characteristic of having two axes of different lengths, giving crystals in this system a characteristic asymmetry.

6. Triclinic System

Crystals in this system are the most irregular, with three unequal-length axes intersecting at oblique angles. They're often called *pinacoids* because their irregular shape looks like it has been pinched at the top. Examples of this system include feldspars, kyanite, and labradorite. Apart from their asymmetrical shape, crystals in this system are also characterized by the fact that no two faces of the crystal will ever be parallel. In other words, all faces and angles of the crystal in this system will be unique.

Understanding the different crystal systems and how they form is important for anyone interested in working with or collecting crystals. By knowing which system a crystal belongs to, we can better understand how it may form and what properties it may possess. From the isometric system of diamonds to the triclinic system of feldspars and labradorite, each type of crystal system offers a unique way of understanding the beauty and magic of crystals.

Properties of Minerals

Minerals are the building blocks of the Earth, and understanding their properties is vital when studying geology, mineralogy, and gemology. A mineral is defined as a naturally occurring inorganic solid with a crystalline structure and specific chemical composition. Each mineral has a set of properties unique to its chemical composition and crystalline structure. This section will discuss four fundamental properties of minerals: hardness, diaphaneity, cleavage, and piezoelectricity.

Hardness

The hardness of a mineral is its ability to resist scratching. The Mohs Scale of Hardness, named after the German mineralogist Friedrich Mohs, is the most widely used method for measuring a mineral's hardness. The scale ranges from 1 to 10, with 1 being the softest mineral, talc, and 10 being the hardest, diamond. In between, minerals such as quartz, feldspar, and topaz fall at different hardness levels. Hardness is an essential property for mineral identification, and this information is crucial in fields such as mining and mineral exploration.

Diaphaneity

Diaphaneity refers to a mineral's ability to transmit light. Minerals can be classified as transparent, translucent, or opaque. Diamonds are an excellent example of a mineral with high diaphaneity, as they transmit most of the visible light spectrum. Translucent minerals such as agate allow some light to pass through, while opaque minerals like hematite do not. Diaphaneity affects a mineral's value, especially in the precious gemstone industry, where transparency and clarity are highly coveted.

Cleavage

Cleavage is a mineral's tendency to break along planes of weakness, which leaves a clean break in smooth surfaces. The number and angle of these planes of weakness are specific to each mineral. For example, mica has perfect cleavage, meaning it breaks easily along thin, flat sheets. On the other hand, Feldspar has two planes of cleavage at right angles, resulting in a blocky shape when broken. Understanding cleavage is critical for mineral identification, as it can provide clues to the mineral's crystal structure and chemical composition.

Piezoelectricity

Piezoelectricity refers to a mineral's ability to generate an electric charge when subjected to mechanical stress, such as pressure. Some minerals can produce an electric field when subjected to strain, and vice versa, due to the asymmetrical arrangement of atoms within their crystal structure. Quartz is one such mineral that exhibits strong piezoelectric properties, making it useful in electronic devices such as watches and oscillators.

Understanding the properties of minerals is crucial in many fields, from mining to jewelry-making. Hardness, diaphaneity, cleavage, and piezoelectricity are fundamental properties to consider when studying minerals. As beginners, acquiring knowledge of these mineral properties opens up a whole new world of wonder, especially when exploring the many beautiful minerals found around the world.

The Magic of Minerals and Crystal Systems

If you have ever been fascinated by the beauty and mystery of crystals and minerals, you're certainly not alone. For thousands of years, cultures worldwide have revered these geological wonders for their mystical and healing properties. But aside from their allure and intrigue, minerals and crystals are also used as scientific tools for understanding the Earth's history and its processes. Let's delve deeper into the world of minerals and crystal systems and discover the magic behind these amazing substances!

Aesthetic Properties

One of the most interesting aspects of minerals and crystals is their ability to reflect light. This is known as their optical properties and can reveal a lot about their structure and composition. One property, known as birefringence, causes minerals to split light into two rays, revealing stunning patterns and colors when viewed through a microscope. Other properties, such as fluorescence and phosphorescence, cause minerals to emit light when exposed to certain wavelengths, creating a glowing effect that appears almost magical.

Healing Properties

Aside from their aesthetic properties, many minerals and crystals are also believed to have healing properties. This practice, known as crystal healing, is based on the idea that each crystal emits a unique energy or vibration that can interact with the body's energy field to promote physical and emotional well-being. While there is not yet any scientific evidence to support this practice, many people swear by the transformative effects of crystal healing.

Minerals and crystal systems are fascinating entities that hold a great deal of scientific and cultural significance. Whether you're drawn to their aesthetic beauty, their metaphysical properties, or their scientific value, there is no denying the magic and wonder of these amazing geological wonders. So next time you come across a glittering crystal or a unique mineral, take a moment to appreciate its beauty and all that it represents. Who knows what mysteries and secrets it may hold?

Chapter 6: Quartz

If you're at all interested in geology, you've likely heard that quartz is one of the most abundant minerals in the Earth's crust. It's estimated that quartz makes up around 12% of the Earth's surface. But what exactly is quartz, where is it found, and why is it so common? Quartz is a mineral composed of silicon and oxygen atoms with the chemical formula $SiO2$. It comes in many different varieties, including clear quartz, rose quartz, amethyst, and citrine, to name a few. This chapter will explore everything you need to know about this fascinating mineral. By the end of it, you'll have a better understanding of quartz and its many uses.

Fun fact: Quartz crystals can generate electricity when pressure is applied to them. This is known as the piezoelectric effect.

Quartz's Abundance

So, why is quartz so common? One reason is that it forms under a wide range of conditions. It's one of the few minerals that can form at all temperatures and pressures within the Earth's crust. Quartz is most commonly formed in igneous and metamorphic rocks but can also be found in sedimentary rocks. Additionally, quartz is resistant to weathering and erosion, meaning it can survive for long periods and be transported long distances by wind or water. These factors all make quartz one of Earth's most widely distributed minerals.

Another reason for quartz's abundance is its industrial uses. Quartz's unique properties, such as its hardness, chemical stability, and piezoelectricity, make it useful in various industries. For example, quartz is used to manufacture glass, ceramics, semiconductors, and even watches. It's also commonly used as an abrasive in sandpaper and other materials.

Quartz is found worldwide, but certain regions are particularly known for their abundance of quartz. One of the most famous is the Ouachita Mountains in Arkansas, where you can find clear quartz crystals up to a foot long. Brazil is also a major quartz source, with large amethyst and citrine deposits. Other areas where quartz can be found include Madagascar, Namibia, and the Alps in Europe.

Clear Quartz: The Most Versatile Stone

Clear quartz is a perfect choice if you're searching for a versatile stone that adds beauty, balance, and harmony to your life. This enchanting crystal is the most common mineral on Earth and can be found in different places worldwide. Clear quartz has a plethora of wonderful benefits and is treasured in the world of metaphysics. It's no wonder that spiritualists and crystal healers worldwide love this stone.

Characteristics

Clear quartz is a colorless, transparent, six-sided crystal with a prism-like structure. It's known as the "master healer," and it amplifies vibrations around it. Clear quartz is an excellent energy conductor. Thus, it's a stone that enhances spiritual awareness and clarity of thought. Clear quartz's energy encourages thought clarity, spiritual transformation, and overall well-being. It also dilutes negativity and transmutes it into positive energy.

Structure

Clear quartz crystals have a hexagonal structure, which means that each face of the crystal has six sides. Due to the consistency of its six-sided symmetry, it's easy to recognize this crystal. Clear quartz crystals have carefully arranged atoms, forming a lattice grid, which is how the vibrational energy travels through them. The lattice grid arrangements allow clear quartz to store, transmit, amplify, and transform energies.

Hardness

Clear quartz has a hardness rating of 7 on the Mohs Scale of Hardness, making it quite durable. This scale ranges from one to 10, with one being the softest and 10 being the hardest. Clear quartz's durability is essential when using it for daily wear and is perfect for making crystal rings, necklaces, and other jewelry.

Ways to Identify

Clear quartz is relatively easy to identify as it's transparent and colorless. It is non-magnetic and doesn't conduct electricity, so it won't interfere with magnets or conduct electricity. When held under bright light, clear quartz may project a rainbow of colors, which makes it even more captivating.

Clear quartz crystals are an extraordinary gift to humanity from the Earth's womb. Its healing properties make it popular for spiritual awakening and raising vibrations. Clear quartz is simple yet powerful and can greatly help focus and mental clarity. Overall, the world's love for clear quartz is not without reason, as it's a versatile stone in its vibrational properties, resilience, and beauty which make it one of the most beloved stones in the crystal kingdom.

Rose Quartz: A Gemstone with Many Benefits

Rose quartz is a beautiful, semi-precious gemstone found in abundance around the world. It has many qualities that make it highly sought after for its beauty and healing powers. From its lovely pink color to its heartwarming energy, rose quartz is a stone that has been used for centuries in a variety of ways.

Rose Quartz.[70]

Characteristics

Rose quartz ranges in color from pale pink to deep rose. Its color comes from traces of titanium, iron, or manganese. The most desirable shade is a pure, slightly pink color, free of any orange or gray hues. It has a vitreous or glassy luster and is translucent to opaque. The stone is highly prized for its color, associated with love and passion. It is often used in jewelry, especially in necklaces and bracelets.

Structure

Rose quartz is a member of the quartz family of minerals, which includes other well-known stones such as amethyst, citrine, and smoky quartz. It's a silicon dioxide mineral, a hexagonal crystal system, and a pyramidal termination. It contains tiny inclusions of pink fibers or needles, which give it a unique look.

Hardness

Rose quartz has a hardness of seven on the Mohs scale, which means that it is relatively hard and durable. It can be scratched by harder minerals such as topaz, sapphire, and diamond. Remember that while rose quartz is hard, it can still be chipped or damaged if exposed to extreme heat or pressure.

Ways to Identify

Color and structure are the ways in which this stone is identified. It should be pale to deep pink without any gray or orange inclusions. It should also have a hexagonal shape and pyramidal termination. You can also use a loupe or magnifying glass to look for inclusions in the stone. It is worth noting that synthetic rose quartz is also available on the market, so purchasing from a reputable dealer is crucial.

Benefits

Rose quartz is known for opening the heart and healing emotional wounds. It is often used in meditation to promote love, compassion, and peace. It is also believed to have physical benefits such as improving circulation, reducing wrinkles, and easing tension headaches. Rose quartz is a versatile stone that can help promote emotional and physical health.

Rose quartz is a beautiful gemstone with many benefits. It has a lovely pink color and heartwarming energy that make it highly prized in the jewelry world. Its hexagonal structure and pyramidal termination make it easy to identify, and its hardness ensures that it will last for many years. Whether you are seeking emotional healing or physical health benefits, rose quartz is a stone that can help you achieve your goals.

The Magic of Amethyst

Amethyst is one of the most fascinating stones known to man. Its unique purple color and spiritual associations have given it a special place in mystical history as both a decorative stone and a healing crystal. They can be found worldwide, but some of the most ancient and revered specimens have come from Southern Brazil, Uruguay, Madagascar, and Zambia.

Amethyst.[71]

Characteristics

Amethyst belongs to the mineral quartz group. It's sometimes called the "Stone of Spirit" because of its spiritual and calming properties. The color can range from pale lilac to deep purple, and it often features natural color zoning. Amethyst is known for its high purity, and it doesn't contain any visible inclusions or impurities. It's also a relatively common mineral, with sizable deposits found all over the world.

Structure

Amethyst has a trigonal crystal system, which forms six-sided prisms with pointed tips. It has a hexagonal, prism-shaped lattice structure that gives it its unique and iconic look. This structure makes it easy to identify, and once you've seen one, you'll have no trouble recognizing amethyst ever again.

Hardness

The hardness of amethyst is seven on the Mohs Hardness Scale. This means it's a relatively durable stone that will resist scratching and wear normally. However, it's still vulnerable to more extreme shocks and scratching from harder materials. So, if you're looking to wear an amethyst ring or pendant, avoiding activities that could put it at risk is best.

Ways to Identify

One of the easiest ways to identify an amethyst is by its color. If you see a purple crystal that's translucent to opaque, then it's worth further investigation. Some other characteristics you should look for in an amethyst include its refractive index, birefringence, and its pleochroism. Amethyst also has a specific gravity of 2.66, which can be used to distinguish it from other minerals.

Amethyst is a beautiful and highly sought-after stone that has fascinated people for centuries. Its unique purple color and spiritual properties have made it a popular choice for jewelry, home decor, and meditation. Hopefully, the in-depth exploration of amethyst's characteristics, structure, hardness, and ways to identify it have given you greater insight and a newfound respect for this incredible stone. If you've never owned an amethyst before, maybe it's time to treat yourself to one and experience its magic for yourself.

Smoky Quartz

Are you looking for a crystal that can help you stay grounded and focused while also providing protection? Look no further than smoky quartz. This beautiful crystal is known for its unique color and powerful properties. In this section, we'll explore smoky quartz's characteristics, structure, and hardness and ways to identify it. By the end, you'll have a greater appreciation for the many benefits of this special crystal.

Smokey quartz.[73]

Characteristics

Smoky quartz is a variety of macrocrystalline quartz that ranges in color from a light gray to a deep, rich brown. Its color comes from the presence of aluminum impurities in the crystal structure. Smoky quartz is known for its transparency and is often found in clusters or as individual crystals. It is also said to have a powerful grounding energy.

Structure

Smoky quartz has a hexagonal crystal system and is composed of silicon dioxide. Its chemical formula is SiO_2. The crystal structure of smoky quartz is formed by the orderly arrangement of atoms and molecules that make up the crystal lattice. This crystal system is what gives smoky quartz its unique properties and energy.

Hardness

On the Mohs scale of mineral hardness, smoky quartz has a rating of seven. This means that it is relatively hard and durable, making it suitable for many different uses. Smoky quartz is often used in jewelry because of its beauty and durability. It is also used in various industrial applications, such as in high-precision optics.

Ways to Identify

Smoky quartz is identified by its characteristic color, transparency, and crystal structure. It is often found in clusters or as individual crystals. Smoky quartz can also be distinguished from other types of quartz by its brownish-gray color and its unique energy properties. When held, smoky quartz is said to provide a sense of calm and grounding.

Uses

Smoky quartz has many different uses, from jewelry to industrial applications. It is also often used in meditation to help promote a sense of calm and focus. It is also believed to provide protection from negative energy and to ground the wearer. Smoky quartz is also used in various healing modalities, such as crystal healing and Reiki.

Smoky quartz is a powerful and versatile crystal that offers many benefits to its users. From its unique color and structure to its powerful energy properties, it is an excellent choice for those who are looking to stay grounded and focused while also staying protected from negative energy. Whether used in jewelry, meditation, or healing, smoky quartz will surely provide you the benefits you're looking for.

Herkimer Diamond: A Rare Gem

Herkimer diamond is a unique mineral that is found in Herkimer County, New York. These rare gemstones are not diamonds but are quartz crystals that resemble diamonds. They are often used in jewelry making and have become increasingly popular over recent years.

Herkimer diamond.[78]

Characteristics

One of the most significant characteristics of the Herkimer diamond is its clarity. These quartz crystals are known to be very clear, and they are often found in pairs with perfectly symmetrical shapes. Herkimer diamonds are also double-terminated, meaning that they have two terminations, or points, on each end. This characteristic makes them unique compared to other quartz crystals.

Structure

The structure of Herkimer diamond is one of the things that make this mineral different from other quartz crystals. They have a hexagonal crystal system and belong to the trigonal crystal class. The crystal lattice of the Herkimer diamond is also unique because it is structurally perfect. The absence of any inclusion or impurity makes them one of the most beautiful crystals in nature.

Hardness

Herkimer diamond has a hardness level of seven-and-a-half to eight on the Mohs hardness scale. This makes it a very durable mineral and resistant to scratches. It also means that it can be used in jewelry for daily wear with minimal care. The durability of Herkimer diamond also makes it a popular choice for industrial applications such as optical devices.

Ways to Identify

There are several ways to identify Herkimer diamonds. The first is its double-terminated shape, which is unique compared to other quartz crystals. Another way is the clarity of the crystal. Herkimer diamonds are known for their excellent transparency and are often used as a substitute for diamonds. Finally, Herkimer diamonds are specific to Herkimer County in New York. Therefore, if you discover a clear double-terminated quartz crystal outside this region, it is unlikely to be a Herkimer diamond.

Herkimer diamond is a unique and rare mineral with several characteristics that set it apart from other quartz crystals. Its clarity, perfect structure, and double-terminated shape make it a sought-after gemstone for jewelry making. The fact that it is exclusive to a single region in New York also adds to its appeal to rock collectors. There are several ways to identify Herkimer diamonds, including their signature double-termination and crystal clarity. If you ever have the chance to hold a Herkimer diamond, you will appreciate it for its beauty, rarity, and history.

The Lustrous World of Aventurine

Glistening with radiant beauty, aventurine is a sparkling gemstone that arouses the senses of anyone who lays their eyes on it. Whether you're a gem collector or a jewelry lover, aventurine is an irresistible gemstone to which you will find yourself drawn. With its sparkling characteristics, structure, and hardness, aventurine has become one of the world's most valued and sought-after gemstones.

Characteristics

Aventurine is a member of the quartz family and is known for its shimmering luster and captivating sparkles. The stone resembles marble and has a shiny, rainbow color. This is because it contains tiny pieces of

Aventurine.[74]

fuchsite or mica. These minerals refract light which gives aventurine its distinctive glow. Depending on the number of mineral deposits, aventurine comes in a range of colors, including green, yellow, orange, blue, and red. It is also commonly found with black, gray, and white patterns running through it.

Structure

The structure of aventurine is crystalline, and its lattice is hexagonal. Its six-sided prism shape gives it a distinct geometric appearance, which makes it easily recognizable. The lattice structure in aventurine is what gives it its hardness and durability, making it perfect for carving and creating jewelry. The hexagonal arrangement of atoms gives aventurine its strength, meaning it can withstand daily wear and tear without cracking or breaking.

Hardness

Aventurine is a moderately hard gemstone with a Mohs hardness scale in the range of six-and-a-half to seven. However, its hardness can vary slightly depending on the color and quality of the stone. For instance, aventurine with more mica flakes or mineral deposits tends to be slightly softer than those with fewer deposits. Nevertheless, aventurine is still one of the most durable gemstones in the quartz family.

Ways to Identify

To accurately recognize aventurine, look for its unique color, inspect the structure of the stone, and gauge its hardness. Its characteristic luster and sparkle are a dead giveaway that its aventurine. When you hold it up to the light, it should also have a translucent quality, with its internal inclusions and mineral deposits visible. Additionally, its relatively high density can differentiate aventurine from glass or plastic stones.

Aventurine is a gemstone that adds a touch of glimmer to any piece of jewelry or collection. With its brilliant shine, unique characteristics, and durability, it's no wonder that aventurine has become a favorite choice amongst gem enthusiasts. Its hexagonal lattice structure and crystalline framework make it innovative and adaptable. Additionally, inclusions and mineral deposits tend to give it a natural and organic feel. When identifying an aventurine, look for its unique glow and hexagonal structure. If you're looking for a gemstone that possesses unparalleled splendor and remarkable durability, aventurine is a perfect choice.

Exploring the Alluring World of Citrine

If you're a fan of gemstones, you must have heard of citrine. This golden-colored crystal is adored for its beauty and energy-healing properties. But what exactly is citrine? Where does it come from? How can you identify it? From the characteristics of citrine to its structure and ways to identify it, we've got you covered. So, let's dive into the alluring world of citrine.

Citrine.[75]

Characteristics

Citrine, a popular variety of quartz, is a yellow to golden-orange-colored gemstone. Citrine's unique color comes from the iron present in its crystal structure. It is found in many countries worldwide, including Brazil, Russia, Madagascar, and the United States. A fully natural citrine is rare, and most citrine available in the market is heat-treated to enhance its color. Citrine is widely known as the "merchant's stone" as it is believed to bring prosperity and success.

Structure

The structure of citrine follows other varieties of quartz. It has a hexagonal crystal system and is commonly found in crystal clusters, geodes, and drusy. Citrine can be distinguished from other gemstones, such as amethyst, smoky quartz, and topaz, by its orange-to-brown color. Citrine is known for its unique lattice structure, which can help facilitate better concentration, enhance mental clarity, and promote inner peace.

Hardness

Citrine is a hard mineral and falls at seven on the Mohs scale of hardness, which means it is relatively tough and not easily breakable.

However, despite its hardness, it is still scratchable by harder minerals such as diamond and corundum. Thus, keeping your citrine away from abrasive materials that can scratch or damage it is advisable.

Ways to Identify

Identifying citrine is relatively easy as the gemstone is distinct in color and structure. Due to its color and clarity, citrine is commonly mistaken for topaz or golden beryl. However, you can differentiate citrine from other gemstones by examining its structure and color. Topaz typically has a different crystal structure and is more transparent, whereas golden beryl is a lighter shade of yellow. Additionally, the presence of inclusions in citrine distinguishes it from other gemstones.

Uses

Apart from adorning jewelry, citrine is widely used in energy healing practices. Its healing properties include bringing positivity, boosting self-esteem, and promoting inner balance. Citrine can also be useful in feng shui practices to attract wealth and abundance into your life. If you're interested in meditation, citrine's energy can support achieving greater spiritual awareness.

In a nutshell, citrine is a beautiful gemstone with distinctive properties that separate it from other crystals. Whether you're a metaphysical enthusiast or a gemstone collector, owning a citrine can be a valuable addition to your collection. Remember to handle your citrine carefully and avoid exposing it to harsh conditions that can affect its beauty and properties. Overall, it's safe to say that citrine is a fantastic gemstone with much to offer, so add it to your collection today!

Quartz isn't just interesting because of its abundance or industrial uses. It has been valued for centuries for its beauty and metaphysical properties. Clear quartz, in particular, is believed to have healing properties and the ability to enhance mental clarity and focus. Rose quartz is used for promoting love and compassion, while amethyst is said to aid in spiritual growth and stress relief. These beliefs may not have scientific backing, but they certainly add to the allure of this fascinating mineral.

Quartz is a mineral that is both incredibly common and endlessly fascinating. The unique properties of quartz and its wide range of uses make it an important part of our everyday lives, whether we realize it or not. So next time you come across a quartz crystal or a piece of quartz jewelry, take a moment to appreciate the beauty and wonder of this amazing mineral.

Chapter 7: Chalcedonies and Agates

Agates and chalcedony are amazing stones that have been prized for centuries. Both of these classes of rocks are part of a greater family, the majestic quartz. Although agate and chalcedony are similar, each one has its unique charm and appeal. Agate is a beautiful, banded stone, often with captivating swirls or patterns. On the other hand, chalcedony is usually a solid color, ranging from an almost pastel pink to an intense dark blue. Despite having different characteristics, both of these stones are incredibly desirable.

Jewelers prize the durability and interesting features which they bring to accessories and artwork. With such stunning natural elements to work with, it's no wonder that people have enjoyed gems like agate and chalcedony for so long. This chapter will provide an introduction to the two stones, their properties, examples of both types, and tips on how to care for them. By the end, you'll be an expert on agate and chalcedony!

Introduction to Chalcedonies

Chalcedony is one of the most stunning gems in the world of jewelry. The gemstone comes in different variations of colors, including blue, white, gray, pink, and peach. It is popular for its various healing properties, which make it an excellent addition to any crystal healing regimen.

Chalcedony.[76]

What Is Chalcedony?

Chalcedony is a mineral that belongs to the quartz family and comprises microscopic crystals. It is generally found inside volcanic rocks, and its color variations depend on the minerals contained in the environment of its formation. This gemstone is considered one of the oldest minerals used for decorative purposes and has been a popular gemstone throughout history.

Properties of Chalcedony

1. **Color:** Chalcedony comes in various colors, including blue, white, gray, pink, and peach. Blue chalcedony is the most popular among them. It's a beautiful, serene, and calming color that helps bring peace and calmness to the wearer.
2. **Hardness and Durability:** Chalcedony has a hardness of six to seven on the Mohs scale, making it a relatively durable gemstone. It's essential to keep in mind that the gemstone can fracture easily, so it's important to handle it with care.
3. **Banding:** Banded chalcedony is a beautiful variation of the gemstone that comes with unique patterns and swirls. These patterns occur when the chalcedony forms next to another mineral, creating lines and swirls of color inside the stone.
4. **Healing Properties:** Chalcedony is known for its healing properties, making it an excellent choice for anyone seeking emotional balance, peace, and tranquility. This gemstone is

believed to help overcome feelings of inferiority and bring out the inner strength and confidence of the wearer. Additionally, chalcedony is thought to provide physical benefits such as improving gut health and blood circulation.
5. **Metaphysical Properties:** In the world of spirituality, chalcedony is associated with the throat chakra, which governs communication and self-expression. This gemstone is believed to help the wearer speak their truth, improve their communication skills, and eliminate fear and anxiety associated with public speaking.

Types of Chalcedony

Chalcedony, with its beautiful and special characteristics, is truly one of the most fascinating minerals to ever exist. This type of mineral belongs to the quartz family and can come in various types. One of the most amazing characteristics of chalcedony is that it can form in a wide range of colors, each with unique properties. This section will explore some of the most popular types of chalcedony gems. From carnelian to onyx, we look forward to taking you on a journey to discover these wonderful types of chalcedony.

A. Carnelian

Carnelian is a gorgeous orange-to-reddish-brown mineral. It is a semi-precious stone and one of the most sought-after varieties of chalcedony. Its distinctive reddish-brown color is due to the presence of iron oxide within the mineral. Its properties include inner strength, courage, and creativity. When wearing carnelian, people can tap into their natural intuition and manifest their desires more easily. It is known to activate the second and third chakras, which enhance physical and mental vitality, renewed energy, increased creativity, and improved self-esteem.

B. Chrysoprase

Chrysoprase has a delicate green color that is reminiscent of fresh foliage in the spring season. It is known for its healing properties and is considered a powerful cleansing stone. Wearing chrysoprase can help you release negative thoughts and emotions while grounding your spiritual journey. The healing energy of chrysoprase can also recharge your energy field, attracting abundance, prosperity, and good luck.

C. Heliotrope

Heliotrope, also known as bloodstone, is a striking green mineral with streaks of red that can resemble a blood spatter. It is considered a powerful healing stone, believed to help purify the blood and relax the mind. It is also a popular stone for those trying to overcome emotional pains such as sadness, stress, and anxiety. Heliotrope can balance emotions and promote inner peace.

D. Chrome Chalcedony

One of the most unique varieties of chalcedony is chrome chalcedony. It has a stunning green color and can be transparent or translucent. Its properties include calming the mind while increasing intuition and emotional balance. When wearing it, one can feel their third eye chakra opening and their emotional center aligning with their spiritual journey. It can help release past emotional traumas and bring clarity and focus to the present.

E. Tiger's Eye

Tiger's eye is a rich golden-brown color with streaks of yellow and red. It is a powerful stone that can boost confidence and self-esteem and can help bring success to one's personal or professional life. Its properties include a mind-calming effect that balances negative emotions such as anxiety and insecurity. Tiger's eye is a practical stone that can help manifest the desired goals of those who wear it.

F. Jasper

Jasper can come in various colors, each with unique properties. It is considered a stabilizing stone that can help balance one's physical, emotional, and spiritual aspects. When wearing it, jasper carries nurturing energy that can promote comfort and security. It can help one release energy blocks, promoting positivity and drawing abundance to one's life.

G. Onyx

Onyx is a black mineral with a glossy finish. It represents strength, protection, and self-confidence. It is said to aid a person in controlling and focusing their energy while releasing negative emotions such as anxiety, depression, and anger. Wearing onyx can provide strength during mental or physical stress, making it a popular choice for those working in fast-paced or high-stress environments.

The different types of chalcedony are both beautiful and meaningful in their unique way. Each stone carries properties that can help enhance one's energy and well-being. Carnelian, chrysoprase, heliotrope, chrome chalcedony, tiger's eye, jasper, and onyx are just a few of the many types of chalcedony. Take the time to discover which one resonates with you and aids in your spiritual journey. Remember, chalcedony has something to offer everyone, making it a timeless and essential mineral to explore.

The Marvelous World of Agates

Agates are some of the most stunning, colorful, and intriguing crystals. You may have heard of them before, or maybe you haven't. But have you ever wondered what these rocks are and how they are formed? Well, this section will introduce you to the enchanting world of agates, from their basic properties to their intricate formations and how they are treasured by collectors, jewelry makers, and geology enthusiasts.

Agate.[77]

What Is an Agate?

Agates are a type of chalcedony mineral, which is composed of microcrystalline quartz formed from volcanic or sedimentary rocks. This mineral holds many secrets that give each agate its unique personality, ranging from striking bands of colors, subtle hues, or even translucent or opaque variations. The colorful and detailed designs in the rocks come from minerals like iron, manganese, and silica. These minerals enter the rock through tiny holes and cracks. The mix of these minerals creates a latticework of banding or other forms of inclusions that make each agate one-of-a-kind.

Properties of Agates

1. **Color:** Agates come in a wide spectrum of colors, ranging from fiery reds, oranges, and yellows to serene greens, blues, and purples, and subtle grays, whites, and browns. Some agates are solid in color, while others display intricate patterns that resemble landscapes, eyes, seascapes, and many more. Expert lapidaries and jewelers often use the color and patterns of agates to create stunning pieces that highlight the natural beauty of these stones.
2. **Hardness and Durability:** Agates are relatively hard minerals, with a rating of six-and-a-half to seven on the Mohs hardness scale. This makes them a popular choice for use in jewelry, decorative objects, and even sculptures due to their durability and resistance to scratches or chipping. They also have a high chemical corrosion resistance, making them ideal for use in chemical apparatus, such as test tubes, flasks, and mortars.
3. **Banding:** The banding of agates is one of the most distinctive features that make them so prized by collectors and enthusiasts. Banding is a series of alternating layers of minerals that create a wavy or straight-line pattern that runs across the agate. The patterns can be asymmetrical, symmetrical, or radial, often resembling natural landscapes, waves, or other natural phenomena. Sometimes smaller inclusions like an "eye" or "bloat" (where gas bubbles were trapped during the formation of the agate) break up the banding in some places.
4. **Varieties:** There are many types of agates, each with its own properties, colors, and patterns. Some of the most popular types of agates include fire agate which displays a brilliant range of orange and red hues; blue lace agate, known for its delicate blue to white lacy pattern; and Botswana, featuring a distinct grey to darker gray banding. Other notable types of agates include crazy lace and landscape. Plume agates are also stunning and coveted by collectors and enthusiasts alike.

Types of Agate

If you are a gemstone lover or a believer in the healing properties of crystals, you may already be familiar with the mystical agate. This unique mineral is widely popular for its rich colors, intricate patterns, and metaphysical properties. But did you know that agate also comes in various types that exhibit distinct features and meanings?

A. Blue Lace Agate

Blue lace agate is a stunning variety of agate characterized by its delicate blue and white striped pattern. This crystal is revered for its calming and uplifting energy, which helps to soothe stress, anxiety, and emotional turmoil. Blue lace agate is also believed to enhance communication, clarity, and creativity, making it an ideal stone for artists, writers, and speakers. This crystal is often used in meditation, spiritual healing, and chakra balancing, as it can help to calm the mind and promote inner peace.

B. Fire Agate

Fire agate is a mesmerizing variety of agate that displays a rainbow-like iridescence and a fiery glow. This crystal is known for its grounding and protective properties, which help to stabilize energy, foster courage, and ward off negative energies. Fire agate is also regarded as a creativity and manifestation stone that can help to amplify one's desires and manifest their dreams into reality. This crystal is popular among jewelers and crystal collectors due to its unique appearance and powerful energy.

C. Moss Agate

Moss agate is a distinctive variety of agate with beautiful green moss-like patterns on its surface. This crystal is highly regarded for its connection to nature and its ability to promote growth, abundance, and harmony. Moss agate is believed to facilitate communication with plants and animals, as it is said to embody the spirit of the natural world. This crystal is popular among gardeners, environmentalists, and outdoor enthusiasts seeking to align with the Earth's energy and promote ecological balance.

D. Dendritic Agate

Dendritic agate is a captivating variety of agates with unique brown or black dendritic inclusions resembling ferns, trees, or other organic forms. This crystal symbolizes growth, stability, and balance, as it embodies the essence of nature's creative power. Dendritic agate is often used for enhancing visualization, intuition, and connection with the natural world. This crystal is ideal for nature lovers, healers, and environmentalists who seek to promote personal and planetary healing.

Agates vs. Chalcedonies: What Makes Them Different?

Agates and chalcedonies can easily be mistaken for each other. Both are stunningly beautiful and come in breathtaking colors, but what exactly sets them apart? Understanding the difference between these two gems can help you choose the perfect one for your collection.

Differences in Structure

One of the main differences between agates and chalcedonies is their internal structure. Agates have a distinctive banding pattern that is caused by the deposition of minerals in layers or rings around the walls of the hollow cavity where the stone formed. Chalcedonies, on the other hand, do not have this banding pattern, but they often have microcrystalline structures that create a waxy surface.

Color Variations

Agates and chalcedonies come in a wide range of colors, but each stone's colors and patterns differ. Agates have distinct patterns, including eye-shaped markings, stripes, and concentric rings that come in different colors, ranging from earthy browns and greens to vibrant reds, blues, and purples. On the other hand, chalcedonies are usually solid in color, with light blue, gray, and white being the most common colors.

Different Uses

Agates are often used for beads, tumbled stones, and cabochon cut gems because of their distinctive bands of colors. They are also used for decorative items such as bookends, coasters, and vases. Chalcedonies are often used for carvings, cameos, and intaglios because of their dense structure and waxy luster. They are also used for beads, pendants, and other jewelry pieces.

Caring for Chalcedonies and Agates

Taking care of chalcedonies and agates is both simple and rewarding. The most important part of caring for these beautiful stones is keeping them clean to help maintain their stunning colors and unique patterns. Cleaning with a soft, damp cloth is the safest way, as harsh detergents can damage them. Avoid using any type of chemical exposure, such as cleaning solutions or steam cleaners, when caring for your collection. When storing them, ensure they are kept in a cool, dry place away from direct sunlight to protect the beauty of these precious stones. Anytime you wear jewelry containing agates or chalcedonies, be sure to remove it before participating in activities that may be too strenuous for the delicate metals used in settings. Following these few steps is all it takes for these gems, which boast incredible variety in their color pallets and luster, to last for many years.

Chalcedony is a stunning gemstone that is rich in beauty and healing power. Whether you're seeking emotional balance, personal strength, or a way to improve your overall well-being, there is much to gain from this gemstone. With so many variations and benefits, it's no wonder that chalcedonies have remained a popular choice among jewelry enthusiasts throughout history. So, if you're looking for a gemstone that is as beautiful as it is beneficial, chalcedony is undoubtedly the perfect choice for you.

Agate is a fascinating mineral that has a wide variety of patterns, colors, and metaphysical properties. Whether you are drawn to the calming energy of Blue lace agate, the protective energy of fire agate, the harmonizing energy of moss agate, or the growth-oriented energy of dendritic agate, there is an agate variety that can suit your needs and enhance your life. So, next time you come across an agate stone or a piece of agate jewelry, take a closer look and try to discover its type and meaning. Who knows, you may just find the perfect crystal to support your spiritual journey and personal growth.

Chapter 8: Precious Gemstones

Precious gemstones have been treasured since antiquity and are admired for their dazzling colors as well as their rarity. Over the centuries, these gems have been a status symbol, exchanged as gifts of love or worn to bring good luck. Whether you appreciate the beauty of a deep sapphire blue, a joyful yellow topaz, or an elegant pink diamond, there is something timeless and magical about gemstones that continues to captivate us today. Their luxurious allure makes them desirable items that are worthy investments in any jewelry collection.

This chapter will discuss the four precious gemstones. It will cover their characteristics, how to identify them, as well as mining and polishing techniques. Lastly, it will explain what makes these stones so precious in the first place. By this chapter's end, you will better understand these rare and valuable gems.

Precious Gemstones: The Shimmering World of Elegance

Gemstones have been a part of human civilization for centuries. From royalty to commoners, everyone has been fascinated by precious gemstones. These colorful, sparkling, finest examples of Mother Nature symbolize elegance, luxury, and status. Each precious gemstone has its beauty, origin, and cultural significance.

Origins of Gemstones

Gemstones are formed deep inside the Earth, under extreme pressure and heat over millions of years. Each precious gemstone has a unique origin story. For example, emeralds are formed in the metamorphic rocks of Colombia, while sapphires originate from Sri Lanka's alluvial deposits. The rarity and origin of gemstones determine their value.

Classification of Gemstones

Gemstones are categorized based on their chemical composition and optical properties. The four categories of precious stones are diamonds, emeralds, rubies, and sapphires. While other gemstones like turquoise, amethyst, and garnet are considered semi-precious, they hold significant value in the jewelry industry.

Significance of Gemstones

Gemstones have cultural significance and are considered an expression of one's personality. For example, sapphires are considered a symbol of wisdom, loyalty, and truth. Similarly, rubies represent courage and passion, emeralds represent fertility and prosperity, and diamonds symbolize love and commitment. Gemstones are also associated with astrological properties and are believed to have healing powers.

Price of Gemstones

The cost of a gemstone depends on several factors, like how rare it is, its quality, how big it is, and where it comes from. Diamonds are the most expensive and valuable gemstones, followed by emeralds, sapphires, and rubies. The quality of a gemstone is judged based on the four Cs- cut, clarity, carat, and color.

Caring for Gemstones

Gemstones are delicate and require proper care to maintain their luster and value. Exposure to heat, chemicals, or rough handling can damage them. It is crucial to store them in a cool, dry place and avoid wearing them during strenuous activities like exercise, swimming, or gardening. Regular cleaning and maintenance are essential to keep the gemstones looking their best.

Emeralds: The Gemstone of Royalty

Emeralds have been known to be one of the most exquisite and sought-after gemstones for centuries. The vibrancy of their green color pays homage to life, nature, and growth. Wearing an emerald gemstone can bring the wearer happiness, peace, and prosperity. This section will discuss the characteristics and identification of emeralds so you can understand and appreciate the value and luxury of owning them.

Characteristics

Emeralds belong to the beryl family of minerals and are characterized by their vivid green color, transparency, and luster. The color of emeralds is due to the presence of chromium ions in them. These stones may have visible inclusions called "jardin," French for *garden*, and can be seen as moss-like formations inside the gem. The inclusions do not necessarily diminish the beauty of the emerald, as they may enhance its unique character.

Identification

Identifying an emerald gemstone requires a bit of experience and technical knowledge. Below are some common ways to identify an emerald stone:

1. **Color:** Emeralds are known for their distinct green color. However, it is not merely green, so make sure to look for their tone, saturation, and hues. The most sought-after color is an intense green with hints of blue.
2. **Clarity:** Inclusions are typical in emeralds, but make sure they are not too prominent to be seen with the naked eye. Professionals can use magnification tools to observe the gemstone's clarity.
3. **Cut:** Emeralds are delicate, so they should be cut to enhance the stone's natural beauty. The emerald cut is the most common, which reveals the stone's clarity and establishes a distinct yet elegant appeal.
4. **Carat:** An emerald is measured in carats, with good quality, and a smaller emerald is worth more than a larger and inferior quality stone. Consider carat weight, color, clarity, and cut when purchasing an emerald.

Emeralds have long been admired by royalty and are still considered to be one of the most valuable gemstones. The beauty, rarity, and significance of this gemstone are undeniable. If you intend to purchase an emerald, exercise caution and seek professional guidance to ensure the stone's authenticity. Owning an emerald enhances the aura and brings the wearer happiness, peace, and prosperity.

Diamonds

Diamonds have symbolized love and devotion for centuries – and it's easy to see why. Their dazzling sparkle, durability, and rarity make them one of the most sought-after gemstones in the world. But what exactly makes a diamond so special? Let's explore the characteristics and identification of diamonds, so you can learn everything you need to know about these stunning gemstones.

Characteristics of Diamonds

Diamonds are created in the Earth's mantle under extreme pressure and heat and are made of a single element: carbon. They are the hardest naturally occurring substance on Earth, so they are highly resistant to scratching and breaking. Additionally, diamonds have a unique ability to refract light, giving them their signature sparkle and fire.

How to Identify a Diamon

There are a few crucial characteristics to search for while identifying diamonds. The "four Cs" — carat weight, cut, color, and clarity — come first. "Carat weight" refers to the diamond's weight, with one carat equaling 0.2 grams. The term "cut" describes how the diamond has been fashioned, and it significantly impacts the diamond's worth and brilliance. The diamond's color describes how colorless or yellow it appears, with perfectly colorless diamonds being the most expensive. The presence of imperfections or flaws within the diamond is called *clarity;* fewer inclusions results in greater value.

In addition to the four Cs, there are a few other ways to identify diamonds. One is using a loupe, a specialized magnifying glass that lets you see the diamond up close. You can also use a diamond tester, which uses thermal conductivity to test if a gemstone is a real diamond. However, the best way to ensure you're getting a real diamond is to purchase it from a reputable jeweler who has certified the diamond's authenticity.

Not all diamonds are created equal. Some diamonds are treated with high heat or radiation to enhance their color or clarity, which can impact their value. Also, diamonds can be ethically sourced or come from conflict zones, so it's critical to research and purchase from a jeweler who sources their diamonds responsibly.

Diamonds are truly special gemstones with unique characteristics and rich history. Understanding the four Cs and other identification methods can help ensure that you're getting a high-quality diamond. And when purchasing a diamond, always choose a reputable jeweler who sources them ethically. With this knowledge, you're ready to explore the world of diamonds and find the perfect piece of jewelry to treasure for years to come.

Rubies

Rubies are one of the most sought-after gemstones in the world. A gemstone that is fiery, passionate, and captivating in every possible way. Rubies have been prized for their vibrant color, rarity, and history for thousands of years. From royals to commoners, rubies have always been revered and sought after.

Characteristics

Rubies are most well-known for their striking red color. But not all rubies are created equal. Rubies can vary in color from deep red to pinkish-red and even purple-red tones. The color of rubies is caused by the presence of chromium within the crystal structure. The more chromium, the deeper and richer the red color of the ruby.

Identifying Rubies

Rubies are one of the hardest gemstones and are also very durable. They rank nine on the Mohs hardness scale, indicating their superior toughness. This makes rubies perfect for everyday wear jewelry, including engagement rings or other frequently worn pieces. Rubies are usually found in metamorphic rocks but may also be found in sedimentary rocks or igneous.

Significance

Did you know that rubies have a rich history? The first recorded ruby dates back to ancient India, where they were used as talismans to ward off evil spirits. Today, they are still considered a symbol of love and passion and are often gifted for romantic occasions such as anniversaries, Valentine's Day, or engagement presents. Additionally, rubies have been associated with prosperity, peace, and power throughout history.

Rubies are also incredibly rare, and their scarcity is another reason for their high value. The most significant supply now comes from Burma, Sri Lanka, and Thailand. However, it is important to note that not all rubies are natural. Many are now created in laboratories, and it can be difficult to distinguish between natural and lab-created rubies. Synthetic ruby is made to be the same as natural ruby and has excellent clarity, which is why some people prefer them over natural rubies because it is not as expensive.

Sapphires: The Timeless Beauty

When it comes to precious stones, sapphires are among the favorites. Known for their stunning beauty and durability, sapphires are popular for engagement rings, anniversary gifts, and other special occasions. But what exactly are sapphires, and what makes them so special? This section will take a closer look at sapphires, including their characteristics and how to identify them correctly.

Characteristics

Sapphires are a type of corundum mineral that is second only to diamonds in terms of hardness. They come in various colors, but the most well-known color is blue. Sapphires are often synonymous with blue, but they can come in other colors like pink, yellow, orange, green, and even white. The color of sapphire is caused by different impurities or the presence of specific minerals, such as iron or titanium.

Identifying Sapphires

One thing that makes sapphires unique is their ability to change color depending on the lighting conditions. A sapphire that looks blue under natural light can appear purple or violet in incandescent light. This phenomenon is called pleochroism, and it is a characteristic that is only present in certain gemstones, such as sapphires. Another way to identify a sapphire is by its luster, which is the way it reflects light. Sapphires have a brilliant or vitreous luster, which means that they shine brightly under the light. However, this is not unique to sapphires, as many other minerals have similar luster.

The most effective way to distinguish a sapphire is through its clarity and its cut. High-quality sapphires have excellent clarity, free from any inclusions or blemishes that can affect their sparkle and shine. The cut of sapphire can also affect its overall beauty, as it can enhance or diminish the stone's color and brilliance. The carat weight of a sapphire does not necessarily dictate its value, as other factors like color, clarity, and cut play essential roles in determining its worth. However, sapphires that are larger than four carats are rare and can command a high price.

Sapphires are truly timeless and remain a favorite among gemstone enthusiasts. Their unique characteristics, including their stunning colors, pleochroism, luster, clarity, and cut, make them a popular choice for jewelry making. Whether in the market for an engagement ring or a special gift, sapphires are always an excellent option. Remember, when purchasing a sapphire, always check for its color, clarity, cut, and luster to ensure that you're getting value for your money.

Mining, Cutting, and Polishing

Precious gemstones are fascinating and hold a special place in everyone's hearts. We have used these stunning gems for jewelry, decor, and even medicinal purposes for centuries. But have you ever wondered how these gems are sourced, cut, and polished to make them so dazzling?

Mining

Gemstones are found in various places worldwide. They can be excavated from the earth, mined from underwater beds, and even found in meteorites.

There are four methods of mining gemstones:

- Alluvial mining
- Open-pit mining
- Seabed mining
- Underground mining

Open-pit mining is used to access shallow deposits of gemstones that can be easily extracted. Alluvial mining involves extracting semi-precious stones from sediment deposited on riverbeds. Underground mining is when gems are extracted from deep under the Earth's surface. Lastly, seabed mining is used to extract gems from ocean sediments.

Cutting

Once the gemstones have been extracted, they are sent to a cutting facility. Here, skilled artisans use various tools to shape the gemstones into desired shapes and sizes. The most common tools used for cutting gemstones include saws, grinding wheels, and polishing wheels. It takes years of training and experience to become a skilled gemstone cutter.

Polishing

Once the gems have been cut, they are handed over to the polishers. The goal of polishing is to give the gemstones a mirror-like finish. Polishers use a series of abrasive materials, such as diamond powder, to remove the scratches and create a smooth surface on the gemstone.

Finally, the polishing wheel is used to create the final mirror finish on the gemstone.

The Importance of Ethical Sourcing

With the growing concern about unethical mining practices, we must ensure that the gemstones we buy are ethically sourced. The Kimberley Process Certification Scheme (KPCS) is an international certification scheme that ensures that rough diamonds are mined, cut, and exported ethically. Furthermore, many gemstone companies have joined hands to create responsible sourcing initiatives that address environmental and social issues.

Mining, cutting, and polishing precious gemstones is an arduous process but one that produces beautiful and timeless gems. It takes an experienced team of miners, cutters, and polishers to create the perfect gemstone. Knowing about ethical sourcing is crucial to ensure that the gemstones we buy are conflict-free. The world of precious gemstones is fascinating, and understanding the process of mining, cutting, and polishing makes us appreciate these beautiful gems all the more.

Gemstones are a mesmerizing creation of nature that has been admired and treasured throughout history. Their beauty, rarity, and cultural significance make them valuable and cherished possessions. From birthstones to engagement rings, gemstones have a special place in our hearts and have become an integral part of the jewelry industry. However, their value extends beyond their monetary worth, as they remind us of our emotions, beliefs, and aspirations. So, the next time you admire a sparkling gemstone, remember that it is not just a piece of jewelry but a symbol of elegance, luxury, and individuality.

Chapter 9: Semi-Precious Gemstones

Semi-precious gemstones are some of Earth's rarest and most beautiful items, often found in gorgeous blues, pinks, purples, and more. Semi-precious stones offer an intriguing insight into the world of geology, with each stone one-of-a-kind in its composition and shape. Not only do semi-precious gemstones make striking pieces to be used for jewelry, but they also introduce a wonderful element of luxury and class to any space. Used as part of home decor, these stones can add an air of subtle sophistication that is truly something special.

This chapter will cover the different types of semi-precious gemstones. It'll dive into the different gemstone families, from quartz to turquoise, and explain their characteristics, structure, and identification. Images of the different stones in each family will be included so you can get an up-close and personal look at their beauty. By the end of this chapter, you'll better understand the different semi-precious gemstones and be able to distinguish them from one another.

Overview of Semi-Precious Gemstones

There's something about gemstones that has always captured our fascination. Few things come close to the allure of these shimmering, iridescent natural gems that never seem to lose their charm. Amongst these jewels are semi-precious stones, often underrated but no less beautiful. Although they might lack the heart-stopping price tags of precious gemstones, they are nothing short of splendorous!

What Are Semi-Precious Gemstones?

Semi-precious stones are natural gemstones that don't fall into the "precious" category, which comprises diamonds, emeralds, rubies, and sapphires. These stones are also called colloquial "gemstones" or "semi-precious gems." However, they can be just as gorgeous, sparkling, and valuable as their precious counterparts. The market for semi-precious stones is vast and varied, so there's a huge range of stones to choose from at all price points.

Types of Semi-Precious Gemstones

Unlike precious stones, limited to a select few, semi-precious stones offer a wide range of colors and varieties. Most semi-precious stones come from mineral deposits in the Earth's crust, while others are organic or man-made. The variety of semiprecious stones is staggering, from aquamarine, amethyst, topaz, and jade to tourmaline, citrine, garnet, and many more!

Symbolism and Meaning of Semi-Precious Gemstones

Throughout history, semi-precious gemstones have acquired symbolic and mystical meanings and properties associated with them. These meanings tend to be based on spiritual, cultural, and personal beliefs. For instance, the garnet symbolizes peace and prosperity, while the amethyst is thought to offer protection against negative influences. Other stones carry more specific symbolism, such as rose quartz, which represents love, and moonstone, which is thought to bring good luck.

How to Care for Semi-Precious Gemstones?

As with precious stones, taking care of your semi-precious gems is important to preserve their beauty for years to come. While some of these stones are sturdy and can withstand daily wear, others are more delicate and require proper care. Here are some tips to ensure that you're taking good care of your gemstones:

- Handle gemstones with a clean cloth or gloves to prevent oil from your fingers from sticking to their surface
- Store them separately in their pouches or lined boxes to avoid scratches or damage from other jewelry
- Avoid exposing them to intense heat or sunlight
- Avoid subjecting them to harsh chemicals or cleaning agents

Semi-precious gemstones are a vibrant and fascinating world unto their own. They carry a plethora of symbolism and are available in so many varieties that it's impossible to pick just one favorite. So, whether you're a seasoned collector or a newbie on the hunt for your first piece of gemstone jewelry, consider the many possibilities semi-precious stones offer. Simply put, the splendor of these gems is your own to explore and enjoy.

Beryl Family Gemstones

If you're a fan of gemstones, you might have already heard about the beautiful and exotic beryl family of gemstones. Ranging from colors like yellow, green, blue, pink, and white, these gemstones are famous for their unique properties and characteristics. If you want to know more about the beryl family gemstones, their characteristics, structure, and how to identify them, read on to explore fascinating information about them and why they are ideal jewelry pieces.

Characteristics

Beryl is a mineral family consisting of several varieties of gemstones. While the most famous beryl gemstone is emerald, other gemstones, including aquamarine, morganite, heliodor, and goshenite, are also known to belong to the beryl family. The physical and chemical properties of beryl gemstones vary, with properties such as hardness, color, clarity, and transparency depending on the variety of beryl. For instance, while emerald belongs to the beryl family and typically exhibits a green color caused by the presence of chromium or vanadium, beryl gemstones like aquamarine have a distinct blue color.

Structure

In terms of structure, beryl family gemstones are hexagonal crystals composed mainly of beryllium aluminum silicate. They are characterized by their high refractive index of more than one-and-a-half and their ability to split light into two as it enters the crystal. These properties give beryl family gemstones a sparkling and bright appearance, making them an ideal choice for designers looking for radiant and vivid jewelry pieces. Moreover, beryl gemstones are known for their excellent toughness and resistance to scratches, making them perfect for everyday jewelry wear.

Identification

Identifying beryl family gemstones typically involves using a standard gemology testing process. Typically, gemstones' hardness and chemical and physical properties are used to identify them accurately. Beryl gemstones typically have a hardness rating of seven-and-a-half to eight, meaning they are hard to scratch. Depending on the gemstone variety, you can also identify beryl family gemstones through their characteristic color, which varies from deep green to light yellow or pink. Additionally, beryl gemstones have a distinctive crystal structure that makes them stand out from other minerals.

Uses

When it comes to jewelry, beryl family gemstones provide an excellent option for creating unique pieces that are both beautiful and durable. From rings, necklaces, and bracelets, beryl gemstones come in different colors and shades that can complement any outfit or skin tone. Whether you prefer a classic emerald cut emerald or a contemporary cushion cut morganite, beryl family gems are perfect for creating jewelry that tells a story and makes a statement.

Corundum Family Gemstones

As a gemstone enthusiast, you might have encountered the term "corundum family." But do you know what it means, its characteristics, and how to identify the different types? Corundum family gemstones are a group of minerals that belong to the oxide family, and their distinguishing feature is their high hardness. The hardness of corundum ranges between nine and 10 on the Mohs scale; the only mineral that is harder than corundum is diamond. Some of the most famous gemstones in the corundum family are sapphires and rubies, which are widely sought after for their stunning colors, durability, and rarity.

Structure

The corundum's structure is hexagonal, and its crystal pattern is usually flat and tabular. Corundum's color typically ranges from transparent to opaque; in some cases, it may contain small inclusions or surface blemishes. The color of corundum is mainly determined by small amounts of impurities in the crystal lattice. For instance, red corundum, the most valuable variety of corundum, is caused by the presence of chromium.

Identification

Identifying corundum family gemstones can be a bit tricky, particularly when they are not faceted. You can use several factors to identify corundum, including its hardness, density, and color. One of the most straightforward methods of identifying corundum is to use a refractometer that measures the light's refractive index as it moves through the gemstone. Due to the unique crystal structure, each gemstone has its distinctive refractive index, which can be used to identify its type.

Another critical characteristic of corundum family gemstones is their pleochroism, which means that it exhibits different colors when viewed from different angles. This trait is particularly noticeable in sapphires, which may appear blue from one angle, but purple from another. Rubies also exhibit a similar phenomenon but tend to show red to pinkish-red hues from most angles.

Tourmaline Family Gemstones

Tourmaline is a fascinating gemstone that comes in an array of colors and is known for its unique properties. Its crystal structure makes it a complex mineral species that has become popular in jewelry making. But, with so many colors and varieties, it can be challenging to differentiate between them.

Characteristics

The tourmaline family comprises 12 different mineral species ranging in color from black to pink, green, blue, yellow, and even bi-color or tri-color. Due to tourmaline's pleochroism, the color can vary based on the viewing angle. One of the most prized varieties is the Paraiba tourmaline, discovered in Brazil in the 1980s and had a unique, vivid blue-green color. Tourmaline is also known for displaying electric properties, creating pyroelectricity and piezoelectricity. This unique feature means that when you rub a tourmaline, it becomes electrically charged and can attract dust or even small pieces of paper.

Structure

The crystal structure of tourmaline is quite interesting, as it is classified as a cyclosilicate mineral. This means that the crystal structure is composed of rings of SiO_4 tetrahedrons. Each tourmaline crystal is a long, thin, three-sided prism with grooves and bumps along the sides. Mineral inclusions and the presence of other chemical elements can alter the shape of these prisms, resulting in a unique appearance for each tourmaline.

Identification

When it comes to identifying tourmaline, it can be quite challenging, as each species can have different physical and chemical characteristics. One of the most helpful tools in identifying tourmaline is its heightening color characteristics which can reveal the presence of specific elements. In addition, using a polariscope can help distinguish between different types of tourmaline, as some may show birefringence or even color zoning.

Another noteworthy aspect of tourmaline is its use in alternative medicine. This gemstone is believed to possess various healing properties, including mental clarity, anxiety relief, and energy balance. It is thought to help release negative ions and absorb electromagnetic radiation from electronic devices. Many people wear tourmaline jewelry during meditation or place tourmaline under their pillow to promote peaceful sleep.

Spinel Family Gemstones

These gemstones are often overlooked, but they hold an unmatched beauty equal to that of any other gemstone family and are just waiting to be discovered.

Characteristics

Spinel family gemstones are mineral-based, and they belong to a group of gemstones that are made up of various elements. These gemstones can be found in many colors, such as blue, green, pink, and yellow. Spinel gemstones are known for their durability and hardness, which ranges from seven-and-a-half to eight on the Mohs scale. The spinel family of gemstones comprises magnesium aluminate, a mineral that forms crystals in a cubic system.

Structure

Spinel family gemstones feature unique structures, which makes them different from other gemstones. The crystal structure of Spinel gemstones consists of a series of octahedral octets meaning that there are eight ions in each octahedron. This structure makes the gemstones denser and more robust than many other types. Spinel family gemstones also contain high amounts of chromium, which contributes to the gemstones' coloration.

Identification

Now that we know the spinel family's structure and what comprises them, let's look at how to identify them. It can be challenging to identify spinel gemstones, as they often get mistaken for other gemstones, such as ruby or sapphire. However, a few unique features distinguish spinel gemstones from other gemstones. One such feature is their single refraction, differentiating them from double-refracting gemstone types. Spinel gemstones also register twinned or interpenetrating spinel crystals, which is a characteristic that is unique to them.

In addition to their unique features, spinel family gemstones have a fascinating history. The gemstones were named after the Latin word *spina*, meaning "thorn." During ancient times, spinel gemstones were believed to have properties such as healing illness and protecting their wearer from harm. The gemstones also played a significant role in many royal jewelry pieces throughout history, such as being a centerpiece gemstone in the British crown jewels.

Other Semi-Precious Gemstones

The world is full of beautiful gemstones that never cease to amaze us with their exquisite beauty and unique characteristics. Amongst the most beautiful and enigmatic of them are the garnet, opal, turquoise, and peridot. These gemstones have a rich history, and their popularity in jewelry continues to skyrocket steadily. Here are some more details about each of these precious gems.

Garnet Family Gemstones

The garnet comes in a variety of colors, including red, green, and yellow. This gemstone is a silicate mineral with six variants: grossular, spessartine, andradite, uvarovite, pyrope, and almandine. These variations give garnets different chemical compositions and, therefore, different hues. Garnets are easily identified by their crystal structure and are usually found in the metamorphic rocks of the Earth's crust. Additionally, it is not easily scratched, making it a perfect choice for jewelry.

Opal Family Gemstones

Opals come in different colors ranging from white to black. Most opals have a rainbow-like play of colors, making them highly sought after in the jewelry world. These gemstones are formed from silica gel that seeps into cracks and crevices of rocks, hardening over time. Opals are not durable gemstones, and that's because they contain a lot of water, making them more prone to cracking and chipping. To identify an opal, look for the unique play of colors and its pearly luster.

Turquoise Family Gemstones

Turquoise is a blue-green gemstone that is highly valued for its mid-blue color. It is a relatively soft gemstone, ranking just below quartz on the Mohs hardness scale. Turquoise occurs in arid regions and is often found in association with copper deposits. The gemstone has a granular structure and is easily identifiable by its waxy luster.

Peridot Family Gemstones

Peridot is a green gemstone with a yellowish-green color. It is a mineral found in ultramafic rocks such as peridotite and meteorites. Peridot is relatively hard, ranking six-and-a-half to seven on the Mohs scale of hardness. It is easily identified by its high refraction index and double refraction.

Garnet, opal, turquoise, and peridot gemstones are a representation of the Earth's beauty and diversity. Each gemstone has unique features that make it stand out in the jewelry world. While garnets are known for their rich colors and exquisite beauty, opals are loved for their unique play of colors. Turquoises are valued for their unique blue-green color, and peridots for their yellow-green color. Whether you're a lover of gemstones or just getting started on collecting them, these gemstones should make it to your list.

Semi-precious gemstones are some of the most sought-after gemstones in the jewelry world. Each gemstone has unique characteristics that make them stand out from each other and make them all the more special. Whether you're looking for a piece of jewelry with a pop of color or something classic and timeless, these gemstones will surely be the perfect addition to your collection. With their beauty, durability, and unique characteristics, these gemstones will bring a sparkle of joy to you and your loved ones. So, don't hesitate to add these beautiful semi-precious gems to your collection today!

Chapter 10: Meteorites and Tektites

Meteorites and tektites are two amazing space features that fascinate the modern world. Meteorites are comprised of pieces of rock or metal that have traveled from space and landed on Earth's surface. Conversely, Tektites are generally rounded rocks and pebbles created when meteorites impacted Earth's surface and melted part of the planet's crust. The individual elements found in these two types of cosmic occurrences allow scientists to better understand how our universe operates.

Understanding more about meteorites and tektites opens up a unique window into an unseen world and is truly an exciting prospect for those seeking further knowledge about our time in the cosmos. This chapter will focus on the definition of meteorites and tektites, the various types of each, and ways to identify them. Examples of well-known specimens of meteorites and tektites will also be discussed. By the end of this chapter, you will be more familiar with the fascinating world of meteorites and tektites.

Definition of Meteorites and Tektites

Meteorites and tektites are two components of *meteoritics*, the study of objects that originate from space. Meteorites are pieces of solid material that have fallen to Earth from outer space, typically formed when an asteroid or comet enters the atmosphere. Tektites are glassy objects found on Earth that, it is speculated, have resulted from the impact between Earth and extraterrestrial objects. While meteorites come in various sizes and forms, ranging from small stones to large chunks of rock, tektites are generally dark greenish or brownish with a glossy appearance. Both meteorites and tektites are valuable sources of knowledge. Studying them can give us insight into the origin of our solar system and help scientists understand the impact of collisions between asteroids in space.

Types of Meteorites

Meteorites have been recorded since ancient times. These solid pieces of debris from outer space have traveled across the vast expanse of our universe before finally ending up on our planet. The study of meteorites has given us valuable information into the formation and evolution of our solar system.

Meteorite.[78]

A. Iron Meteorites

Iron meteorites are the easiest to recognize among the three types. These are made up of over 90% iron-nickel alloy and have a distinctive metallic appearance. They are believed to have formed in the core of a planetesimal, a small protoplanet formed from dust and gas in the early stages of the solar system. Iron meteorites are rich in minerals such as kamacite and taenite, which are responsible for the Widmanstätten patterns that can be observed when slicing a polished iron meteorite. These patterns are unique to iron meteorites and can be used to determine their origin.

B. Stony-Iron Meteorites

Stony-iron meteorites, also known as pallasites, are a combination of both iron and silicate minerals. They are believed to have formed at the boundary between the core and the mantle of a planetesimal. The silicate minerals in stony-iron meteorites are usually olivine and pyroxene and are located in the metal matrix, which gives the meteorites their unique appearance. Pallasites are one of the rarest types of meteorites, accounting for less than one percent of all known meteorites.

C. Stony Meteorites

Stony meteorites are the most abundant of the three types, accounting for over 90% of all meteorites ever found. They comprise silicate minerals such as olivine and pyroxene, similar to those found in the Earth's mantle. Stony meteorites can be further classified into two groups: chondrites and achondrites. Chondrites are the most primitive meteorites and are believed to be remnants from the early stages of the solar system. On the other hand, Achondrites have undergone some degree of differentiation, meaning they have experienced some form of geological processing.

Types of Tektites

Tektites are unique, beautiful, and visually stunning. But have you ever wondered about their origin or types? Tektites are formed when a meteor strikes the Earth's surface, and the impact causes a pressure wave that melts the surrounding rocks. This molten material then cools and solidifies into a glassy structure commonly referred to as a tektite.

27. Tektite.[79]

1. Microtektites

This type of tektite is incredibly small, typically measuring less than one millimeter across. Microtektites are created when a meteor impact occurs and sends tiny glass fragments into the atmosphere. Microtektites do not originate from the melting of rocks or other materials on the Earth's surface. This type of tektite can float in the atmosphere for a long time, creating a phenomenon called tektite rain. It also reminds us of the catastrophic events that have occurred in our planet's history.

2. Muong-Nong Type Tektites

This type of tektite was first discovered in Vietnam in 1938. It is primarily found in Indochina, Cambodia, and Laos. The muong-nong-type tektites are dark brown or black and shaped like irregular droplets. They are about ten times heavier than a typical meteorite and comprise various elements like aluminum, silicon, magnesium, and more. Scientists believe that the muong-nong type tektites might be one of the oldest forms of tektites that exist on our planet.

3. Splash-Form Tektites

These tektites are the most abundant form across the planet. The splash-form tektites are formed when a meteorite strikes the Earth with such force that molten glass is created from the melting of rocks on the ground. The type of splash-form tektite found worldwide is based on the location of the meteorite impact. For example, Ivory Coast tektites are found in West Africa, while the North American tektites can be found around the Great Lakes region.

4. Australites

The australite tektites are unique because they were formed by multiple meteor impacts that hit several locations in southern Asia and around Australia. The australite tektites have a sleek, aerodynamic shape which is quite different from the other types of tektites. They are typically dark green, black, or brown and are found strewn in fields in Australia and Laos.

Famous Specimens of Meteorites and Tektites

- The night sky has always fascinated humans, and we have always been captivated by the amazing things that fall from it. One such thing is meteorites, which are pieces of asteroids or comets that reach the Earth's surface. Tektites, on the other hand, form from impact events on Earth, resulting in glassy rocks that are incredibly rare and valuable. Here are some of the most famous meteorites and tektites known to us:

- **Allende Meteorite:** The Allende meteorite is the largest carbonaceous chondrite ever found, weighing over two tons. It was first discovered in 1969 in the Chihuahuan Desert of northern Mexico. This meteorite is fascinating because it contains pre-solar grains, which are grains of stardust that predate our Solar System. These grains give insight into the universe's conditions before the formation of our own Solar System.

- **Fukang Meteorite:** The Fukang meteorite was discovered in 2000 in the Gobi Desert in China. It's a type of pallasite meteorite, which means it is made up of iron-nickel and silicate materials. This meteorite is unique because it contains some of the largest olivine crystals ever found, some up to 10 centimeters across. It's also one of the most visually stunning meteorites, with a beautiful green and yellow coloration.

- **Esquel Meteorite:** The Esquel meteorite was discovered in 1951 in Argentina and is one of the few meteorites composed entirely of nickel-iron metal. It's also a fantastic example of a meteorite's Widmanstätten pattern, which is a unique crystalline structure that forms due to the slow cooling of an iron-nickel alloy. The pattern is a visually stunning reminder of the meteorite's journey through space.

- **Moldavite Tektite:** Moldavite is a glassy green rock that is thought to have formed around 15 million years ago when a meteorite hit the Earth. It's found mainly in the Czech Republic and is one of the most valuable tektites in the world. What makes moldavite so fascinating is its unique composition, which contains rare elements not found on Earth. It's also believed to have mystical properties and is valued by collectors and spiritualists.

- **Libyan Glass Tektite:** The Libyan glass tektite is a type of tektite that formed around 26 million years ago when a meteorite hit the Earth in what is now Western Egypt. It's a rare and valuable specimen due to its unique composition and the fact that it's believed to contain evidence of water on the moon. It's also been found to contain high levels of helium-three, a rare isotope that's highly valuable for scientific research.

- **Darwin Glass Tektite:** The Darwin glass tektite is a type of tektite found in Tasmania, Australia. It's named after Charles Darwin, who first discovered the glassy rock in 1838 during his voyage on HMS Beagle. This tektite is fascinating because it is believed to have formed from a meteorite impact over 800,000 years ago. It is also one of the most visually stunning tektites, with a deep green color and natural bubble patterns that make it highly sought after by collectors.

Ways to Identify and Test a Meteorite

1. **Shape:** One of the easiest ways to identify a meteorite is by its shape. Meteorites are typically very irregular in shape and often have a pitted or grooved surface. If you find a rock that has a smooth, rounded shape, it is likely not a meteorite.
2. **Color:** Another way to identify a meteorite is by its color. Meteorites are often darker in color than other rocks due to their high iron content. If you find a rock that is very light in color, it is likely not a meteorite.
3. **Weight:** Meteorites are also much heavier than other rocks due to their high density. If you find a rock that is very light in weight, it is likely not a meteorite.
4. **Magnetism:** One way to test if a rock is a meteorite is by using a magnet. Meteorites are attracted to magnets due to their high iron content. If the rock you are testing is not attracted to a magnet, it is likely not a meteorite.
5. **Acid Test:** Another way to test if a rock is a meteorite is by using acid. Meteorites contain high levels of iron, which will react with acid. If the rock you are testing does not react with acid, it is likely not a meteorite.

Meteorites and tektites are fascinating remnants of our solar system's past. These rocks are valuable not just for their scientific value but also for their aesthetic beauty. Meteorites provide insight into the formation of our planets, and tektites provide clues about ancient impacts on the Earth. By studying meteorites and tektites, we can learn more about our solar system's history and better understand the amazing forces that shaped it. From the visually stunning Widmanstätten pattern to the mystical properties of moldavite, these rocks offer a window into our universe's past.

Appendix: A-Z of Rocks, Crystals, Gems, and Minerals

Now that you have familiarized yourself with the basics of rocks, crystals, gems, and minerals, let's dive a little deeper. Below is an alphabetical list of various types with quick reference details:

Amber - A fossilized tree resin that is often found in the form of a gemstone. It can be between 30 and 90 million years old.

Agate - A variety of chalcedony with various patterns and colors, often formed in cavities of other rocks.

Amethyst - A type of quartz, often purple, used to make jewelry and other decorative objects.

Apatite - A phosphorous mineral that is the main component of teeth and bones.

Azurite - A copper mineral that ranges in color from deep blue to green.

Beryl - A family of minerals that includes emeralds and aquamarine.

Chalcedony - A form of quartz that is found in a variety of colors.

Diamond - A hard, clear mineral that is the hardest natural substance known.

Fluorite - A mineral composed of calcium and fluorine atoms with a variety of colors.

Garnet – A group of minerals that come in a range of colors and are used in jewelry.

Hematite – A mineral that is often black or steel-gray and used as a pigment in paint.

Jade – An ornamental stone, usually green, used for centuries to make jewelry and sculptures.

Kyanite – A blue or green mineral that is often used as a gemstone.

Labradorite – A mineral with an iridescent quality, typically gray.

Lapis Lazuli – A rock composed of several minerals, including lazurite, pyrite, and calcite.

Malachite – A green mineral that is often found in the upper layers of copper-bearing ores.

Opal – A type of mineraloid composed of silica and water molecules with a variety of colors and iridescent qualities.

Quartz – A mineral composed of silicon and oxygen atoms with a variety of forms and colors.

Sapphire – Corundum in its purest form, typically blue, but can be found in other colors.

Tiger's Eye – A chatoyant gemstone often used for jewelry and ornamentation.

Topaz – A mineral that comes in many colors, including yellow and blue.

Turquoise – An opaque, green-blue mineral often used for jewelry and ornamentation.

Zircon – A hard, durable mineral with a variety of colors, such as yellow and red.

We hope this list has provided useful reference information about the various types of rocks, crystals, gems, and minerals available. Happy collecting!

Conclusion

Rocks, gems, and minerals are intricate geological features that have captivated the imagination of humans for centuries. We marvel at their stunning beauty, exquisite texture, and complex composition. They provide us with an endless source of entertainment while also informally educating us on the processes of creation and erosion. There is something special about standing in awe of a beautiful landscape or precious stone. All these geologic wonders unveil secrets of our natural world to those curious enough to find them.

Geology is an endlessly fascinating science with a world of natural wonders that never fails to amaze. Whether it's the seemingly infinite varieties of rocks, or the bright and dazzling gems and minerals, each is a unique specimen that requires thousands of years to form and create. A single rock can tell you a multitude of stories about its journey. Every crystal and gem has an almost magical beauty. It's no surprise that they have been credited with ancient powers since time immemorial. Taking the time to explore geology is sure to provide you with an educational experience like no other.

From the basics of why each is important to uncovering unique and precious stones from different parts of the world, no stone has gone unturned. We take an exciting journey through each geological process that leads us to discoveries for different types of rocks, including igneous, sedimentary, and metamorphic. Whether it be research or simply gathering knowledge out of curiosity, this guide provides a comprehensive path to understanding more about our Earth's wonders with its valuable content.

This book is a treasure trove of knowledge, giving readers an in-depth look into the fascinating world of crystal systems and quartz formations. With this resource, we've learned about both precious and semi-precious gemstones and discovered the mysterious buried secrets tektites and meteorites keep. Lastly, the helpful A-Z guide at the end of this book makes it easy to identify which rocks are valuable minerals and which aren't.

Exploring the natural world can be a great way to find rocks, gems, crystals, and minerals that can all serve as special treasures. Whether hiking in the woods or rummaging through your local farmers market, you never know what you might find. Rocks and gemstones have been prized for centuries as sources of beauty and power. Crystals are also said to have healing properties and can serve as powerful energizers when placed in specific areas of your living space. Lastly, minerals can often be found in everyday elements unusually rich in certain metals or other elements. Have fun exploring the crystal realms and see what magical discoveries you might stumble upon!

Here's another book by Mari Silva that you might like

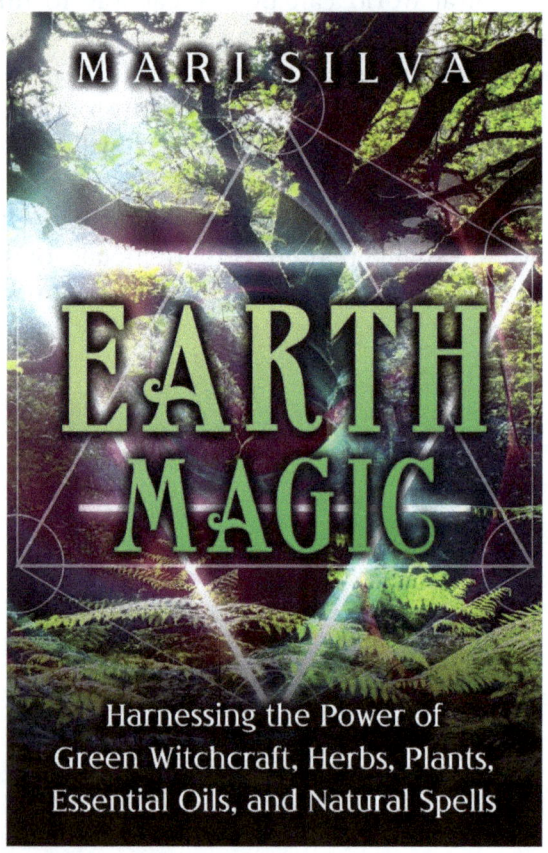

Your Free Gift
(only available for a limited time)

Thanks for getting this book! If you want to learn more about various spirituality topics, then join Mari Silva's community and get a free guided meditation MP3 for awakening your third eye. This guided meditation mp3 is designed to open and strengthen ones third eye so you can experience a higher state of consciousness. Simply visit the link below the image to get started.

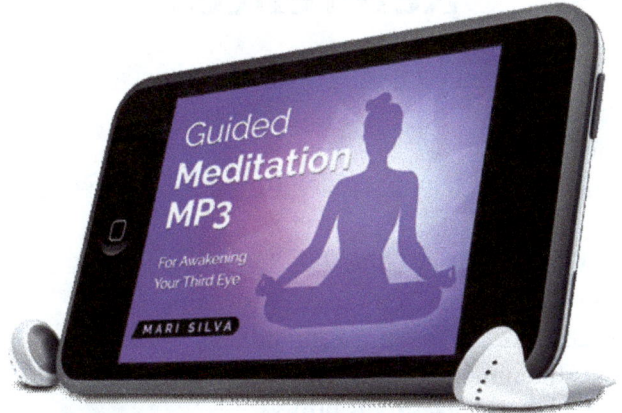

https://spiritualityspot.com/meditation

Or, Scan the QR code!

References

(N.d.). Amnh.org. https://www.amnh.org/explore/ology/earth/if-rocks-could-talk2/three-types-of-rock

(N.d.). Mindat.org. https://www.mindat.org/article.php/1782/Tips+and+Tricks+For+Rockhounds

(N.d.). Usda.gov. https://www.fs.usda.gov/Internet/FSE_DOCUMENTS/stelprdb5385347.pdf

(N.d.-a). Johnbetts-fineminerals.com. http://www.johnbetts-fineminerals.com/jhbnyc/articles/minclean.htm

(N.d.-b). Johnbetts-fineminerals.com. http://www.johnbetts-fineminerals.com/jhbnyc/articles/tools.htm

10 Most Popular Crystals. (n.d.). FossilEra. https://www.fossilera.com/pages/most-popular-crystals

Aloian, M. (2010). What Are Metamorphic Rocks? Crabtree Publishing Company.

Basic rock and mineral cleaning at home. (n.d.). Arkansasstateparks.com. https://www.arkansasstateparks.com/articles/basic-rock-and-mineral-cleaning-home

CK-12 Foundation. (2016, August 10). Types of fossilization. Ck12.org. https://www.ck12.org/earth-science/types-of-fossilization/lesson/fossils-ii-types-of-fossilization/

Dutfield, S., & How It Works magazine. (2021, May 17). The 5 mass extinction events that shaped the history of Earth – and the 6th that's happening now. Livescience.com; Live Science. https://www.livescience.com/mass-extinction-events-that-shaped-Earth.html

Fossil identification guide. (2022, November 17). The Burren and Cliffs of Moher UNESCO Global Geopark | People, Place, Learning, Livelihood; The Burren and Cliffs of Moher UNESCO Global Geopark.
https://www.burrengeopark.ie/learn-engage/fossil-identification-guide/

Fossil types & Fossilization process, importance, and divisions. (2014, August 21). Biology Boom – It's All about Zoology, Botany and Biology.
https://biologyboom.com/fossil-and-fossilization/

Fossil. (n.d.). Nationalgeographic.org.
https://education.nationalgeographic.org/resource/fossil

Fossils. (2020, May 5). British Geological Survey.
https://www.bgs.ac.uk/discovering-geology/fossils-and-geological-time/fossils/

Guzei, I. (2015, November 8). How are crystals formed? Morgridge Institute for Research. https://morgridge.org/blue-sky/how-are-crystals-formed/

handbook, A. (n.d.). types of gemstones. Anpeateliercph.com.
https://anpeateliercph.com/files/Types-of-Gemstones-Booklet_Printing.pdf

Health benefits of element collecting. (n.d.). DoveMed.
https://www.dovemed.com/healthy-living/wellness-center/health-benefits-element-collecting/

Helmenstine, A. M. (2004, January 26). How to grow crystals – tips and techniques. ThoughtCo. https://www.thoughtco.com/how-to-grow-great-crystals-602157

How to plan a rockhound road trip. (2022, December 12). Rockngem.com; Rock & Gem Magazine. https://www.rockngem.com/how-to-plan-a-rockhound-road-trip/

How to start rockhounding: The ultimate beginner's guide. (2020, September 8). How to Find Rocks. https://howtofindrocks.com/how-to-start-rockhounding/

How to start rockhounding: The ultimate beginner's guide. (2020, September 8). How to Find Rocks. https://howtofindrocks.com/how-to-start-rockhounding/

How to start rockhounding: The ultimate beginner's guide. (2020, September 8). How to Find Rocks. https://howtofindrocks.com/how-to-start-rockhounding/

Igneous rocks. (n.d.). Nationalgeographic.org.
https://www.nationalgeographic.org/encyclopedia/igneous-rocks/

In, G. (n.d.-a). How to Identify Common Minerals? Geologyin.com.
https://www.geologyin.com/2017/02/how-to-identify-common-minerals.html

In, G. (n.d.-b). What Is the Difference Between Minerals and crystals? Geologyin.com. https://www.geologyin.com/2016/03/what-is-difference-between-minerals-and.html

Koppes, S. (2022, September 12). The origin of life on Earth, explained. University of Chicago. https://news.uchicago.edu/explainer/origin-life-earth-explained

List of gemstones: Precious and semi-precious stones – gem society. (2016, June 8). International Gem Society; International Gem Society LLC. https://www.gemsociety.org/gemstone-encyclopedia/

MacMillan, K. (2021, October 14). Where to find crystals and minerals in your home town? The Stone Circle. https://www.thestonecircle.co.uk/post/where-to-find-crystals-and-minerals-in-your-home-town

Matlins, A. (2016). Colored gemstones: The Antoinette matlins buying guide -- how to select, buy, care for & enjoy sapphires, emeralds, rubies & other colored gems with confidence & knowledge. Gemstone Press.

Mineral varieties and other names A-Z – the mineral and gemstone kingdom. (n.d.). Minerals.net. https://www.minerals.net/mineralvarieties.aspx

Mowers, S. (2018, September 28). Nevada adventure, on The Rocks. Travel Nevada. https://travelnevada.com/mines-prospecting/nevada-adventure-on-the-rocks/

Panchuk, K. (2022). 1.5 three big ideas: Geological time, uniformitarianism, and plate tectonics. In Physical Geology – H5P Edition. BCcampus.

PRO tips for beginner & experienced rockhounds + safety tips. (2020, August 9). How to Find Rocks. https://howtofindrocks.com/best-tips-for-rockhounding/

Rhea, M. (2020, October 15). Where to find crystals – A helpful guide. Rockhound Resource. https://rockhoundresource.com/where-to-find-crystals-a-helpful-guide/

Rock and mineral collecting is an exciting hobby, and we've been helping collectors for years. If you're just starting, here are helpful tips for your collection. (n.d.). Irocks.com. https://www.irocks.com/rock-and-mineral-collecting-for-beginners

Rock-forming minerals. (2019, February 1). Geological Society of Glasgow. https://geologyglasgow.org.uk/minerals-rocks-fossils/rock-forming-minerals/

Rockhounding 101: Must-have tools for a safe, productive rock collecting. (n.d.). Stonebridge Imports. https://stonebridgeimports.com/a/700-rockhounding-tools-for-safe-productive-mineral-collecting

Rockhounding rules. (n.d.). Oakrocks.net. https://www.oakrocks.net/rockhounding-rules/

Rockhounding, J. (2021, October 12). How to clean rocks and minerals (tips and techniques). Just Rockhounding. https://justrockhounding.com/how-to-clean-rocks-and-minerals/

rockseeker. (2019, February 18). What is rockhounding: An intro to my favorite hobby (rock hunting). Rock Seeker. https://rockseeker.com/rockhound/

Sedimentary rocks. (2018, April 12). Geology Science; Mahmut MAT. https://geologyscience.com/rocks-2/sedimentary-rocks/

Sedimentary rocks. (n.d.). Nationalgeographic.org. https://www.nationalgeographic.org/encyclopedia/sedimentary-rock/

Seeker, R. (2021, May 27). How to clean rocks and minerals (ultimate guide to cleaning rocks and minerals). Rock Seeker. https://rockseeker.com/how-to-clean-rocks-and-minerals/

Seeker, R. (2022, August 29). The ultimate guide to rockhounding tools and supplies. Rock Seeker. https://rockseeker.com/ultimate-guide-to-rockhounding-tools/

Shambhavi, S. (2016, October 20). List of top 15 sedimentary rocks. Your Article Library. https://www.yourarticlelibrary.com/geology/sedimentary-rocks/list-of-top-15-sedimentary-rocks-geology/91311

Significance – fossils and paleontology (U.S. National Park Service). (n.d.). Nps.gov. https://www.nps.gov/subjects/fossils/significance.htm

The Best Ever Tips for a great rockhounding experience. (n.d.). Gatorgirlrocks.com. http://www.gatorgirlrocks.com/resources/the-best-ever-tips-for-a.html

The best places in the world to go fossil hunting. (n.d.). Worldwalks.com. https://www.worldwalks.com/walking-holidays/best-places-world-go-fossil-hunting/

Unearthed Store. (2019, May 2). Beginner's guide to rockhounding. Unearthed Store. https://www.unearthedstore.com/blogs/guides/beginners-guide-to-rockhounding

Veloz, L. (2018, March 13). Importance of fossils. Sciencing; Leaf Group. https://sciencing.com/importance-fossils-2470.html

Warren, S. (2021, November 22). How the Earth and moon formed, explained. University of Chicago. https://news.uchicago.edu/explainer/formation-earth-and-moon-explained

Wendorf, M. (2020, November 17). Nine beautiful crystals you can grow at home. Interesting Engineering. https://interestingengineering.com/diy/nine-beautiful-crystals-you-can-grow-at-home

What are Gemstones? (n.d.). Riginov. https://riginov.com/education-guidance/gemology/what-are-gemstones.aspx

What is rockhounding? How do I get started with the hobby? (n.d.). Stonebridge Imports. https://stonebridgeimports.com/a/696-what-is-rockhounding-how-to-get-started

What is rockhounding? How do I get started with the hobby? (n.d.). Stonebridge Imports. https://stonebridgeimports.com/a/696-what-is-rockhounding-how-to-get-started

(N.d.). Thekidshouldseethis.com. https://thekidshouldseethis.com/post/gems-minerals-crystals-and-rocks-whats-the-difference

Farndon, J. (2017). Rocks, Minerals, and Gems. Australian Geographic.

Gem & mineral identification. (n.d.). Treasure Quest Mining. https://treasurequestmining.com/treasure-identification/gems/

Identifying minerals. (n.d.). Google Arts & Culture. https://artsandculture.google.com/story/QgXh9pyyxhIYKQ

King, H. M. (n.d.). Gemstones. Geology.com. https://geology.com/gemstones/

List of gemstones: Precious and semi-precious stones - gem society. (2016, June 8). International Gem Society; International Gem Society LLC. https://www.gemsociety.org/gemstone-encyclopedia/

Minerals and gems. (2017, January 15). National Geographic. https://www.nationalgeographic.com/science/article/minerals-gems

Somarin, A. (2014, March 20). Where did those gemstones come from? Advancing Mining. https://www.thermofisher.com/blog/mining/where-did-those-gemstones-come-from/

Using characteristics of minerals to identify them. (n.d.). Illinois.edu. https://isgs.illinois.edu/outreach/geology-resources/using-characteristics-minerals-identify-them

Image Sources

[1] https://commons.wikimedia.org/wiki/File:Geologic_Clock_with_events_and_periods.svg

[2] M.Bitton, CC BY-SA 3.0 <https://creativecommons.org/licenses/by-sa/3.0>, via Wikimedia Commons: https://commons.wikimedia.org/wiki/File:Tectonic_plates_(2022).svg

[3] https://www.pexels.com/photo/photography-of-stones-1029604/

[4] https://pixabay.com/photos/fossil-rock-hammer-geology-2312/

[5] https://pixabay.com/photos/walking-boots-boots-leather-3583017/

[6] https://unsplash.com/photos/8sjBzL1IyMo?utm_source=unsplash&utm_medium=referral&utm_content=creditShareLink

[7] https://www.pexels.com/photo/closeup-photo-of-black-framed-brown-sunglasses-978808/

[8] https://www.pexels.com/photo/master-hitting-instrument-with-hammer-in-carpentry-5974328/

[9] https://www.pexels.com/photo/person-using-google-maps-application-through-black-android-smartphone-35969/

[10] https://www.pexels.com/photo/crop-man-with-reflecting-crystal-ball-in-forest-3721533/

[11] KarlaPanchuk, CC BY-SA 4.0 <https://creativecommons.org/licenses/by-sa/4.0>, via Wikimedia Commons: https://commons.wikimedia.org/wiki/File:Hematite_streak_plate.jpg

[12] File:Bar magnet.jpg: Photo taken by Aney / derivative work: MikeRun, CC BY-SA 3.0 <http://creativecommons.org/licenses/by-sa/3.0/>, via Wikimedia Commons: https://commons.wikimedia.org/wiki/File:Bar_magnet_crop.jpg

[13] https://www.pexels.com/photo/map-of-the-world-book-laid-open-on-brown-wooden-surface-32307/

[14] https://www.pexels.com/photo/antique-compass-on-a-table-6593994/

[15] https://www.pexels.com/photo/man-using-black-binoculars-near-forest-trees-at-daytime-1181809/

[16] https://unsplash.com/photos/9uISZprJdXU?utm_source=unsplash&utm_medium=

referral&utm_content=creditShareLink

[17] https://unsplash.com/photos/npxXWgQ33ZQ?utm_source=unsplash&utm_medium=referral&utm_content=creditShareLink

[18] https://www.pexels.com/photo/first-aid-kit-on-white-background-5664736/

[19] https://pixabay.com/photos/whistle-attention-warning-referee-2475470/

[20] https://unsplash.com/photos/R13RJX_V42A?utm_source=unsplash&utm_medium=referral&utm_content=creditShareLink

[21] https://unsplash.com/photos/VKLJ-BJlszE?utm_source=unsplash&utm_medium=referral&utm_content=creditShareLink

[22] https://unsplash.com/photos/Talnaz9Bug0?utm_source=unsplash&utm_medium=referral&utm_content=creditShareLink

[23] https://unsplash.com/photos/IKJ8k8cfHnY?utm_source=unsplash&utm_medium=referral&utm_content=creditShareLink

[24] https://unsplash.com/photos/ToDanUwG4vs?utm_source=unsplash&utm_medium=referral&utm_content=creditShareLink

[25] Moha112100, CC BY-SA 3.0 <https://creativecommons.org/licenses/by-sa/3.0>, via Wikimedia Commons: https://commons.wikimedia.org/wiki/File:Garnet_Andradite20.jpg

[26] Didier Descouens, CC BY-SA 3.0 <https://creativecommons.org/licenses/by-sa/3.0>, via Wikimedia Commons: https://commons.wikimedia.org/wiki/File:Topaze_Br%C3%A9sil.jpg

[27] https://www.pexels.com/photo/clear-stone-2363577/

[28] Dave Dyet http://www.shutterstone.com http://www.dyet.com, Public domain, via Wikimedia Commons: https://commons.wikimedia.org/wiki/File:Feldspar_1659.jpg

[29] https://unsplash.com/photos/ppmiXmhHHyc?utm_source=unsplash&utm_medium=referral&utm_content=creditShareLink

[30] Rob Lavinsky, iRocks.com – CC-BY-SA-3.0, CC BY-SA 3.0 <https://creativecommons.org/licenses/by-sa/3.0>, via Wikimedia Commons: https://commons.wikimedia.org/wiki/File:Halite-Picromerite-mrz114a.jpg

[31] GOKLuLe 盧樂, CC BY-SA 3.0 <https://creativecommons.org/licenses/by-sa/3.0>, via Wikimedia Commons: https://commons.wikimedia.org/wiki/File:Tourmaline_sample.jpg

[32] https://www.pexels.com/photo/white-stone-56030/

[33] https://commons.wikimedia.org/wiki/File:Montblanc_granite_phenocrysts.JPG

[34] Ji-Elle It feels nice and warm It feels like a _____, CC BY-SA 3.0 <https://creativecommons.org/licenses/by-sa/3.0>, via Wikimedia Commons: https://commons.wikimedia.org/wiki/File:Lipari-Obsidienne_(5).jpg

[35] https://commons.wikimedia.org/wiki/File:BasaltUSGOV.jpg

[36] Didier Descouens, CC BY-SA 4.0 <https://creativecommons.org/licenses/by-sa/4.0>, via Wikimedia Commons: https://commons.wikimedia.org/wiki/File:Dolomite-Magn%C3%A9site-Navarre.jpg

[37] I, Jonathan Zander, CC BY-SA 3.0 <http://creativecommons.org/licenses/by-sa/3.0/>, via Wikimedia Commons: https://commons.wikimedia.org/wiki/File:Millet-Seed_Sandstone_Macro.JPG

[38] James St. John, CC BY 2.0 <https://creativecommons.org/licenses/by/2.0>, via Wikimedia Commons: https://commons.wikimedia.org/wiki/File:Chattanooga_Shale_(Upper_Devonian;_Burkesville_West_Rt._90_roadcut,_Kentucky,_USA)_25_(40541681100).jpg

[39] Gabriel Haute Maurienne, CC BY-SA 4.0 <https://creativecommons.org/licenses/by-sa/4.0>, via Wikimedia Commons: https://commons.wikimedia.org/wiki/File:Quartzite_Solli%C3%A8res.jpg

[40] Luis Miguel Bugallo Sánchez (Lmbuga Commons)(Lmbuga Galipedia)Publicada por/Publish by: Luis Miguel Bugallo Sánchez, CC BY-SA 3.0 <http://creativecommons.org/licenses/by-sa/3.0/>, via Wikimedia Commons: https://commons.wikimedia.org/wiki/File:Mineral_M%C3%A1rmore_GDFL021.jpg

[41] No machine-readable author provided. Siim assumed (based on copyright claims)., CC BY-SA 3.0 <http://creativecommons.org/licenses/by-sa/3.0/>, via Wikimedia Commons: https://commons.wikimedia.org/wiki/File:Gneiss.jpg

[42] Postdlf, CC BY-SA 3.0 <http://creativecommons.org/licenses/by-sa/3.0/>, via Wikimedia Commons: https://commons.wikimedia.org/wiki/File:Smilodon_californicus.jpg

[43] Francesco Bandarin, CC BY-SA 3.0 IGO <https://creativecommons.org/licenses/by-sa/3.0/igo/deed.en>, via Wikimedia Commons: https://commons.wikimedia.org/wiki/File:Fossil_Hominid_Sites_of_South_Africa-113352.jpg

[44] https://unsplash.com/photos/7ByfI6Fpi90?utm_source=unsplash&utm_medium=referral&utm_content=creditShareLink

[45] https://www.pexels.com/photo/white-soft-satin-fabric-7717488/

[46] https://www.pexels.com/photo/crop-woman-with-eco-brush-and-soap-bar-7262410/

[47] https://www.pexels.com/photo/similar-cotton-ear-buds-on-wooden-sticks-on-table-4202350/

[48] https://www.pexels.com/photo/eyelash-extension-tweezers-on-gold-tray-5128316/

[49] Hannes Grobe, CC BY 3.0 <https://creativecommons.org/licenses/by/3.0>, via Wikimedia Commons: https://commons.wikimedia.org/wiki/File:Bandelin-sonorex_hg.jpg

[50] https://www.pexels.com/photo/black-and-red-canister-vacuum-cleaner-on-floor-38325/

[51] https://www.pexels.com/photo/brown-handle-magnifying-glass-268460/

[52] https://unsplash.com/photos/RLw-UC03Gwc?utm_source=unsplash&utm_medium=referral&utm_content=creditShareLink

[53] https://unsplash.com/photos/yCdPU73kGSc?utm_source=unsplash&utm_medium=referral&utm_content=creditShareLink

[54] https://unsplash.com/photos/66BgmIglPhM

[55] James St. John, CC BY 2.0 <https://creativecommons.org/licenses/by/2.0>, via Wikimedia Commons https://commons.wikimedia.org/wiki/File:Granite_26_(49199871943).jpg

[56] Smithsonian Institution, CC0, via Wikimedia Commons https://commons.wikimedia.org/wiki/File:Basaltic_Andesite_from_Paricutin_volcano_in_Mexico_-_Smithsonian_Rock_Sample.jpg

[57] James St. John, CC BY 2.0 DEED <https://creativecommons.org/licenses/by/2.0/>https://www.flickr.com/photos/jsjgeology/49943337113

[58] James St. John, CC BY 2.0 <https://creativecommons.org/licenses/by/2.0/>, via Wikimedia Commons https://commons.wikimedia.org/wiki/File:Peridotite_mantle_xenoliths_in_vesicular_phonotephrite_(Peridot_Mesa_Flow,_Middle_Pleistocene,_580_ka;_Peridot_Mesa,_San_Carlos_Volcanic_Field,_Arizona)_7_(14992925414).jpg

[59] James St. John, CC BY 2.0 DEED <https://creativecommons.org/licenses/by/2.0/> https://www.flickr.com/photos/jsjgeology/36690094351

[60] James St. John, CC BY 2.0 DEED <https://creativecommons.org/licenses/by/2.0/> https://www.flickr.com/photos/jsjgeology/16638766949

[61] Didier Descouens, CC BY-SA 4.0 <https://creativecommons.org/licenses/by-sa/4.0>, via Wikimedia Commons https://commons.wikimedia.org/wiki/File:Dolomite_Luzenac.jpg

[62] Manishwiki15, CC BY-SA 3.0 <https://creativecommons.org/licenses/by-sa/3.0>, via Wikimedia Commons https://commons.wikimedia.org/wiki/File:Fossiliferous_Limestone.JPG

[63] https://commons.wikimedia.org/wiki/File:Sandstone(quartz)USGOV.jpg

[64] https://pixabay.com/es/photos/esquisto-roca-roto-textura-rocoso-2255022/

[65] James St. John, CC BY 2.0 <https://creativecommons.org/licenses/by/2.0>, via Wikimedia Commons https://commons.wikimedia.org/wiki/File:Phyllite_(French_Slate,_Paleoproterozoic;_Snowy_Range_Road_roadcut,_Medicine_Bow_Mountains,_Wyoming,_USA)_8_(45625222381).jpg

[66] James St. John, CC BY 2.0 <https://creativecommons.org/licenses/by/2.0>, via Wikimedia Commons https://commons.wikimedia.org/wiki/File:Sioux_Quartzite_(Paleoproterozoic,_1.65_to_1.70_Ga;_Transcontinental_Arch,_USA)_17.jpg

[67] James St. John, CC BY 2.0 <https://creativecommons.org/licenses/by/2.0>, via Wikimedia Commons https://commons.wikimedia.org/wiki/File:Marble_(Murphy_Marble,_Ordovician;_quarry_near_Tate,_Georgia,_USA)_(16268833583).jpg

[68] James St. John, CC BY 2.0 <https://creativecommons.org/licenses/by/2.0>, via Wikimedia Commons https://commons.wikimedia.org/wiki/File:Garnet-chlorite_schist_(Lake_Martin,_Alabama,_USA)_2_(33367535678).jpg

[69] James St. John, CC BY 2.0 <https://creativecommons.org/licenses/by/2.0>, via Wikimedia Commons https://commons.wikimedia.org/wiki/File:Gneiss_2_(33239757534).jpg

[70] James St. John, CC BY 2.0 <https://creativecommons.org/licenses/by/2.0>, via Wikimedia Commons https://commons.wikimedia.org/wiki/File:Rose_quartz_(32132819430).jpg

[71] James St. John, CC BY 2.0 <https://creativecommons.org/licenses/by/2.0>, via Wikimedia Commons https://commons.wikimedia.org/wiki/File:Amethyst_(purple_quartz)_15.jpg

⁷² *Rob Lavinsky, CC BY 3.0 <https://creativecommons.org/licenses/by/3.0>, via Wikimedia Commons https://commons.wikimedia.org/wiki/File:Smoky-quartz-TUCQTZ09-03-arkenstone-irocks.png*

⁷³ *James St. John, CC BY 2.0 <https://creativecommons.org/licenses/by/2.0>, via Wikimedia Commons https://commons.wikimedia.org/wiki/File:Quartz_(%22Herkimer_Diamond%22)_(near_Herkimer,_New_York_State,_USA)_8.jpg*

⁷⁴ *Mahdikarimi70, CC BY-SA 4.0 <https://creativecommons.org/licenses/by-sa/4.0>, via Wikimedia Commons https://commons.wikimedia.org/wiki/File:%D8%B3%D9%86%DA%AF_%D8%AF%D9%84%D8%B1%D8%A8%D8%A7-Aventurine_01.jpg*

⁷⁵ *https://pixabay.com/es/photos/citrino-cristal-roca-cuarzo-joya-1093454/*

⁷⁶ *Rob Lavinsky, iRocks.com – CC-BY-SA-3.0, CC BY-SA 3.0 <https://creativecommons.org/licenses/by-sa/3.0>, via Wikimedia Commons https://commons.wikimedia.org/wiki/File:Chalcedony-121273.jpg*

⁷⁷ *James St. John, CC BY 2.0 <https://creativecommons.org/licenses/by/2.0>, via Wikimedia Commons https://commons.wikimedia.org/wiki/File:Agate_(Adrasman_City,_Tajikistan)_(32755918215).jpg*

⁷⁸ *Doug Bowman from DeKalb IL, USA, CC BY 2.0 <https://creativecommons.org/licenses/by/2.0>, via Wikimedia Commons https://commons.wikimedia.org/wiki/File:Oriented_Meteorite.jpg*

⁷⁹ *James St. John, CC BY 2.0 <https://creativecommons.org/licenses/by/2.0>, via Wikimedia Commons https://commons.wikimedia.org/wiki/File:Indochinite_tektite_(Pleistocene,_783-803_ka;_Australasian_Tektite_Strewn_Field,_southeastern_Asia)_6.jpg*

www.ingramcontent.com/pod-product-compliance
Lightning Source LLC
Chambersburg PA
CBHW051843160426
43209CB00006B/1131